DISCARD

VISIONS OF CULTURE

VISIONS OF CULTURE

VOLTAIRE
GUIZOT
BURCKHARDT
LAMPRECHT
HUIZINGA
ORTEGA Y GASSET

By KARL J. WEINTRAUB

UNIVERSITY OF CHICAGO PRESS

CHICAGO & LONDON

Library of Congress Catalog Card Number: 66–13893

THE UNIVERSITY OF CHICAGO PRESS, CHICAGO & LONDON
The University of Toronto Press, Toronto 5, Canada

To
Christian W. Mackauer
Mentor—Friend—Mirrorbearer

Acknowledgments

The basic idea underlying this study came to me through my participation in the Western Civilization course at the University of Chicago. Work in this eminently rewarding educational undertaking has forced upon me — more than any other historical labor — a lasting awareness of the problems faced by the historians of civilization and culture. No excitement compares with the challenge to give coherence and meaning to the interpretation and presentation of a rich tradition; nothing has taught me as well the need for intellectual courage in the face of the inadequacy of all our understanding. My thanks go to the questioning students and my helpful colleagues. Above all I am indebted to the man to whom this book is dedicated. His wisdom, incisive criticism, and friendship sustained me throughout my labors in the course and on the book; that I willfully disregarded some of his criticism helps to account for the weaknesses of the book.

I derived much profit from the advice and suggestions of my former teachers Louis Gottschalk, James Cate, and Donald Lach and from such colleagues as William H. McNeill, Walter Johnson, and Alan Simpson. Through the generosity of the Willett Fellowship I had a chance to do some of the research without interruption. There was a time when I wondered why authors thank their wives. I no longer do. Without my wife's English style, patience, good sense, and her willingness to bear with me when I must have been unbearable, this book never would have been finished.

Contents

Introduction

This book is composed of six essays; each essay is self-contained, but the six taken together are intended to form a whole that is greater than the sum of its parts. Each essay discusses one writer who made a substantial contribution in the field of cultural history or the history of civilization (I use these two terms without making any technical distinction).[1] One of the authors, Ortega y Gasset, is a philosopher of history; the other five — Voltaire, Guizot, Burckhardt, Lamprecht, and Huizinga — are professional historians; but they are not less concerned with defining their tasks and the principles that guided them. It is my hope that from an analysis of their writings some light may fall upon the matter itself with which they tried to deal: how can a civilization or a culture be understood and presented in all its complexity and yet as an intelligible and structured whole?

---

[1] The elaborate survey of definitions provided in Alfred L. Kroeber and Clyde Kluckhohn, *Culture: A Critical Review of Concepts and Definitions* (New York: Random House, 1963) — originally published in 1952 as Vol. XLVII, No. 1, of the Papers of the Peabody Museum of American Archaeology and Ethnology, Harvard University, but here cited in the paperback edition — makes eminently clear how nearly impossible it is to provide a clear definition of either term considering the present state of theory. I also consider their statement justified that "it is evident that the contrasting of culture and civilization, within the scope of a larger entity, was mainly an episode in German thought" (p. 29). For the English usage of the terms see the discussion in Raymond Williams, *Culture and Society, 1780–1950* (New York: Columbia University Press, 1958). I do in no way deny that the terminological issue is of profound importance, and so may be the differentiation between culture and civilization under certain aspects; but I did not consider it advisable to burden this study further by its inclusion.

1

Since the eighteenth century there have been historians who have dealt with those social worlds we call cultures or civilizations. The comprehensive scope of their subject is obvious. It pulls together all the varied material on which the political, the military, the economic, the social, and the art historian work separately. The historian of a civilization is interested in the total way of life, in the style of life by which men gave unified expression to their manifold activities. He pursues that elusive collective individuality in which distinctive human groups have worked out their specific human form.

Many of the details with which the cultural historians must concern themselves are, moreover, subtle and baffling matters. The historians look for the spirit underlying all the expressions of life. They try to understand the mental habits and attitudes of an age or a people. Prejudices, values, moral commitments, and aesthetic preferences are unavoidable parts of their study. They try to take the pulse of the prevailing moods and temper of societies. And some probe the inclinations of men's hearts, their aspirations, the dreams and hopes of whole societies — all matters from which the political, military, and economic historian is happy to escape.

Sheer scope and the esoteric subtlety of subject matter pose problems, but the historian of culture is in addition challenged by its complexity. He sees a culture not as a mere aggregate of traits but as forming an intricately interrelated pattern. In this delicately fashioned network the arts may have their ties to religion and economic values, morality may affect the constitutional arrangements and in turn be affected by political realities, a mood reflected in literature may also come to the fore in a social custom, and a scientific insight may work back upon a religious belief. Any one of these numberless interrelations alone can baffle the historian's skill. There is a challenge to his ingenuity, for instance, in tracing the nexus between economic behavior and epidemics, or in seeking to explain the stylistic traits of Gothic architecture by reference to the mental habits of scholasticism. Even to outline a dominant pattern of interrelations in the total cultural complex presents enormous difficulties.

And the historian of civilization must confront these tasks twice, so to speak, on two levels. He studies what a culture is and also how it develops. He must be able to see a culture in the total, relatively static, configuration attained at a given time; but he must trace as well its gradual transformation through time. This double concern with what has been called by anthropologists the synchronic and the diachronic mode of culture implies, on the one hand, the study of connections between cultural factors in their structural relationship, and, on the other hand, the study of the gradual changes, either by the introduction of new factors or by a shift in emphasis among the existing relations, resulting in a modification of the cultural configuration. In the world of the cultural historian all things touch one another. He is compelled to keep track of a host of intricately interrelated matters simultaneously.

In the face of all these difficulties those who are either so foolhardy or so wise as to pursue this particular historical task have two objectives. (1) The cultural historian must disentangle the relationships among matters tightly interwoven in the fabric of life he studies and then bring together, in his mind, all these matters as a unified whole. (2) He must present to a reader this constructed totality in a sequence of aspects. According to Burckhardt, who understood such problems well: "It is the most serious difficulty of the history of civilization that that which forms a great continuum of the mind must be broken up into single, and often into what seem arbitrary categories, in order to be in any way intelligible." [2] In many respects the historian of culture shares methodological difficulties with all other historians. But in so far as he concentrates more upon the understanding and descrip-

---

[2] Jacob Burckhardt, *Die Kultur der Renaissance in Italien* (Vienna: Phaidon, n.d.), p. 1.

tion of general conditions, and not as others upon sequentially ordered events, the problems described above under points 1 and 2 loom especially large for him.[3] These two interrelated problems form a major concern of this study.

The historian of culture defines his subject rather vaguely as the "total way of life characteristic of a given social group at a given time." He can only give form to it by conceiving this totality as a structured whole. It would be interesting to discuss how the historian discovers the past by the judicious use of such a heuristic device as the "ideal type." But this problem is of subordinate importance in the context of this book; only occasionally shall I touch upon it. Whether the cultural historian discovers an actually existing ordered configuration of a civilization or whether he more or less imposes such an order upon an essentially chaotic group of experiences is a question of historical epistemology that I do not care to enter upon. We may just posit the assumption — naïvely, if one likes — that the cultural historian arrives through detailed investigations at an understanding of his subject as an ordered configuration. Somehow, under his hands, what first presents itself as a vast multiplicity of actions, attitudes, and institutions turns into an interrelated whole. Seemingly disparate matters become part of a continuous pattern. And this continuum, to be more than a blur, must have discernible regions standing in definite relation to one another and to the whole. Or — to use almost inevitable visual terms — before his mind's eye the cultural historian should have a vision of a civilization as a vast tableau. A tableau is seen from a vantage point and has its own perspective, thus bearing out Jacob Burckhardt's assertion that every vision of a civilization is *a* vision and not *the* vision; if it bears an adequate relation to reality it may stand the test of time, but other visions are always possible.

---

[3] The point has been eloquently made by the young Dilthey; see Wilhelm Dilthey, *Die Kultur der Renaissance in Italien: ein Versuch von Jacob Burckhardt* in *Gesammelte Schriften* (12 vols.; Leipzig: Teubner, 1921–58), XI, 71–72.

Like every tableau it will have its foreground and background, its horizon, its subviews, its lighted parts and its shadows, details merely hinted at and details sharply drawn. To the degree to which this visual analogy will hold, it seems permissible, therefore, to say that the historian of culture seeks to give coherent structure to his subject, a civilization. So much about the first task of the historian of civilization to which we shall pay attention again and again in the following investigation: how does the cultural historian create in his mind a "tableau" of a culture in which the confusing multiplicity of details becomes a unified construct, having internal structure, coherence, and meaning?

The second task of the historian is to communicate his vision to others. Unlike the painter, the historian is restricted to descriptive and narrative techniques which permit only a sequential presentation. He therefore now must follow a procedure opposite to the one by which he gained his unified picture. While he has just integrated the multiplicity of detail into a structured whole, he now must break this structure into parts again and present them to the reader in a manner that enables him to rebuild out of these parts the historian's own "tableau." The historian needs all his skill to move the reader's attention from detail to detail, from subsection to subsection, in such a way that each part fits in with each of the preceding and each of the following parts; he must never lose sight of the whole by focusing too sharply on what should remain subordinate in the composite. The periphery of the composition should be discernible without ever drawing attention away from the central plane. Some details must be arresting, others must immediately fade into the background. The various blocks which make up the whole must have the right proportions and must be joined in the right manner. And then the additional complication that we mentioned before: the single "tableau" will not suffice; a sequence of "tableaux" is needed to present the culture in its development. There is a final complication: In directing the reader in his task of reconstruction the historian cannot avoid some abstract argumentation — although a master like Burckhardt reduces such guidance to a minimum and instead relies on careful grouping and cautious hints. It requires all the skill a historical writer can muster to preserve the fresh lifelike atmosphere evoked by the concrete detail from being smothered by cold dialectic. This is then the second sense in which the historian of civilization faces the problem of structure: an intricately constructed whole must be taken apart and presented as a differently arranged structure. It is a problem which through the very nature of his subject is for him much more difficult and complex than for the political historian or the historian of ideas whose subject matter more naturally fits a sequential mode of presentation.[4]

These problems of "structure" and structured presentation will play a large role in each of the following essays. In each we shall investigate the "organizational centers" around which the historian built his structure and which he induces his reader to discover and make the mainstay of his own understanding and reconstruction. And we shall study the conceptual and artistic devices used by the different authors in their structural task.

Every historian of culture uses an enumerative principle to some extent. The experience of life itself leads to the distinction of some "natural" categories under which man subsumes a civilization, for example, social customs, political and economic institutions and attitudes, artistic production, or thought and beliefs. The historian is in his right when he accepts and uses these concepts as "building blocks" out of which he erects his own structure; these regions of fundamental human concerns will be discernible in every cultural history. But every cultural historian worth his salt will try to present the civilization he has selected for his investigation as a unity of interdependent parts, even if full of tension and contradiction. He therefore will search for a center, or for a

---

[4] *Ibid.*, pp. 70–76.

cluster of interrelated foci, from which the totality can be understood and presented as a unified whole. The more he considers all historical actualities as manifestations or expressions of one complete whole, the more he will adhere to the point made by Wilhelm Dilthey: "Like the individual, every cultural system, every community, has a focal point within itself. In it, a conception of reality, valuation, and production of goods, are linked into a whole."[5] With such a focal point, such a center of organization, the vision of a civilization and its presentation can attain that structural quality whereby all that seemed loosely related, or not related at all, has become an integral part of a whole.

The choice of such a focal point largely determines the historian's work of analysis and construction. Some emphasize the external conditions of the human existence: climate, soil, geographic position, inherent racial characteristics. Others find their guiding principle in the interaction of man's inventiveness with such natural data. In one entire historiographic school the key to the understanding of every civilization would be each society's mode of production. For some of the earliest historians of civilization the focus was on the growth of rationality in human institutions and customs. For a more modern analysis the center may lie in man's psychological needs and the means used for their satisfaction. But the choice of a fulcrum for the historian's analysis and construction does not always fall on what he considers the dominant causal factor in the historical process. He may put in the center of his work an especially representative cultural phenomenon. He may look instead for some particularly representative sphere of cultural life which with great sensitivity registers all shades of cultural change and may find it, for instance, in literature and the fine arts. Another group of historians may select the laws and the political institutions of a society as the

---

[5] Wilhelm Dilthey, *Pattern and Meaning in History*, ed. Hans P. Rickman (New York: Harper & Bros., 1961), pp. 129–30; this book was originally published by Allen & Unwin, London, in 1961 under the title *Meaning in History*.

most reliable embodiment of social aspirations, customs, and attitudes. For still another group the focal point may lie on that set of most basic convictions which men of a particular culture have formed about their own reality, the heart of their *Weltanschauung*. Finally, a historian may place at the center of his understanding and presentation the specific human type, the particular historical personality type, in whom he sees the carrier and the best expression of all cultural aspirations and achievements.

A particular concern of this study, therefore, has been the question of how different methods of organization have affected the understanding and presentation of cultural complexes. The reasons for the historian's particular choice of a focus are far from arbitrary. They are to be found rather in the historian's values, temperament, and world view. He who believes that a way of life is but the outgrowth of objective needs that dictate men's course will not choose the same center as he who holds that men are free players with cultural forms. A historian convinced that culture is man's self-willed answer to a chaotic and meaningless universe will make different choices from the historian trusting that culture is a process through which God educates men toward His ways. The perspectives under which culture is treated differ where the one views man as a Protean creature who periodically restyles his way of life in order to give untried expression to all the potential modes of human existence, and the other sees in all cultures the unfolding of analogous forms according to a uniformly valid pattern of psychological development. Because such individual differences help to account for different centers and different modes of understanding and presenting a civilization, an attempt will be made, wherever possible in the following chapters, to illuminate the methodological peculiarities of each author through a short presentation of his personality, even his moods and prejudices.

The selection of historians included in this book must be justified. Represented here are five historians of civilization —

Voltaire, Guizot, Burckhardt, Lamprecht, and Huizinga — and a non-historian, the philosopher Ortega y Gasset. Of these, Voltaire, Burckhardt, and Huizinga, I hope, seem logical choices. More controversial may appear the selection of Guizot, Lamprecht, and Ortega. Some readers may object that Gibbon, Herder, Moeser, Goethe, Condorcet, or Buckle either wrote more interesting histories or contributed more to the development of the discipline than did Guizot. Others may think that almost anyone is more deserving of attention than Lamprecht, who, according to some, was wrong on every important issue; so, why not instead treat Gustav Freytag, Macaulay, Taine, Spengler, or Toynbee? Some will make the case that Dilthey and Max Weber had more profound thoughts about historical problems than did Ortega y Gasset.

My criteria for selection result, of course, from the particular problem chosen for analysis. By the nature of the question I asked I was led to those writers who had tackled one culture, at least, in its total complexity. Given my own preoccupation with western civilization, I have preferred authors in the western tradition on subjects basically western. This does not mean, however, that the authors chosen must deal with western civilization as a whole, as one indivisible historical individual. But I chose only authors who approach their selected period as an entity which can be understood as a comprehensive "way of life." This excluded all those who narrowed their conception of culture to that segment of life comprising the "finer things of the mind," to what in the German tradition has at times been considered the proper subject of *Kulturgeschichte*. The same considerations shut out all those works that take as their subject separate branches of history such as mere history of manners (or *Sittengeschichte*), intellectual history (even in its somewhat broader form of *Geistesgeschichte*), history of ideas in the Lovejoy tradition, or any form of history concerned with but one single cultural phenomenon such as religion, literature, or the fine arts. Nor should the historian's effort restrict itself to a special sector of society. By this I mean chiefly that it should not be cultural history of the English working class or the seventeenth-century French bourgeoisie or medieval chivalry. But my criterion does not exclude cultural histories which seem to confine themselves to the lives led and the thoughts thought by cultural elites. Almost all the material from which the historian can reconstruct a way of life consists in statements made by and about a small cultural minority. If we ignore the most modern times, the cultural history of any age will, of necessity, have to work with this kind of material and with almost no other. This is not the place for discussing the vexing question whether and to what degree the cultural historian must work on the assumption that those with the gift of formulation and expression convey what is valid for the voiceless as well; I have chosen only historians who made the most penetrating use of the broadest range of evidence, available in their sources, for social existence as a whole.

For my purpose it seemed advisable to concentrate on historians who consciously accepted the task of writing the history of a culture. There have always been some historians — Gibbon and Macaulay are examples — who wrote basically political history but placed it within a framework of the total culture of the time. Their actual focus, however, was not upon the totality of culture. On the other hand, Dilthey, for instance, had a fundamental concern for the values, the world views, and the mental habits, in short the *Geist*, which pervaded the life of periods. Yet, profound and stimulating as Dilthey's thoughts are, his theoretical discussions remain fragmentary and he certainly did not write a comprehensive cultural history of any epoch. In contrast, Voltaire and Guizot each dwelt heavily upon political matters; but their declared objective was to treat a civilization. Neither may have succeeded in writing integrated cultural history; but one senses in all their work that they had their vision trained upon this entity, civilization. Their repeated programmatic statements indicate that they were searching for a way to deal with it. On the surface, Lamprecht may appear to have written the history of a people merely, in the vein of Michelet or Green; but he consciously conceived his *Deutsche Geschichte* as a model for dealing with a culture and, more than anyone else, theorized about the task and method of the cultural historian. The deliberate intent with which a man asked himself, How can one cope with such a complex reality historically? weighed so heavily as a criterion of selection that I elected to include Ortega y Gasset, who, strictly speaking, wrote no history but who clearly and purposely asked that question.

I frankly admit that some kind of personal prejudice accounts for another selective criterion. Works based on a strictly deterministic explanation of culture were rejected in favor of others which see man as the relatively free creator of a social and cultural cosmos. No historian worth our interest will have either a completely deterministic or a completely voluntaristic view of civilization. But those of us who, in Voltaire's tradition, devote our years to the study of civilization for reasons transcending mere intellectual curiosity will join in the great *philosophe*'s credo that culture is man's justification, the creative effort by which he saves himself from chaos, boredom, vice, and barbarism. For all six authors discussed in this book, civilization was man's creation and responsibility, although Guizot, with his latent providential view, and Lamprecht, with his belief in psychogenetic patterns of development, rest their case on a higher degree of determinism than the other four.

Given these considerations and prejudices, my choice of authors to be selected was not too difficult.

The active concern with the history of civilization is barely two hundred years old. Its first real spokesman and practitioner was Voltaire. But he had to be included for more reasons than just his priority in time and impulse. For one, he believed in civilization, not civilizations. That conception in the singular, with its peculiar structural problems, prevailed with many eighteenth-century thinkers and in the next century is discernible in those influenced by positivism. In Voltaire's historical work one encounters a mind fired by new questions and sensitive to the intricate interrelations of cultural phenomena yet still searching for an effective form to present this complex whole. Essentially he used an enumerative technique and gave much room to the narrative of political events, but his agile curiosity spiced everything with the most interesting observations. He was strong in his condemnation of barbarism and a superb fighter for civilized existence, and his weapon was often history. But, in a sense, he was weak in working out the developmental side of civilization and was not primarily interested in history as a process. He formulated a new program for historians, he struggled, as the first to do so, with the perpetual problems of cultural history, and the courage with which he advanced along untrodden trails remains an inspiration for others attacking such problems. He designed such a rich program and he set the objectives so well that he could serve as a guide for many who came after him. Much has been written about him and his histories, but, as far as I can see, nothing that deals with them in the perspective of the questions chosen in this book. So, Voltaire had to be my starting point.

Several of the other eighteenth-century historians would but have presented some contrast to Voltaire's outlook and the problems raised in his work. Gibbon was the greater historian, but his frame of reference does not seem very different from that of his enlightened predecessor. His subject is the story of an empire, and through half of the book only the Byzantine part of the empire, although he knew how to enrich his political narrative with social, religious, and cultural matter. Condorcet may have been even closer to Voltaire's position. When he differed from the old master, as in his demand for creating a history of the common man (a subject I have treated in another place), he left us his thought in fragments. Justus Moeser, in his *Osnabrückische Geschichte*, exhibited an awareness of the interrelations of social, administrative, and economic issues exceeding that of Voltaire, but his neglect of all other fields of civilization excludes him from this survey. A real and important contrast to Voltaire could be found in Herder's work. He discovered cultures as existing in the plural. He knew of the manifoldness of human existence which expresses itself in a series of characteristically different collective individualities. He came to history with a deep sense of its genetic direction. He gave the historian a rich and fresh formulation of his tasks. But the inclusion of Herder would have raised problems I preferred to avoid at this time. One would have been the problem of presenting two different phases of the man's thought. For, what the young Herder of *Auch eine Philosophie der Geschichte zur Bildung der Menschheit* suggested with enthusiastic fervor, the disciple of Kant took back, in part at least, in his later *Ideen zur Philosophie der Geschichte der Menschheit*. Herder, anyway, was less a historian of civilization than a philosopher of history. His creative suggestions found their superb concrete fulfilment in the work of Jacob Burckhardt.

From Burckhardt came my main inspiration in planning and writing this book. He was the cultural historian par excellence, and — for me — he remains the most illustrious representative of the genre. He was fully aware of the problems — most of all, the structural problem facing the historian of culture — and the way in which Burckhardt tried to solve them remains highly instructive for anyone who puts his hand to this task. He lightly disavowed any theory and any methodological preoccupation. But in his early and lasting devotion to the aesthetic and historical understanding of the graphic arts, he developed skills and techniques which he transferred with astonishing success to the writing of cultural history. This interlocking of Burckhardt the art historian with Burckhardt the historian of culture has been my particular concern in writing the chapter on him. He had learned from the painters, sculptors, and architects how to look, to visualize, and to compose. With these master skills he gave form, in analysis and presentation, to his vision of cultures in a manner that no man after him has been able to equal.

The choice among the other historians of the nineteenth century was in part conditioned by the central position of Burckhardt. Since he so clearly represented the historian who solves the structural problems by artistic devices rather than by reliance on theory and conceptual schemes, I preferred two flanking contrasts to him rather than other historical artists such as Macaulay, Mommsen, or Treitschke. The temptation to include Ranke never was strong. Despite the wide span of his interests, especially in the *Deutsche Geschichte* and the *Päpste*, Ranke remains chiefly the political historian.

Among the early nineteenth-century historians, Guizot most explicitly addressed himself to the problems of civilization. And he elaborated aspects of the problem which happily supplemented Voltaire's approach. He strove for a coherent view of the evolution of the West; he saw western history as one continuous process, as one decisive chapter in the growth of civilization. In a striking manner he fused into a clearly perceived personal equation such diverse ingredients as his commitment to Calvinism and Providence, the social thought of Robertson and Montesquieu, touches of German idealistic philosophy, and some of the ideas of the legal-historical school as it emerged during the Romantic movement. He so strongly emphasized the political and institutional aspects of civilization that some may deny him the title of a genuine cultural historian. Yet he developed a noteworthy conception of civilization which, despite all idiosyncratic elements, strongly appealed to his fellow bourgeois. That he has been so neglected as a historian, as well as a statesman, is hard to explain.

Among the later nineteenth-century historians I decided to treat Karl Lamprecht rather than such other candidates as Gustav Freytag, Fustel de Coulanges, Riehl, Buckle, Taine, or Renan. Some of these never presented themselves as serious possibilities because I was not sufficiently familiar with their work; on the other hand, a reading of Lamprecht, several years before the conception of this book, had drawn my attention to this controversial figure. He more and more seemed a fruitful contrast both to Burckhardt and to Huizinga. He was an arch-systematizer, an ardent "methodologist" and historical "scientist," and a vociferous advocate of cultural history, though more successful among the reading public than among his fellow historians. He aroused great hostility against his person as well as against the overly ambitious claims he made in defense of cultural history; he fought tenaciously; he rarely acknowledged his mistakes even when they were forced upon his attention. Many of his fundamental assumptions now seem wrong; but it is exactly from his errors that one can learn. Perhaps no other historian — except Spengler, to whom he was in many ways similar — can illustrate so well as Lamprecht the size of the tasks and problems facing the historian of civilization. His work points to the vicious dangers inherent in this branch of historical scholarship, but also to its potential rewards and to tasks which should not be shunned. Many strains of the rich historiographic developments of the nineteenth century met in this man. Despite (perhaps even because of) his controversial quality, it seemed better to include him than Buckle or Taine.

Huizinga is as clear a choice among the men of the twentieth century as Burckhardt is among those of the preceding one. His greatness lies in the sensitivity with which he conceived and the artistry with which he executed his cultural histories. But he supplemented these qualities by his sagacious speculations about the nature of culture and the tasks and habits of the cultural historian. It seemed to me especially challenging to attempt an analysis of *The Waning of the Middle Ages* in the light of the theoretical thought. But though this helped toward understanding the complicated structure of the book, it seems in retrospect to be both dangerous and even unfair to such a historian to bring his own, much less succinct, theoretical reflections too closely to his masterwork. Here, as with

Burckhardt, it becomes clear that the mode of working of a great cultural historian can hardly be expressed in a theoretical formula — not even by the historian himself. Unlike the works of Voltaire, Guizot, or Lamprecht, the works of the Swiss and the Dutchman do not easily yield their secrets to the analyst. But the search for these secrets remains ever challenging.

With Ortega y Gasset I was handicapped because, unlike the others, I was not able to read his work in the original language. Ortega wrote no history of civilization, although one can discern in several of his works how he might have done it. His importance for my investigation lies in his almost constant preoccupation with questions directly relevant to the problems of this book. He sought to understand what gives unity to human life and how a society acquires coherent interdependence of its parts. He thought much about culture as an expression of human needs and never tired of searching for unexpected interrelations among its different manifestations. He tried to suggest — perhaps without convincing most of his readers — how to account for the constant change in culture and society through the use of the idea of successive generations. He was, in all likelihood, the philosopher most deeply convinced of the basic historical nature of human existence. One may treat with justifiable skepticism his proud claims to originality where the parentage of the ideas often seems obvious; one may lament that he too frequently succumbed to the temptation to produce a sparkling metaphor instead of putting forward a simple, clear, and modest formulation of an idea; and one may admit that at times the verbal fireworks hide mere commonplaces. But despite such faults, Ortega y Gasset had a deliberate manner of philosophizing which incites independent thinking along some interesting avenues. I may be prejudiced in his favor; for many of the concerns underlying this book are derived from suggestions gleaned from his thought when I first encountered it during some difficult times in World War II. All of this may help to explain a choice that otherwise might have fallen upon Dilthey or

Max Weber, who probably made more original contributions to the thinking of twentieth-century historians. But there is a more objective justification of my choice. Weber's thoughts on history represent an ever renewed struggle with a recalcitrant matter upon which — when his untimely death interrupted his work — he had not yet imposed an order satisfying his own rigorous demands. This is true of his analysis of historical causation as well as — for our purpose so immensely relevant — of his forging of the conceptual instrument of the "ideal type." Fascinating insights, of direct relevance to the problems discussed in this book, can be found in Weber's *Ancient Judaism,* for instance, although he leaves unanswered the vexing question to what degree sociology of religion and cultural history are comparable in their methods. And although Dilthey's methodological conceptions are of extreme fruitfulness for any historian, his focus was upon *Geistesgeschichte* rather than *Kulturgeschichte.* Many of his relevant contributions, moreover, are duplicated in Ortega y Gasset. Probably the most fascinating and relevant line of thought flowing directly and implicitly from Weber's and Dilthey's work involves the use of representative men, or of specific personality types, as the focus of historical configuration. Aside from the fact that this is a vital matter in the earlier chapter on Burckhardt, a thorough critical discussion of it would be a treatise in itself.

From what I just have said, it should be obvious that I do not claim for the six essays brought together in this book any more subtle unity than the fact that all six men were faced with a common problem: how can one understand and present a complex cultural entity as a unified whole? Since, as I have pointed out, personal preferences and the basic frame of reference influence individual solutions to this problem, each chapter tries to establish briefly how the historian looked at life and why the problem of culture was important to him. But I restrict myself to a minimum of relevant information;

I do not aspire to any thumbnail intellectual biographies. Where the historian himself provided a set of programmatic statements, I condensed these statements into a summary. The core of each chapter consists of an analysis of the manner in which the historian conceived of the unity and the inter-relations of parts within a civilization; this is followed (except with Ortega y Gasset) by a look at his mode of presenting his vision as a full-length picture of civilization. The book is almost exclusively based on a textual analysis of the works of these six historians. It was not planned as a systematic survey of cultural historiography. I have taken notice of contributions made by other scholars; but I have refrained from polemical discussion in order to concentrate on my proper task.

1 : *Voltaire*
1694 - 1778

Throughout many centuries western men accounted for their past by telling the fate of empires and the works of "God's people." By the eighteenth century this customary view of history had been seriously weakened by the stretching of the European horizon to encompass the entire world. Man's knowledge of civilized and uncivilized peoples had increased substantially. It was time "to stop insulting all sects and nations"[1] as if they were mere appendages to the history of a chosen people. Knowledge of other traditions, especially that attained from the Chinese records, necessitated a rethinking of chronology.[2] "Exotic" peoples became more interesting than those Greeks and Romans whom the humanists had raised to divine stature for centuries. "What the telescope was for astronomy, became for history the enlarged view over Israel, Hellas, Rome, Turks, Hindus, Persians, and Chinese, and even the noble savage of America who had occupied the minds of men since the days of Montaigne."[3] Heathens could no longer be treated as neglected children of God. Acquaintance with great systems of thought such as Confucianism, and the civilized modes of life built on them, raised doubts about the superiority of Europeans. The perspectives of a wider horizon and the comparison of cultures had undermined the traditional views of the past.

---

[1] Voltaire, *Essai sur les moeurs*, in *Oeuvres complètes*, XI, 192 (hereafter cited as *Essai* and *O.C.*).

[2] A major point in Kaegi, *Historische Meditationen*, I, 239. See also *Essai*, in *O.C.*, XI, 151.

[3] Johan Huizinga, "Natuurbeeld en historiebeeld in de achttiende eeuw," in *Verzamelde Werken* (9 vols.; Haarlem: Tjeenk Willink, 1948–53), IV, 352.

Social and intellectual changes in European life also contributed to the gradual decline of traditional historiography. Those who were aware of the social transformation, who recognized the weakness of an old aristocracy and the rising strength of a middle class, who perceived that industry and commerce affected the course of history more decisively than the acts of heroes, could not be satisfied with traditional accounts of political and military history. The growing sense of material and cultural well-being, a respect for work and ingenuity, rising hopes for a better future — all increased man's self-respect and self-reliance. He was inclining toward the pursuits of this life and was less willing to accept life as a mere pilgrimage. Man's own works interposed themselves between him and the hereafter. The providential explanation of events had lost its hold over the minds of men who took personal pride in the accomplishments of civilized existence and who had learned to understand the universe by reference to three simple Newtonian laws.

This reversal of man's orientation had been in preparation for a long time. By the early decades of the eighteenth century the historical discipline was as ripe for a new comprehensive formulation as physical science had been at the times of Galileo and Newton, or philosophy at the time of Bacon and Descartes. Intellectual revolutions are rarely wrought by single men, and yet there is reason for beginning the "new history" with Voltaire. The separate strands of a drawn-out development came together in his work. He broke with that traditional providential history last expressed in Bossuet's great synthesis. He also turned away from the style and form of humanist historiography. He pulled together the methodological discussions of the age of erudition and overcame the Pyrrhonic skepticism left in the wake of Bayle's incisive questions.[4] But, most important, Voltaire focused historical atten-

---

[4] The best discussion of Voltaire's historical method is in John H. Brumfitt, *Voltaire, Historian*, and in Paul Sakmann, "Die Probleme der historischen Methodik"; for a succinct discussion of Bayle's influence on method see the chapter on history in Ernst Cassirer, *Die Philosophie der Aufklärung.*

tion upon a newly conceived unit of study by replacing the history of empires and God's people with the history of civilization. His work has long since been assessed. Yet, in the context of my investigation, I must ask once more: What was his conception of man? What was his conception of civilization? How were these two conceptions related? And how did he use them to make the course of history comprehensible to his audience?

What was left to men who could no longer find a meaningful explanation of their existence in the traditional Christian view? Voltaire answered this question often during his long life, but he never condensed his answer into a short formula.[5] He drew practical consequences from the revolution brought about by Copernicus and Newton. *Sub specie stellarum* man lived on an insignificant speck of cosmic mud. A reasonable man would smile at the assertions that this atom is the center of the cosmos, or that every part of the magnificent celestial clockwork turns around this puny planet. Nor was there cause to think this earth a garden prepared for men. Three-quarters of this tiny globe is water, and the remainder is largely desert, swamp, mountains, jungle, and forest. The belt around the middle is parched by the sun and the poles are buried under ice. The crust is occasionally shaken by quakes which thoughtlessly and mercilessly entomb the work of man. Pouring rain and melting ice can flood arable land, and hail and wind destroy harvests. Nature cares not for man's wishes but follows its own inexorable laws.

Man is a complicated and brittle mechanism, smaller than the whale, weaker than the tiger, slower than the gazelle, and so awkward compared to the bird. He is subject to death and the inevitable transformation of matter. On the average he is but five and one-half feet tall — even when a Prussian king

---

[5] The subsequent summary of Voltaire's view of man is based largely on the letters, the *contes*, the *Dictionnaire philosophique*, the *Mélanges*, and the poems. I shall give citations only for quotations and some statements of special importance.

puts a high grenadier hat on him. Instinct explains most human motion: hunger must be gratified, and self-love stimulates the desire for preservation and propagation. But men are also endowed with a sense of compassion and beneficence. They are social creatures by instinct and they can communicate. Above all, man is a sentient being and he reasons about his sense experiences. He can count, measure, judge right from wrong, and feel both pain and pleasure. His reason is sufficient to unravel the mechanical laws of the universe and the moral law in men. If he uses his reason correctly, he can see things for what they are. He can understand that "he marches with his feet, digests with his stomach, feels with his body and thinks with his head." [6] If he is wise, he learns to resign himself to stay within these limits of his capacities. Such cautious resignation, to be sure, is not easy; many disturbing questions remain unanswered. What is the soul? And is it immortal? Where do I come from and where do I go? Why and how can I think? Why am I so imperfect and why is there evil in this garden? Desperate over the inability of reason and experience to solve these riddles, men unbridle their reason and escape into superstition and mystical nonsense. They substitute pretense of knowledge for the wisdom of resignation. Freed from the restraint of doubt, and intoxicated with answers unjustified by reason, men become a plague to themselves and others. They becloud the mind, which needs clarity to see, and endow their hocus-pocus with the sanction of fabled divinities. They impose their errors and false gods on gullible brothers and drive truth into hiding at the bottom of a well. They pursue the doubter with sword, rack, and torch. With superstition and fanaticism, those two "denatured daughters of religion," we make society a hell.

In inimitable stories, Voltaire led charmingly innocent earthlings through the chaotic experiences of life. Suffering illness and pain, endangered by earthquakes and storms at

---

[6] *Dictionnaire philosophique*, in *O.C.*, XVII, 163 (hereafter cited as *Dictionnaire*).

sea, they learn that this globe was not created as their paradise. And after nature has unleashed all her evils, they yet have to cope with man-made disasters: unrequited love, arbitrary exercise of power, unpredictable reactions of irrational men, bad cooking, the idiocies of Bulgar wars, crimes committed in the name of justice, the overweening pride of stultiloquent fools, the life-endangering encounter with superstitious fanatics, and the soul-endangering exposure to bad poetry — to say nothing of the rack or auto-da-fé. Good-natured and to the end trusting in man's humanity, our better Voltairian selves — Candide, Zadig, the Huron Ingénu — tumble from one human experience into another, clearly demonstrating that man, though good within measure, is but precariously endowed for the good life. On a heap of mud, lost in the immense universe, a universe not made for him, in an environment at best indifferent, often hostile, man must live within his means.

We vainly seek for a given meaning in this chaotic life. We must provide it ourselves and we have but one way to save ourselves: we can build civilization. Voltaire summed up the meaning of human existence in an overquoted but ever significant remark: we must cultivate our garden.[7] By pooling years of labor, humanity may form a social life which blends wisdom, morality, material welfare, order, and aesthetic well-being.

Man can acquire a measure of wisdom by using his reason properly. He must be skeptical without hanging himself on the gibbet of hyperskepticism. Though plagued by tempting and unanswerable questions man can safely assure himself that "two and two make four."[8] He can avoid gross error by using his senses prudently. With careful observation, discriminating argument, and constant testing, science can furnish a realistic understanding of the surrounding world. Through

---

[7] This, of course, is taken from the very last lines of *Candide*; as the reader can see, my argument is heavily based on the assumption that Voltaire meant these lines as a defense of civilization against chaos and not merely as advice for attaining a peaceful personal life.

[8] *Dictionnaire*, in *O.C.*, XIX, 548, and XX, 120.

Newton's disclosure of the inner mechanics of the celestial clockwork man can humbly orient himself in the universe. And with a clear concept of the physical realities he can try to arrive at a fruitful accommodation with the globe on which he has been placed. The haunting disaster of Lisbon's earthquake in 1755 challenges the assumption that we ever can become nature's master, but we can attempt to carve out a small realm for our own work. We can learn to live with nature and can persuade her to work for us. By painstaking labor we can coax nature to release some of her bounty. The silkworm can be made to spin for us. Our ingenuity can supply us with artifacts; and by constructing watches, we can even imitate the greater marvels of creation. Work is life's greatest blessing, the best antidote for boredom, vice, and sorrow; and work is the creative force that wrests our "garden" from nature. Like Candide, tempted by the irrepressible *raisonnements* of Dr. Pangloss, we must summon ourselves to work again and again with the exhortation, "But we must cultivate." The question of conscience is always: "Do you build? and do you plant?" [9] As the landlord of Ferney, Voltaire proudly answered, Yes, I care for my tenants of Gex, my mulberry trees feed the silkworms who give work to my silk spinners, and my little colony of watchmakers has a market for its ingenious product among my princely friends.

When man follows reason, he is a moral and a social being. The moral law for him is simple: Adore God and be just and do not do unto others what you would not wish to have done unto yourself.[10] An undistorted view of the world mechanism

[9] *Lettres*, I, 369. Several decades later, Goethe's Faust, after a long search for a meaning of human existence, also resigned himself to useful work (in this case gaining land from the sea) as the only way of human self-fulfilment. For Voltaire's own account of his work at Ferney see *Lettres*, II, 199, 211, 268, 289, 298, and "Défense de Louis XIV contre l'auteur des Ephémérides," in *Oeuvres historiques*, p. 1283 (hereafter cited as *O.H.*).

[10] When Voltaire discussed Confucius in the *Essai*, he expressed his preference for the positive formulation of the golden rule: "Il ne dit point: Ne fais aux autres ce que tu ne voudrais pas qu'on te fît; mais: Fais aux autres ce que tu veux qu'on te fasse" (*O.C.*, XI, 176).

tells of a wise geometer and master watchmaker. "A catechist announces God to children and Newton has demonstrated him to the wise." [11] Man's morality depends on recognizing this fact. A society of atheists seemed to Voltaire an impossibility.[12] We know little of God but all thinking men have acknowledged him. He may not be a moral lawgiver; it is sufficient for man to be endowed with compassion for his fellows and with an instinctive sense of justice. If we neither overrate men as angels nor underrate them as animals,[13] we can make life bearable by helping and tolerating one another. We must practice tolerance because wisdom on many questions is hardly attainable; and there is surely nothing sillier for a weak creature, moving over the shifting sands of existence, than to believe himself correct all the time. And in addition, we must be left free to fulfil our social task. Since the good life depends on that tiny measure of knowledge open to us, we must be free to think, free to believe, and free to move. Within the limits of order and common justice, we must be free to use our energies and gifts for our own and others' benefit.

Voltaire did not believe in the actual equality of all men. As the world goes, not all can play the same role, though we all play under the same rules. The multitude can do little more

---

[11] *Dictionnaire*, in *O.C.*, XVII, 476; see also *Essai*, in *O.C.*, XI, 180, and *Lettres*, I, 252. The sincerity of Voltaire's belief in God has often been questioned; among the mildest doubters is Louis Gottschalk: "One sometimes feels that the old rascal was an atheist, but too fearful of public opinion to admit it" (*The Era of the French Revolution* [Boston: Houghton Mifflin, 1929], p. 65). Personally I lean toward the conviction that Voltaire was a deist and that he was fearful of an atheistic society; see also Ira Owen Wade, *Voltaire and Candide*, p. 261.

[12] Among many remarks see *Essai*, in *O.C.*, XI, 180, XII, 322; *Dictionnaire*, in *O.C.*, XVII, 456, 462, 472; and *Mélanges*, in *O.C.*, XXVI, 315–29, XXIX, 282.

[13] ". . . l'homme enfin qui n'est pas bête, et qui ne croit point être ange" (*Dictionnaire*, in *O.C.*, XX, 416); and "Inexplicables humains . . . comment pouvez-vous réunir tant de bassesse et de grandeur, tant de vertus et de crimes?" ("Le monde comme il va," in *Romans et contes*, p. 75). That man is a paradox is nicely stated in the title of Voltaire's story "Micromegas" — the little-big one.

than be good husbandmen and skilful artisans. Let us not expect more from them than that they love God and their neighbor and that they sell their vegetables at reasonable prices.[14] They fulfil their necessary social task and can hope for God's mercy, if they act as good husbands, good fathers, good neighbors, good subjects, and good gardeners. Without the simple virtues and the discipline of good laws they degenerate into meddlesome *canaille*. Since men are so rarely worthy of governing themselves,[15] the best hope for a decent society lies with the good mandarins who devote themselves to making life tolerable for all. If magistrates are wise, they make a few good laws — clear, uniform, and concise — and administer these justly. The more their actions accord with a deep respect for the humanity of man, the more enlightened their rule. If, as a result, they preserve peace and order and promote men's material welfare, their part is perfectly played.

When peace and just order are preserved, when fanatic superstition is curbed, when men are assured of a measure of the good and useful things, then some can devote themselves to the task of elevating human existence to a higher level. There are those who cultivate the garden of the mind and heart by refining thought and sentiment, by writing and reading, by experimenting on nature and inventing useful things, and by giving ever more adornment to human life. Though they are the privileged of leisure, their function is a profoundly social one. This community of *esprit* and *goût* (good taste)[16] leavens the commonwealth with cultural accomplishments. True society is formed by the refinement of the art of communication. Thus cities, with their ease of communication, are the home of this aristocracy of the mind. In the polished atmosphere of salons, men of equal standing exchange thoughts and sentiments while genteel ladies, with

---

[14] "Catechisme du jardinier," *Dictionnaire*, in *O.C.*, XVIII, 86–88.

[15] *Dictionnaire*, in *O.C.*, XIX, 33, XX, 185; *Essai*, in *O.C.*, XI, 528.

[16] The notion of *goût* is of central importance in any discussion of Voltaire; for the best treatise on the subject see Raymond Naves, *Le goût de Voltaire*.

their highly civilizing influence, guard the whole. And the exquisitely developed art of letterwriting unites a widespread community of cultured minds.[17] A careful concern for the elegance and norms of language is as much a ticket of entrance as are propriety of thought and sentiment and gentility of manners. And the theater, rather than a mere distraction and an escape into a world of make-believe, is a means for expressing and propagating perfectly blended reason and sentiment. It is not a time-killer for lazy parasites but the symbol of culture. For culture is the work of art whereby men rescue themselves from senseless chaos. Culture is men's great drama. By an urbanized, refined human intercourse, where each subtly attuned fiber of the *esprit* and sentiment vibrates, where polished manner has banished all grossness, we achieve a worthy existence. If the sober mind, unwilling to deceive itself, even then cannot say that this is the best of all possible worlds, at least it can admit that "all is passable." [18]

Voltaire dedicated a long, long life and the sweat of his genius to the spread of civilization. Yet he had no such words as "civilization" or "culture." The abstract noun civilization, as a collective term for the total civilized condition of society, remained apparently uncoined during most of Voltaire's life.[19] Probably it did not appear before 1766. After 1770 the word gains some currency and appears, though sparsely used, in the writings of Badeau, Raynal, Diderot, Helvetius, Holbach, and Grimm. The word is equally young in the English language. In 1772 Dr. Johnson still prefers "civilty" as the

---

[17] The best road of access to Voltaire himself is his correspondence.

[18] "Ituriel . . . résolut de ne pas même songer à corriger Persépolis, et de *laisser aller le monde comme il va.* Car, dit-il, *si tout n'est pas bien, tout est passable*" ("Le monde comme il va" in *Romans et contes,* pp. 87–88; Voltaire's italics).

[19] Most of the following rests on a paper by Lucien Febvre, "Civilisation, évolution d'un mot et d'un groupe d'idées," in *Civilisation; le mot et l'idée* (Paris: Centre International de Synthèse, Première semaine internationale, fasc. 2, 1929), pp. 1–55.

less "barbarous" term. Robertson was one of the first historians to use the word; but in 1771 a French translation of his book substituted the word *raffinement*. The French Académie included the word *civilisation* for the first time in the 1798 edition of its normative dictionary. Voltaire knew the word *culture* (which has a much more complicated history)[20] but did not use it in quite the modern sense. It was not considered a collective noun for either the total cultured condition of a society or a society characterized by cultured conditions. With such a connotation the word culture first seems to have been used by the German philologist Johann Christoph Adelung after 1774.

Voltaire resorted to a variety of other terms. He utilized such notions as "society," "nation," and "people" when speaking of entities which possessed civilized traits. The word *siècle* served to indicate periods characterized by a specific state of cultured life. He used the verb *civiliser* and the adjective *civilisé*, already used by Montaigne and Descartes in this sense, in contrast to everything barbarous. He favored the term *policer* in a variety of usages; as *politesse* it described for him an urbane mode of life befitting the most cultivated circles. The notion of *raffinement* appeared largely in connection with matters of taste and manners. Stages in the development of thought and opinion were usually measured against the term *éclairer* and its derivatives. Like other thinkers of the Enlightenment, Voltaire characterized certain aspects of a man-worthy existence by the complex Latin concept *humanitas* in its French near-equivalent *humanité*. And he employed the word *culture* in its old meaning of *cultura*, "care" and "cultivation." Occasionally he applied it to matters which

---

[20] E. Tonnelat, "Kultur, histoire du mot, évolution du sens," *ibid.*, pp. 61–73; and see above all Joseph Niedermann, *Kultur: Werden und Wandlungen des Begriffes und seiner Ersatzbegriffe von Cicero bis Herder*, Biblioteca dell' Archivum Romanicum, Ser. 1, Vol. XXVIII (Florence: Bibliopolis, 1941). As a *Sammelbegriff* for a human group with a specific mode of existence the word was rarely used before the nineteenth century. The later distinction between civilization and *Kultur* is inappropriate for Voltaire.

require the carefully cultivating hand of the good husband-man. One can cultivate letters, good taste, good sentiments, and good manners. The young poet used it in the sense of education or upbringing when he blamed Charles IX's despicable behavior on his "funeste culture." [21] If the old landlord of Ferney meant to summarize the meaning of human existence in his final sentence of *Candide* ("Mais il faut cultiver notre jardin"), he used his agricultural term in a wonderfully concrete and transcendent sense.

But while Voltaire had to shift without the verbal concept, he had a concrete conception of civilization. While his discussion of the phenomenon of civilization seems unsystematic in method and concept to moderns, Voltaire had a clear, concrete image of the good human life. Voltaire was no utopian and no system-builder. He did not, like some of his contemporaries, propagandize idealized conceptions of a better society. He did not waste his energies on elaborate blueprints for a new Cockayne; nor did he ever revel in the visionary delirium of chiliasts. A sober *philosophe* sees the world for what it is and avoids wishful thinking. Of course, Voltaire was not content to accept the mere status quo; society can always be reformed a little. A wise man's resignation is never moronic submissiveness but acquiescence in the limitations of human existence and the acceptance of a lifelong task. A reform program must be both possible and plausible; it must be more than unsubstantiated speculations about the human potential. There is greater promise in studying man as he is and has been than in the intoxicating suppositions of system-builders who forget the human realities. Civilization, life's saving grace, need not be constructed from the imagination; it is and has been a reality even if only parts of it existed here and there. Any thinking Frenchman — especially if he knew England,

---

[21] *Henriade*, canto 3, verse 11; see also *Essai*, in *O.C.*, XII, 153, on Charles VIII ("Sans aucune culture dans l'esprit"). It is revealing, however, that the usually excellent *Table générale et analytique*, Vols. LI and LII of the *Oeuvres complètes* says under *culture*: "voyez agriculture, terres."

Holland, and Italy as well, and was farsighted enough to understand China, India, and Islam — could see the manifest evidence of cultured life around and in himself. What was civilization if it was not the reality of Racine's refined language, the awesome beauty and clarity of Newton's world view, the sane empiricism of Locke, the enlightened spirit of Diderot or d'Alembert, the humane welfare policy of Colbert or Turgot, the ingenuity of a Swiss watch, the ennobling humor of Molière or La Fontaine, the active commerce of London and Amsterdam, the epic of Ariosto, the prose of Pascal or Bossuet, the sparkling meeting of minds in urbane salons, the humanity of a Chinese emperor as well as of a landlord at Ferney, and the charming solace of contact with refined women like Emilie du Châtelet or Madame Deffand? Most ingredients of the good life could be studied in concrete realizations. And, four times, whole societies approached a pervasive state of civilization so that they could be looked upon as great examples: the age of Alexander (Sophocles, Socrates, Phidias), the age of Augustus (Virgil, Cicero, Horace, Ovid), the time of Leo X (Raphael, Ariosto, Tasso), and the *siècle de Louis XIV*.[22]

The culture of the age of Louis XIV played a very special role in all of Voltaire's thought. His own life reached back into the last decades of Louis's reign. When Voltaire began work on the history of the age, the "ouvrage de toute ma vie," Louis XIV had been in his grave but fourteen years.[23] Many of the great thinkers, statesmen, and artists were alive when Voltaire was a young man. Locke and Newton, his symbols of the new wisdom, died when he was ten and thirty-three,

---

[22] *Siècle de Louis XIV*, in *O.H.*, pp. 616–20 and 1015; and *Défense de Louis XIV*, in *O.H.*, pp. 1285–86. As can be seen from the examples, Voltaire used the term "age" for periods which extended beyond the chronology of the respective eponymus Alexander, Leo, *et al.*

[23] Quoted in Brumfitt, p. 48; the work was apparently begun in 1729 but first published in 1751. Though the *Siècle de Louis XIV* cannot be said to have been Voltaire's life work, he worked all his life at glorifying and defending the age of the great king.

respectively. The living encounter with this historical high point strengthened and colored Voltaire's conception of true civilized existence. To some degree it separated him from the later *philosophes* who never fully shared his admiration. He became increasingly perturbed as he noticed his younger contemporaries turning their backs on the age. Condorcet recounts how Voltaire, as a dying old man, desperately labored on a plan to speak once more to his countrymen about the greatness of Louis XIV's age and to protect it against the rising tide of calumniators.[24]

The *grand siècle* was not a full realization of Voltaire's ideal of civilization although it seemed the high-water mark of men's efforts to lift themselves out of a chaotic existence. Seventeenth-century France was still tainted by too much Christian superstition and too many unwise policies. And yet this age — especially when understood in the broadest sense, which included the accomplishments of the English and the Dutch — brought men nearer to true civilization than any other. "The *siècle* of Louis XIV, *siècle* of great men, of fine arts and *politesse* . . . was like all others marred by public and private calamities which are inseparable from human nature; but it seems as if all that can console men in the misery of their weak and perishable condition was lavished on that century." [25] Innovations in the arts and government, refinement of spirit and manners, veritable revolutions in science which had gradual effects on philosophy, and the great advances in material welfare gave, to western Europe at least, a forceful example of the good life which even the enlightened eighteenth century could surpass and equal only in parts. And in some realms such perfection was attained that the examples became true models. The "arts of life," good manners, and those refine-

---

[24] Condorcet, *Oeuvres*, IV, 207. Much of Voltaire's concern arose over the stir created by the publication of Saint Simon's *Mémoires*. "Il voulait prévenir l'effet que ces Mémoires pourraient produire, s'ils devenaient publics dans un temps ou il ne restera plus personne assez voisin des événements pour démentir avec avantage des faits avancés par un contemporain."
[25] *Précis du siècle de Louis XV*, in *O.H.*, p. 1299 (hereafter cited as *Précis*).

ments of social intercourse (*politesse*)— polished behavior and the sensibilities of decorum and good taste — were so highly developed that France became the school of Europe. Even more outstanding were the heights reached in the fine arts. During that period the French language became a superb instrument of communication, and the great writers taught the nation to think, to feel, and to express itself. Any refined spirit who cared for the arts was bound to admire that age. It was to Voltaire's thinking decidedly a mark of barbarism to remain insensitive to the majestic force of Corneille's beautiful scenes, the inimitable language of Racine, the beautiful *Epîtres* of Boileau and his *Art poétique*, the charming fables of La Fontaine, some of the unequaled operas of Quinault, and, above all, the comic and philosophic genius of Molière.[26] It must be considered an age above ages, when a great king and his refined court, when a soldier such as Condé or Turenne, a practical statesman such as Colbert, and a host of superior men in many fields enriched their daily life by listening to the magnificent heroes of Corneille and Racine, the wit of Molière, the music of Lully, and the elevating prose of Bossuet and Bourdaloue. "Such times will not come again when a Duc de la Rochefoucauld, author of *Maximes*, can come from a conversation with a Pascal or an Arnauld and then go to Corneille's theater."[27] Here were those models frequently forgotten by the young men of the second half of the eighteenth century. Here were the true guides who could introduce men to those finer things which make life bearable. Here were trail-blazers who had prepared the flourishing of good taste and sane sense in all realms of existence and who as poets had created unsurpassed, and perhaps unsurpassable, works. How could this age of genius be explained? What accounted for this burst of brilliance and this unequaled concentration of great men and works? Why did such a constellation of cultural activity occur at that time? How did it

---

[26] *Défense de Louis XIV*, in *O.H.*, p. 1284.
[27] *Siècle de Louis XIV*, in *O.H.*, p. 1012.

compare to the other great creative moments of the past? Why were such civilized periods so rare? What were their consequences? And is it reasonable to count on the indefinite continuation of the present high level of cultivation and on still higher cultural peaks for the future?

These were all questions which Voltaire was not inclined to answer by mere speculation. Answers to such questions could only be attained (if at all) by turning to history. In this eighteenth century of rather ahistorical *philosophes*, the arch-*philosophe* Voltaire turned to history, a discipline over-shadowed at his time by the enormous success of physics. Voltaire, who contributed so greatly to the popularization of Newtonian mechanics by his *Lettres philosophiques* and the *Eléments de la philosophie de Newton*, later became concerned that the intellectual climate might be tyrannized by physics, cosmology, and philosophy (i.e., natural science). "Everyone begins to play the geometer and physicist. One dabbles in speculation [*On se mêle de raisonner*]. Sentiment, imagination, and the graces are banished. . . . I am not annoyed that philosophy is being cultivated, but I do not wish her to become a tyrant who excludes all the rest. She is a fashion in France which succeeds another and will pass in turn; but no art, no science should be a fashion. They all must hold each other by the hand; they must be cultivated all at a time." [28] Although these specific words were meant to rescue the arts, they were uttered at a time when the poet and essayist had become increasingly steeped in historical labors. The more his friend Madame du Châtelet praised science and denigrated history, the more Voltaire was stirred to disprove such historical skepticism.[29] He possessed a sense for the development of human things and the fortuity of events. He knew that the high culture under Louis XIV was both a crea-

---

[28] *Lettres*, I, 154.
[29] See Brumfitt, pp. 24 and 61, on reasons for writing the *Essai sur les moeurs*.

tive act of the moment and the result of long and toilsome preparation.[30] As a poet he was conscious of the centuries needed for the development of language. It takes time to spread truth, good taste, and fine manners.[31] And superstition dies slowly. True, a single heroic "cultivator" like Peter the Great could work civilizing wonders by introducing arts and sciences and reforms into barbarian regions; but Peter was a borrower. Voltaire displayed him as an example to the civilized but less energetic West. "The rulers of states long civilized [policés] will say to one another: 'If in the icy clime of ancient Scythia one man, aided only by his genius, accomplished such great feats, what must we now do in realms where the accumulated labor of several centuries makes everything easy for us.' "[32] Civilization was essentially the accumulated labor of many men. The whys and wherefores of its vicissitudinous career, the specific hows of its development could be answered only through history. And even if a historical understanding of civilization were to shun the innumerable irrelevancies of accident, the accidental still could not be completely discounted. For the fate of civilization often hung in the balance awaiting the outcome of precarious events. Voltaire would probably not have shared Bayle's opinion that a crooked nose on Cleopatra would have changed the course of history; but he understood that a Persian victory at Salamis, a victory of the Guises, a victory of the Armada, would have altered the course of civilization. Unpredictability remains part of life and only historical hindsight enlightens certain issues. "Romulus did not believe that he founded Rome for the Gothic kings or the bishops. Alexander did not imagine that Alex-

---

[30] Lettres, II, 233.

[31] Among many references see Essai, in O.C., XI, 63, 162 ("Il a fallu partout, non seulement un espace de temps prodigieux, mais des circonstances heureuses, pour que l'homme s'élevat au-dessus de la vie animale"), 291, XII, 434 (". . . il faut bien des siècles pour que la société humaine se perfectionne"), and XIII, 122.

[32] Concluding sentence of Histoire de l'empire de Russie sous Pierre le Grand, in O.H., p. 598 (hereafter cited as Russie).

andria would belong to the Turks, and Constantine did not build Constantinople for Mohammed II." [33]

But when Voltaire turned to the historians for an explanation of the course of human development, he found none who told much about what was important for civilization. "There are a thousand chroniclers, but hardly two or three modern historians." [34] The standard historians did not see the real achievement of man. They generally dwelt on the fate of dynasties and the affairs of war. Under those aspects, they wrote some interesting works which Voltaire acknowledged as such,[35] but the true story of man could not be told in terms of the state. Another historical tradition was ecclesiastical history, or providential history in the style of Bossuet. Voltaire revered the great Gallican bishop and tied his own world history to Bossuet's unfinished sketch, but the *Discours sur l'histoire universelle* was the history of "the chosen people." [36] Voltaire could not accept such wilful limitation. How could the story of the Christian God's chosen people be universal history to the cosmopolitans of the eighteenth century? The remaining historical output was devoted to biography, a genre in which Voltaire had made his own entry as historian with his book on Charles XII. What there was of attempts to describe cultural achievements was buried in biographical sketches of artists and scientists. Only during Voltaire's lifetime, but presumably unknown to him, did Johann Joachim Winckelmann make art instead of artists the content of art history. Biography was poorly suited for coping with Voltaire's broad concept of civilization. If he wanted an appropriate form for the true history of man, he had to create it himself.

Voltaire often proclaimed his intention to write *histoire*

---

[33] *Essai*, in *O.C.*, XI, 151. See also *ibid.*, XI, 253, and XII, 110.
[34] "Lettre à Nordberg," in *O.H.*, p. 306.
[35] Brumfitt, pp. 27–30.
[36] See foreword to the *Essai*, in *O.C.*, XI, 158; and also *Siècle de Louis XIV*, in *O.H.*, pp. 1005, 1141, and *Lettres*, I, 332.

en philosophe, and he built an entire program around that phrase.[37] He did not dream of what we would mean by the phrase "philosophy of history" but thought instead of a history viewed in the spirit of an enlightened eighteenth-century *philosophe.* It meant that history had to be written by men who understood the important things in human life. *Homo sum, humani nil a me alienum puto.*[38] Above all it meant that history had to be true and useful (*vrai et utile*). It was time to clear away the immense accumulation of useless fables about the past. "What usually is missing in those who compile history is the philosophic spirit: most write stories for children instead of discussing facts with men." [39] *Soyons en garde contre toute fable!*[40] whether it concerns unbelievable tales by Egyptians, Greeks, Romans, Jews, or Christians. Let us substitute for our customary credulity some sound critical skepticism. Voltaire made no excessive claims about attaining absolute certainty in history; many matters may never be knowable. "The secrets of hearts are so little known": how can we hope to understand the motives of a Constantine; how can we get complete insights into the complex quarrels of Elizabeth and Mary Stuart? [41] Neither the judge nor the historian can ascertain all details. A historian with perspective, therefore, will be content with knowing the great events and the general development of customs. His knowledge will be certain enough when it is probable. "In physics let us admit only that which is proven, and in history only that

---

[37] For use of the phrase see *Nouvelles considérations sur l'histoire,* in *O.H.,* p. 48 (hereafter cited as *Nouvelles considérations*); "Lettre à Dubos," in *O.H.,* p. 607; and Brumfitt, p. 46.

[38] A favorite quotation of Voltaire taken from Terence, *Heautontimoroumenos,* I, 1.

[39] *Remarques sur l'histoire,* in *O.H.,* pp. 41–43.

[40] *Essai,* in *O.C.,* XI, 37; see also *ibid.,* XI, 161, XIII, 174, and "Qu'il faut savoir doubter éclaircissements sur *L'Histoire de Charles XII,*" in *O.H.,* pp. 311–16 (hereafter cited as "Qu'il faut savoir doubter").

[41] "Lettre à Schulenbourg," in *O.H.,* p. 298; "Lettre à Roques," in *O.H.,* p. 1268; and *Essai,* in *O.C.,* XI, 237, XII, 494; see also *Lettres,* II, 234.

which possesses the greatest known probability." [42] The ever ready measuring rod must be the enlightened skeptic's knowledge of nature and man. "Let us refuse our credence to all historians, ancient and modern, who report matters which are contrary to nature and the human heart [*à la trempe du coeur humain*]." [43]

But not everything true or probable is therefore useful as well. And a "philosophic history" must meet the demand of usefulness. "All that has happened does not deserve to be written up." [44] And the man who has an important story to tell cannot worry about useless detail. "It concerns me very little whether Colbert had eyebrows thick and close together, a coarse and common physiognomy, and icy manner; that he joined concern for great things with small trifling vanities. I have kept my eye on the memorable things he did, on the recognition which centuries to come will owe him, not on the way in which he wore his neckband and the bourgeois manner he retained, according to the king, at court." [45] "I want to say useful verities, not verities fit for *historiettes*." [46] Of course sometimes a bagatelle is significant. Pope Julius II was the first to grow a new style of beard; that is a small observation, but of interest to a history of manners. [47] In deciding what is and is not useful, Voltaire made some of his most interesting programmatic statements for a new history. He wishes to receive genuine instruction and not satisfaction for his curi-

[42] *Essai*, in *O.C.*, XI, 164. For other references supporting this point see *ibid.*, XI, 41, 86, and the statement on 152: "The histories of Rome report events which are quite possible but not very likely." See also "Lettre au Journal des Savants," in *O.H.*, p. 303, and "Lettre à Roques," in *O.H.*, p. 1241.

[43] "Qu'il faut savoir douter," in *O.H.*, p. 314; and *Essai*, in *O.C.*, XI, 36, 72.

[44] *Siècle de Louis XIV*, in *O.H.*, p. 620; see also "Notes sur les 'Remarques' de La Motraye," in *O.H.*, p. 284, and "Qu'il faut savoir douter," in *O.H.*, p. 315.

[45] "Lettre à Roques," in *O.H.*, p. 1256.

[46] *Ibid.*, p. 1268.

[47] *Essai*, in *O.C.*, XII, 245.

osity.[48] "What does it matter by which entry Louis the Fat entered the ramshackle houses of Puiset? A citizen wants to know by what degrees the government changed form, what the rights and usurpations of different bodies were, what was being done in the Estates General, and what the spirit of the nation was." [49] Most interesting was Voltaire's attack on the innumerable irrelevancies in Montesquieu's *Esprit des lois*:

I am waiting to learn how decretals changed the entire jurisprudence of the ancient code of Roman law; by what laws Charlemagne ruled his realm; and by what anarchy feudal government toppled it; by what art and audacity Gregory VII and his successors wiped out the laws of kingdoms and great fiefs under the ring of the fisherman, and by what strokes one succeeded in destroying papal legislation; . . . I wish to know the history of the laws under which our ancestors lived; the reasons why they were established, neglected, destroyed, renewed; I seek a thread in that labyrinth; the thread breaks in almost every paragraph. I have been deceived, I found the *esprit* of the author, who has much, and rarely the *esprit* of the laws. He hops more than he marches; he amuses more than he enlightens; he satirizes sometimes more than he judges; and one would hope that such a fine genius would always have sought to instruct rather than astound.[50]

The characteristic remark for the program is the phrase "I seek a thread in that labyrinth." For Voltaire's history this thread was man's struggle for a decent civilized life. He wanted to concern himself with the history of the *esprit humain*, with man's ingenuity, with nations' significant customs, and with the true consolations of life. What was society and family life like? What arts were cultivated? Did war impoverish or enrich this nation? Did Spain really benefit materially from the conquest of the New World? Why did Amsterdam's popula-

---

[48] *Nouvelles considérations*, in *O.H.*, p. 47, and "Lettre à Roques," in *O.H.*, pp. 1265-66.
[49] A critique of the Jesuit historian Gabriel Daniel contained in the *liste raisonnée* of the *Siècle de Louis XIV*, in *O.H.*, p. 1154.
[50] *Idées républicaines*, in *Mélanges* (ed. Heuvel), pp. 523-24.

tion grow from some 20,000 souls to more than 240,000 in barely a century? And how reliable are such figures? What policies make a country strong, and how does the welfare of one affect the well-being of another? The great objective should be the study of laws and customs as the expression of national life. "So that one might know the history of men rather than a tiny part of the history of kings and courts. . . . It is necessary therefore to incorporate with skill this useful knowledge in the tissue of events. This, I believe, is the only way to write modern history *en vrai politique et en vrai philosophe*." [51] Only such history can be read *en citoyen et en philosophe*. And since true civilization is a fairly recent accomplishment, it is best to avoid the impenetrable fog of the origins of people, or the histories known through fables and scripture, and to concentrate on the times when history becomes truly interesting; that is to say, at the end of the fifteenth century. "We cannot make a step which does not remind us of some change which has since then worked upon the world." [52]

Voltaire thus had a revolutionary program for writing history. In what manner did he execute it? In particular, how did Voltaire handle this complex matter for which he had no name but which we call culture or civilization?

Voltaire wrote his major historical works during the middle period of a long life. He was then a mature man whose philosophy of life had been formed.[53] He undertook enormous historical tasks, often in a short time span, and he did not fully develop the new history envisaged in his programmatic utterances. Large sections of his histories are "ordinary" history,

---

[51] *Nouvelles considérations*, in *O.H.*, pp. 47–49; see also *Essai*, in *O.C.*, XI, 66, 267, and XII, 53.

[52] *Remarques sur l'histoire*, in *O.H.*, pp. 43–44; *Essai*, in *O.C.*, XI, 225; *Lettres*, II, 233.

[53] Voltaire changed his mind on several matters after 1750, and some scholars even think that he underwent a profound change from an optimist to a pessimist. I believe that the historical works are generally characterized by a persistent set of basic convictions which make it possible to pay scant attention to the chronological sequence and development of his writings.

heavily focused on political and military events, though written by an extraordinary man who put the stamp of his mind and style on all he touched. Strewn among these sections of traditional history are Voltaire's suggestions for a history of civilization. He asked questions and introduced considerations which oriented historical inquiry toward new concerns. He attempted answers which reveal his profound sense for the value of civilization and his versatility and ingenuity in fixing his attention on the significant and indicative detail. He sketched tableaux, he outlined configurations of cultural concerns, he here or there painted in detail a matter or a figure which caught his fancy, adding his own brilliant dabs of color. Voltaire's histories are never colorless outlines, and never dull reading. And although he wrote no single exemplary history of civilization, his great vision of a new history, focused on the worthy accomplishments of men, is present in all his historical work. A Dutch historian said recently that Voltaire worked in the vestibule (*voorhof*) of the temple of cultural history.[54] Voltaire did more than that: he pushed open the doors to that temple and left suggestions for those cultural historians who labored after him on a new image of the Muse.

Apart from its stylistic liveliness, Voltaire's earliest historical work, the *Histoire de Charles XII*,[55] departed little from traditional histories. But it played a role in his training. Voltaire sharpened his methodology in the controversies over factual details which arose soon after publication. Less tangible concerns, however, are of greater importance for the development of his conception of history. Some passages in this adventure story of a king, "one-half Alexander, one-half Don Quixote," [56] hint at future interests in economic conditions,

---

[54] Jan Romein, *Carillon der tijden*, p. 130.

[55] The *Histoire de Charles XII, roi de Suède* first appeared in 1732 and became immediately popular. More than sixty editions were published during Voltaire's life.

[56] Brumfitt, p. 13, quoting a letter by Voltaire.

population data, and social life. Most fascinating is the emergence of a new hero (if such is the proper term in dealing with a wit little given to hero worship) as opposed to the Swedish conqueror. For while Voltaire was describing the incredible adventures of Charles — the victory at Narva, the deposing and making of Polish kings, the loss of an entire army in the interior of the Ukraine, the weird dealings with Turkish pashas while he was confined at Bender, or the wild ride through central Europe back to Sweden, where he tried to create a new army out of untrained peasants — Peter of Russia captured the author's imagination. That half-barbarian tsar was not a mad conqueror but a builder who suffered a devastating defeat at Narva but returned to construct canals and who used the skills of the Swedish captives taken at Pultava for the westernization of his realm. While Charles exhausted his land, Peter built a capital in the wilderness and he also created a fleet. By his later work on Peter Voltaire may have wanted to atone for the youthful mistake of romanticizing a military hero who contributed nothing to the building of an enlightened society.

Four later works gave Voltaire a greater opportunity to develop his ideas of cultural history: the *Siècle de Louis XIV*, the *Précis du siècle de Louis XV*, the *Histoire de l'empire de Russie sous Pierre le Grand*, and the *Essai sur les moeurs et l'esprit des nations*.[57] A related set of queries about civilization connects them, though they are written as separate works.

---

[57] The *Siècle de Louis XIV* appeared in a complete edition first in 1751 and was often reprinted; the *Précis du siècle de Louis XV* appeared in a completed version in 1769 with the note "servant de suite au Siècle de Louis XIV"; the *Histoire de l'empire de Russie sous Pierre le Grand* came out in 1763 but had been preceded in 1748 by *Anecdotes sur le Czar Pierre le Grand*; for the very involved publication history of these books see *Oeuvres historiques*, pp. 1661–64. The history of the publication of the *Essai sur les moeurs* is even more involved. Fragments of an *Essai sur l'histoire générale* appeared as articles as early as 1745. In 1753 a larger section was published which Voltaire disavowed. In 1756 a seven-volume *Essai sur l'histoire générale et sur les moeurs et l'esprit des nations depuis Charlemagne jusqu'au nos jours* appeared which included the *Siècle de Louis XIV*. Only in 1769 was the work pub-

When, where, why, and in what sense have societies been civilized? How can barbarians become civilized? What has been the fullest expression of civilization? And what has been its further development? Three of these works discussed "modern" civilization, while the longest, the *Essai sur les moeurs*, pondered the question, How has mankind lived before? In the *Essai* Voltaire surveyed in a novel fashion the history of all communities and measured their accomplishments and failures as carriers of civilization. It has been considered both the strangest book written by a historian and the greatest work of Voltaire.[58] Though consistently criticized for omissions and errors, as well as the prejudices of its author, it is an astonishing work especially if the title word *essai* is taken seriously. It is not steeped in knowledge from original sources, but it is a work of enormous erudition. Like many great books, it is paradoxical. It is universal history, from a western point of view; it is the story of man viewed as a whole but from the perspective of civilized existence. The world of its author had become one and interdependent. Voltaire felt the wonder of sitting at Ferney, in the foothills of the Swiss Jura surrounded by books on Aztecs, Muslims, Hindus, Chinese, Greeks, and Romans, beneath a print of Confucius, sipping coffee from Arabia in porcelain from China. He had a sense of space and time which had freed itself from the narrow frame of a Judeo-Christian tradition. The chronology of a world history could hardly be fitted into a Christian timetable; spatially it could not be surveyed from Jerusalem. The emphasis of the *Essai* may still be on the history of the West, but the other experiments in civilization have been woven into it. Occasionally a people was used for "propagandistic"

---

lished under its final title; it included then the *Philosophie de l'histoire* of 1765 as "Discours préliminaire." For more detail see *Oeuvres complètes*, L, 515–16.

[58] John B. Black (*Art of History*, p. 71) thinks highly of the book but finds it strange. For Henry N. Brailsford (*Voltaire*, p. 102), it is the greatest work. Lanson, Dilthey, and Cassirer thought in general more highly of it than Fueter and Meinecke. To some apparently it was little more than a *pasquinade*.

effects. The Jews, those favorite whipping boys when one really wanted to attack a Christian tradition without getting in trouble with a Most Christian Majesty's government, were cruelly pilloried by Voltaire. The Old Testament is a hodge-podge of incredible fables; David was a ruthless bandit; Moses, for forty years unable to find his way in a few square miles of desert, was a ludicrous leader; the Diaspora was a deserved fate for Jewish barbarities.[59] Only when Christians mistreat Jews does Voltaire take them under the protective wing of his historical judgment. The effect of the argument remains that while Chinese, Persians, and Hindus built a way of life with major marks of civilization, the accepted western story of the past was unworthy of much attention. This seems a genuine judgment on the development of civilization rather than a case where "the propagandist has got the better of the historian." [60] As Voltaire had announced in his programmatic utterances, the western world, from a standpoint of civilized existence, becomes a worthy object for the historian only toward the end of the fifteenth century. From that moment on, the *Essai* prepares the reader more and more for the outburst of cultural activities in the seventeenth century. Gradually western men rise above the achievements of the Orient, until the generation of Louis XIV brings forth the greatest flowering of civilization.

In the *Siècle de Louis XIV* Voltaire gave much more than a biography of a great king. "I painted the age and not the person of Louis XIV, nor that of William III, nor that of the great Condé, nor Marlborough." [61] This was to be the history of the human spirit at its proudest moment. This was the story of the near-miraculous advance of the spirit in science, eloquence, poetry, criticism, painting, sculpture,

---

[59] See especially references in the *Essai*, in *O.C.*, XI, 47–49, 67–71, 104–43. Many of the sharpest anti-Jewish remarks can be found in the *Dictionnaire*.

[60] Brumfitt, p. 94, makes this accusation with respect to the comparisons of societies in the introductory parts of the *Essai*.

[61] "Lettre à Roques," in *O.H.*, p. 1255; "Lettre à Dubos," in *O.H.*, pp. 605–6; *Siècle de Louis XIV*, in *O.H.*, p. 616.

music, the goldsmith's art, tapestry, mirror-making, brocade work, and watch-making. Although at least half the book is straight narrative of political and military matters, and although the second half with its disjointed chapters and the unintegrated *listes raisonnées* of great men is anything but a model of cultural history, the book is the monument to an age of genius that its author wished it to be.[62] Despite its faults, which are chiefly structural, no other author has depicted that age's luster with such passion and good sense. Not even the intervening decades of scientific history and of frequently naïve democratic historiography have wiped out this sketch (Voltaire himself called it an *essai*) of a flowering civilized existence. Voltaire did not overlook or pardon the errors of the age; there still was too much Christian persuasion, too many outbursts of fanaticism, too much supercilious snobbery, too little sane philosophy, too few French contributions to science, and too many errors in policy. Yet, whenever Voltaire asked himself, When did men truly exist in the least barbarous manner? he turned to the *grand siècle* and especially its great writers. "I move my eyes over the nations of the world, and I find none which had more brilliant days than the French between 1655 and 1704." [63]

In the *Précis du siècle de Louis XV*, Voltaire presented the sequel to the *Siècle de Louis XIV*.[64] It is an interesting corollary describing modifications of the civilization during the eighteenth century, but it is much less majestic than the *Siècle de Louis XIV* — as Louis XV was much inferior as a king and as a man to his illustrious predecessor. Since parts of the book were written by Voltaire in his capacity as court historian, much of it is mere narration of French foreign policy and

---

[62] "L'auteur du *Siècle de Louis XIV* sentait tout ce qui manquait a ce monument qu'il avait voulu élever à l'honneur de sa nation" ("Lettre à Roques," in *O.H.*, p. 1230).

[63] *Défense de Louis XIV*, in *O.H.*, p. 1287.

[64] Parts of the work had actually appeared as appendixes to the *Siècle de Louis XIV* in 1751 and 1756. Sections of the book were written when Voltaire was the official court historian.

warfare. Even here the narrative may sparkle: the description of the Battle of Fontenoi is unforgettable; the adventures of the Young Pretender, Charles Edward Stuart, are drawn with loving concern; events in faraway India and Canada are interestingly woven into European developments. But aside from short passages on such matters as John Law's financial scheme or Anson's voyage around the world, or a discussion of Beccaria's book on crime and punishment, the theme of cultural history reappears only in the brilliant last chapter. In that final assessment of the development of the human spirit under Louis XV's reign, Voltaire touches on a profound question: Has there been real progress beyond the civilization of Louis XIV's age? It will be seen later that this was a troublesome issue for Voltaire and one to which he gave no clear-cut answer.

A different assault on cultural history is entailed in the *Histoire de l'empire de Russie sous Pierre le Grand*. This somewhat neglected work glorifies the labors of a single man who was striving to lift his barbarous country onto a plateau of civilized existence. It again is filled with lengthy passages of traditional history and is devoid of a discussion of the arts.[65] The stress is on the reforms of a practical half-barbarian, a man great through purpose and will power, who forced his people to become civilized, who forged a nation, who "forced nature in everything, in his subjects, in himself, on the land and on the waters; but he forced her so that he might embellish her."[66] The symbol of Saint Petersburg, where the will and labor of man created a useful work of art in nature's wilderness, pervades the whole book. This was to be instructive and exhortative history, whereas the *Charles XII* was

---

[65] Some of the most interesting aspects of the work involve Voltaire's relation to the sources for a Russian history; a good presentation of this problem is Otto Haintz, "Peter der Grosse, Friedrich der Grosse, und Voltaire; zur Entstehungsgeschichte von Voltaire's *Histoire de l'empire de Russie sous Pierre le Grand*," Akademie der Wissenschaften und der Literatur in Mainz, Abhandlungen der geistes- und sozialwissenschaftlichen Klasse, V (1961), 513–56.

[66] *Russie*, in *O.H.*, p. 597.

merely *amusante*.[67] The book on Peter answered the question, How can barbarians catch up with the higher civilization of their neighbors? It suggested to laggards that the worthwhile life demands man's devoted labor and skill. "Je le répète, on n'a qu'à vouloir; on ne veut pas assez." [68]

The good life which Voltaire equated with civilization, and which he tracked down in man's past, was a composite of many achievements. Its chief components were the political order necessary for civilized activity; the active pursuit of material welfare by means of trade, industrious labor, and the employment of human ingenuity; a set of sane convictions about the nature of the universe, God, and man, resulting in a decent morality; good taste and concern for the refinements of life; and the cultivation of manners and communications whereby the fruits of the good life could be spread. Each of these factors, though not always clearly separated from the others, was a major concern for Voltaire the historian.

Without a protective political order men cannot cultivate their garden of civilization. A state of the wrong kind may seriously hamper civilized concerns; but Voltaire was too practical a man to make high-sounding theoretical pronunciamentos about constitutional forms. *Experientia rerum magistra*; all the hallucinations and speculative schemes concocted in front of Parisian fireplaces are useless.[69] Voltaire judged each government by its accomplishment and not by its theoretical virtues or failures. His ideal state was a *Kulturstaat*, an instrument for the protection of civilization. From that point of view, anarchy is the greatest threat to man, and the rule of law the greatest boon. Voltaire hated feudalism because it was to him barbaric anarchy. It was robbery by the strongest; its alleged constitution was nothing but "a standing ordinance to engage in civil war." [70] Individual men are too

[67] *Ibid.*, p. 353.
[68] *Anecdotes sur Pierre le Grand*, in *O.H.*, p. 330.
[69] *Lettres*, II, 76.
[70] *Essai*, in *O.C.*, XI, 411.

weak to be left to their own discretion; the drive for power among the strong is too real and no illusionary idealist can make it less so; for most men the absence of strong restraint is usually an invitation to superstition and fanaticism. Feudalism condemned Europe to centuries of barbarism. It imposed "the most absurd form of government to which men have ever been subjected." [71] And since this feudal anarchy was aided by actual tryanny, and by the aspirations to absolute power of an intolerant theocracy, Europe was long bereft of conditions under which civilization might have had a chance. On this issue Voltaire was adamant: it is evil to give worldly power to those who have renounced the world.[72] The church never should have enjoyed secular authority. When she becomes a state-within-a-state, factional strife is bound to strengthen the growth of anarchic conditions. The tyranny of one is ultimately preferable to many petty tyrants.[73] The few experiments in self-government have usually come to naught because of factional conflicts; too often democracy was too weak or too lax to protect itself against rapacious neighbors. Among the exceptions, the Swiss have succeeded in "cultivating their rocks in liberty" because every man was a soldier; the Dutch, only after a lengthy struggle, became "perhaps the sole example on earth of the success of indefatigable labor and love of freedom." Venice owed her independence to her lagoons.[74] And, surely, republican government was not for Voltaire an egalitarian democracy, but at best the rule of intelligent citizen-mandarins. He remained skeptical

---

[71] *Ibid.*, p. 517.

[72] *Ibid.*, pp. 294–95.

[73] *Dictionnaire*, in *O.C.*, XX, 544.

[74] *Essai*, in *O.C.*, XI, 526–29; *Siècle de Louis XIV*, in *O.H.*, pp. 625, 629; "L'Homme aux quarante écus," in *Romans et Contes*, p. 318; and *Dictionnaire*, in *O.C.*, XIX, 33: "Je conçois, dit le brame, qu'on ne doit trouver sur la terre que très peu de républiques. Les hommes sont rarement dignes de se gouverner eux-mêmes. Ce bonheur ne doit appartenir qu'à des petits peuples qui se cachent dans les îles, ou entre des montagnes; comme des lapins qui se dérobent aux animaux carnassiers; mais à la longue ils sont découverts et dévorés."

even of the Dutch; factional fanaticism killed Oldenbarnevelt, and in time of crisis the *canaille* revealed its ever lurking barbarism. The De Witts were torn to pieces by the mob. Voltaire resigned himself to the idea that men are rarely worthy and able to govern themselves.[75]

There was more hope in strong centralized government, despite its dangers of tyranny. Anarchy was the greater danger and real tyranny rarer than enlightened propagandists thought.[76] Voltaire believed it difficult to cheat all the people all the time where their true interests are at stake, and extraordinarily difficult to rule a people for a long time against its will.[77] As this world goes, the weak suffer; flies were made to be eaten by spiders, and nary a man escapes being the anvil to a hammer. It cannot be said, alas, that most of those who have held power were good rulers. But rarely does the despot commit only evil, and even more rarely is his tyranny worse than would be the tyranny of the many. The strong at least may keep out rapacious enemies and prevent the *canaille* from going on a rampage. They may accidentally further man's welfare and occasionally they may be persuaded to a good deed "by a mistress, a confessor, or a page boy." [78] Voltaire was a harsh judge of those who pursued power for power's sake, who ruled chiefly by caprice, who conquered simply because they could not resist the desire for a larger domain, or of a strong Charlemagne whose actions proved only that power can succeed. But despotism had entered on the credit side of the historical ledger some enlightened luminaries who had done more for mankind than all other kinds of rulers. A long line of devoted emperors gave China centuries of the stablest, wisest, and best rule. Such benign, parental rule, aided by a corps of dedicated mandarins, genuinely served the welfare of subjects. For a

---

[75] Among many possible references see *Essai*, in *O.C.*, XI, 79, 106, 529, XII, 450, XIII, 45; and *Dictionnaire*, in *O.C.*, XX, 185.

[76] *Essai*, in *O.C.*, XII, 113.

[77] Among many possible references see *Charles XII*, in *O.H.*, p. 99; *Russie*, in *O.H.*, p. 390; and *Siècle de Louis XIV*, in *O.H.*, pp. 848, 861.

[78] *Dictionnaire*, in *O.C.*, XX, 544.

while at least, the Roman emperors ruled with a tolerant paternalism for the good of the *oikumene*. The world of Islam found great benefactors among its strong caliphs, and even the Turkish sultans (attacked, like the Chinese emperors, by Montesquieu) seemed defensible to Voltaire, since they ruled, with admirable toleration, twenty different peoples who seldom revolted because most of their rights were respected. And some tolerable moments in western life occurred under the strong government of Alfred the Great ("I know not whether there has ever been a man on earth worthier of posterity's respect"); [79] the Normans in Sicily, and their successor, Frederick II; an English Norman king, Henry I; a French king, Louis IX ("Never did a man carry virtue further"); [80] an autocrat, Pope Alexander III, who freed Christians at least from one kind of servitude, and Leo X and Sixtus V, under whom "Roman" culture flourished; a gentle, skillful man-in-the-background, William of Orange, and a strong queen, Elizabeth of England; and the most admirable king of all, the great Henry IV of France. If one adds to these the more recent benefactors of mankind, such as Louis XIV, Frederick II of Prussia, and Peter the Great, the case for enlightened absolutism seemed incontrovertible to Voltaire. "On a une patrie sous un bon roi, on n'en a point sous un méchant." [81]

Voltaire uniformly judged governments and rulers by their contributions to culture as he conceived it. His only heroes are those who commit good deeds for the benefit of subjects and mankind. A good ruler governs his realm like a good father his family. Such a model as the young Leopold of Lorraine, though a small prince, maintained peace and order, administered justice justly, promoted material welfare, and above and beyond such basic princely duties he extended his help to persons in debt, provided dowries for his needy subjects' daughters, and rebuilt war-ravaged houses. He founded a uni-

---

[79] *Essai*, in *O.C.*, XI, 309.
[80] *Ibid.*, p. 468.
[81] *Dictionnaire*, in *O.C.*, XX, 182.

versity (which was free of pedants), and helped the sciences and arts, recognizing merit wherever it appeared. "During his entire reign he occupied himself only with providing his nation with tranquility, riches, knowledge, and *plaisirs*." [82] His motto was, "I will resign my sovereignty tomorrow if I cannot do good."

And what this little prince does in Lorraine, a great king like Louis XIV does in France. Although Voltaire never mustered quite the same enthusiasm for Louis that the young poet once had for Henri IV, he admired Louis for the good he did France and mankind. After France had relapsed into feudal anarchy during the Fronde, the young king proved, from the moment of accession, that "France had but one master and the rest were subjects." [83] He taught Europe to respect France. He taught the French to respect their own merits. He employed the best talent France had for implementing policies befitting a great nation. He actively supported the economic and social reforms of Colbert, the military reforms of Louvois and Vauban.[84] He himself worked ceaselessly for his people's welfare and knew how to make others work for France. He was a man of taste whose court became Europe's great school of manners. Above all, he was a patron of the arts and stimulated the unexcelled flowering of France's creative genius. His minister Colbert patronized science and useful inventions. And Louis "not only did good to Frenchmen, he benefited men"; [85] sixty scholars throughout Europe received his gratuities. He was an autocrat, but a wise one who did not abuse the true laws and morality of mankind. He made such mistakes as the Revocation of the Edict of Nantes which cost France dearly; but, all considered, he was a great king. Some surpassed him as a man; others surpassed him in one or another aspect of kingship; no

---

[82] *Siècle de Louis XIV*, in *O.H.*, pp. 790–91, a wonderful vignette of Voltaire's conception of a good ruler.

[83] *Ibid.*, p. 688.

[84] The few pages on the army reforms constitute one of the best examples of Voltaire's admiration for detailed planning; see *ibid.*, pp. 973–76.

[85] "Lettre à Hervey," in *O.H.*, p. 611.

one more deserved to give his name to the greatest age of mankind.

Voltaire looked everywhere in the past for such benefactors of mankind. He glorified a half-barbarian like Peter of Russia, who unfortunately lacked the greatest monarchic virtue, humanity, but who labored like a giant to create a nation, to build a capital in a marsh, to construct roads, hospitals, orphanages; who had a peasant's fear of water, but built a navy and, forcing his nature, taught himself to swim. Though too much a barbarian to exhibit Louis XIV's good taste, he was an illustrious example of a strong-willed man with good sense who shunned idiocies like "verifying passages of Saint Epiphany" [86] and concentrated on everything useful: uniform legislation, trade, manufacture, academies, schools, census figures, and a strong army. Voltaire spared no praise for Peter's efforts to clear the towns of beggars and, especially, to compel useless monks to work for the nation instead of wasting time in monasteries.

Wherever Voltaire turned from these "modern" builders to the great rulers of a more removed past he evinced his conviction that the times must be ripe and right for great reformers. Louis XIV had the help of very great Frenchmen, and Peter the Great and Frederick, though lone workers, could borrow from the high civilization of western Europe. Henri IV, great man though he was, had first to pacify the land and, at best, could only lay foundations for the further growth of France, without himself bringing forth a cultured flowering. Alfred, surrounded by the most abject barbarism, could only for a brief interlude create the conditions of a semicivilized life. His work was a reminder of human dignity amid total chaos. But even those successful rulers, the Chinese emperors, who provided sane, tolerant, beneficial government on the foundations of Confucius' teachings, could not thereby guarantee the continuous expansion of arts and sciences; culturally China remained a plateau surpassed by modern Euro-

[86] *Russie*, in *O.H.*, p. 537.

peans. Good government alone did not bring forth high civilization. But neither could culture bear fruits when the rulers failed it. In a manner which conveys his sadness over the unenlightened abuse of power, mixed with a desperate hope to discover some traces of dedicated labors on behalf of man, Voltaire roamed through the centuries in his *Essai sur les moeurs*, pointing out that Alexander at least built more cities than he destroyed, that another ruler at least passed one good law, that this one at least refrained from tampering with the coinage, that another at least tried to administer justice justly, that this one built a road and defended his bishopric against Vikings and that one gave some recognition to the virtues of industrious burghers.

So Voltaire's survey of history confirmed him in the convictions from which he started: power must be used for higher ends; the human community must have order and stability for its true tasks; power must not be arbitrary; everyone, including the ruler, should know what the few good laws are, what is expected of him, and should submit to these laws; uniformity and consistency of law and rule, and preferably close agreement between law, morality, and national custom, are rational and good; beyond the few good laws and measures necessary to preserve order and well-being, toleration is the only acceptable policy; the state serves men best when it assists them to create a human refuge in an otherwise meaningless, chaotic existence.

The treatment of war in Voltaire's historical works throws some interesting sidelights on his conception of a *Kulturstaat*. By instinct he disliked senseless shedding of human blood. He is said to have experienced fever and severe physical discomfort each year on the anniversary of the Saint Bartholomew massacre.[87] He detested above all those religious wars fought

---

[87] Brailsford, p. 217; the long description of the bloody attack by the Irish battalion during the Battle of Fontenoi (chaps. 15 and 16 of the *Précis*), however, makes one wonder just how sensitive Voltaire was to the shedding of blood.

over unanswerable questions, when the mutual slaughter of fanatics ruined civilization. By Voltaire's calculation such conflicts had, since the time of Athanasius, accounted for more loss in life than all other conflicts (especially since they involved women as well as men).[88] But although he consistently condemned the warring fanatic and lamented the waste of war, Voltaire did not uniformly reject war. Granted that war is a scourge, "it is an inevitable scourge."[89] The affairs of this world are decided by force. "The nation which best employs iron always subjects the one with more gold and less courage."[90] It was easy for the Quakers to be pacifists when others protected them from danger.[91] The Florentines acquired refined tastes and arts but they failed to fight for their way of life like the Greeks at Thermopylae. Some wars are just and are warranted by the laws of nations. Louis XIV was wrong to attack Holland (he had "the glory to repent this"), but his war over the Spanish succession was a most legitimate war.[92] Yet even when Voltaire treated a war as just and respected the testimonials of heroism and self-sacrifice, he did not lose his commitment to the values of civilization. Most indicative is his treatment of one small episode during the War of the Spanish Succession. When this "historical Banker of the Enlightenment"[93] came to the siege of Turin in 1706 he sallied forth on a remarkable little calculation. He interrupted the narrative for a quick accounting maneuver in which he estimated the total expenditure of this siege: 110,000 bullets, 21,000 cannonballs, 27,700 mines, 15,000 sacks of earth, 1,200,000 pounds of powder, and all the quantities of saltpeter, lead, iron, ropes, and so on. "It is certain that the cost

---

[88] *Essai*, in *O.C.*, XIII, 62.

[89] "Guerre," *Dictionnaire*, in *O.C.*, XIX, 321.

[90] *Ibid.*, XVIII, 476; on the other hand, see *Essai*, in *O.C.*, XI, 436, on the proposition that the conquerors are easily conquered culturally by the conquered.

[91] *Essai*, in *O.C.*, XI, 51, and also *ibid.*, XII, 7.

[92] *Défense de Louis XIV*, in *O.H.*, p. 1287.

[93] This fortunate phrase is in Friedrich Meinecke, *Historismus*, p. 104.

of all these preparations for destruction would have sufficed to found and maintain a flourishing colony." [94]

Respect for the practical work whereby men ameliorate their hard existence is obvious in Voltaire's historical view of civilization. This self-nobilitated burgher or bourgeois aristocrat knew the value of work, ingenuity, and merit earned through service. "Work keeps away from us three great evils: need, vice, and boredom." [95] Civilization is the product of work — *il faut cultiver*. Unlike later cultural historians who reacted strongly against the materialistic evils of an acquisitive and utilitarian society, Voltaire admired material welfare, wealth, and everything useful. He himself was a financial genius (what other poet has merited an entire treatise devoted to his financial success?),[96] a landlord, and an entrepreneur on a grand scale. Although he did not like excesses, he did not sneer at luxury and riches (*luxe*) which produced work for the less blessed. He did not share the fashionable glorification of simple men in the state of nature [97] or the virtues of impoverished republics. "What good did Sparta contribute to Greece? Could she ever have had a Demosthenes, Sophocles, Apelles, or Phidias? The riches of Athens resulted in great men of all

---

[94] *Siècle de Louis XIV*, in *O.H.*, p. 841; the treatment of the siege of Turin is a striking example of Voltaire's outlook and narrative art.

[95] *Candide*, in *Romans et Contes*, p. 236.

[96] Léon Kozminski, *Voltaire financier* (Paris: Presses Universitaires, 1929), which is not a small treatise but a substantial book.

[97] See for instance the lines in the poem "Le Mondain," *Mélanges* (ed. Heuvel), p. 204, on Adam and Eve:

> "Avouez-moi que vous aviez tous deux
> Les ongles longs, un peu noirs et crasseux,
> La chevelure assez mal ordonnée,
> Le teint bruni, la peau bise et tannée.
> Sans propreté l'amour le plus heureux
> N'est plus l'amour; c'est un besoin honteux.
> Bientôt lassés de leur belle aventure,
> Dessous un chêne ils soupent galamment
> Avec de l'eau, du millet et du gland;
> Ce repas fait, ils dorment sur la dure:
> Voilà l'état de la pure nature."

genres."[98] Civilized existence implied material well-being and technical ingenuity. In his historical surveying Voltaire paid special tribute to the practical benefactors of mankind. There were some great ones: in his own day, Turgot sought to make the cultivation of the soil more rewarding by wise legislation; Frederick the Great drained marshes for his peasants; Peter learned the skills of an engineer and worked with his own royal hands; and, above all, there was Colbert, who built industries, roads, canals, hospitals, merchantmen, and colonies. Nor did Voltaire forget the lesser ones. Thoroughly characteristic is the story of Anson's vegetables. In the middle of the history of the eighteenth century, provided in his *Précis du siècle de Louis XV*, Voltaire reported on Admiral Anson's voyage around the world.[99] Before leaving the isle of Juan Fernandez, the English sailor planted vegetables for the use of future shipwrecked sailors. May the report of such practical humanitarianism "temper . . . the sadness of a history which consists mainly of slaughter and calamities."

Persistently Voltaire tracked down those moments when the famous and the nameless labored to make life sweeter. He respected those artisans who used their crafty ingenuity for technical wonders long before the scholars understood the principles of mechanics.[100] He wanted to know how hearth and stove affected family life and what men and women wore. He described how people covered their roofs, lighted their houses. When did men begin to use table linen? And was leprosy spread by the use of coarse and unhygienic linen? Amid a devastatingly sarcastic analysis of the Crusades, Voltaire suddenly marveled at the resourcefulness of the Venetians in solving the logistic problems of these senseless and criminal expedi-

---

[98] "Luxe," *Dictionnaire*, in *O.C.*, XX, 17; see also *Siècle de Louis XIV*, in *O.H.*, pp. 699, 988.

[99] *Précis*, in *O.H.*, pp. 1454–61, the quotation following is on p. 1456.

[100] See, for instance, *Essai*, in *O.C.*, XI, 22: "On voit des machines inventées par les habitants des montagnes du Tyrol et des Vosges qui étonnent les savants."

tions. He clearly understood that the invention of cannons, by dooming an aristocratic warrior class, had profound social effects; the same invention, he thought, made henceforth impossible a Mongol threat to civilized societies.[101] But rather than hunting amid the byways of social and economic history for fascinating curiosa, Voltaire concentrated on those unspectacular activities largely responsible for human welfare or misery. Wherever he could find the data, he speculated about the real value of money. He always had a kind word for those who guaranteed standardized weights and measures. He was deeply concerned over the proper relation between population size and economic welfare.[102] The impoverishment of the Spanish and Portuguese monarchies persuaded Voltaire (if he needed such persuasion) that treasures in bullion are worthless unless used. The English knew better and concentrated on the fabrication and trade of essentials like cloth, and the Dutch founded their wealth and freedom on pickled herring.[103] True wealth is founded on cultivators of the soil, on industrious artisans, on ingenious inventions, on the skills of a population, on sound finances, on the genuine guarantee of property, on the absence of too much restraining legislation, and on the wise use of public works. Wherever Voltaire found these rudiments of bourgeois virtues and policies, he found essential conditions for civilized life.

Another major building block of civilization consisted in the element which Voltaire circumscribed by his oft-repeated phrase "sane philosophy." Voltaire had a simple conception of true wisdom. Know the little that is knowable to man and patiently resign yourself to not knowing the unknowable. Remember that two and two is four, that you are mortal and but the insect of a summer's day living precariously on a heap of

---

[101] *Essai*, in *O.C.*, XII, 93 and 431.

[102] For some examples see *Russie*, in *O.H.*, p. 376, and *Essai*, in *O.C.*, XI, 37, 38, 60, XII, 336, 344, 383, XIII, 33.

[103] For examples see *Siècle de Louis XIV*, in *O.H.*, pp. 624, 663; *Précis*, in *O.H.*, p. 1396; and *Essai*, in *O.C.*, XI, 211, 268, 274, 414, XII, 55–56, 121, 424, 467, 486, 551–52, XIII, 92, 116.

mud, that you are meant to obey simple moral laws, and that the world was constructed by a wise geometer whose creation is only partially knowable. The rest is pretentious human swindle and mere speculation under which the wise man places his *non liquet* just as Roman jurists put their N.L. beneath all that was not evident.[104] The real scourge of mankind is not ignorance but superstition and pretense of knowledge. That "other form of ignorance called erudition"[105] is simply useless. It was just because Voltaire's conception of sane philosophy made such modest demands that his desperate search for it in man's past was such a saddening experience. With few exceptions men were ruled by superstition and ignorant fears. Rarely did men see the world as it really is. Their world image was generally distorted by fear of the unknown, or by lack of leisure for careful observation and clear thought, or by poor methods and instruments, or sometimes by the deliberate wish to mislead the weak, or by the deplorable habit of constructing speculative systems from too few facts. The Chaldeans, Chinese, Indians, Greeks, and through these the Arabs, possessed a body of mathematical and astronomical knowledge; but it was not sound enough even to permit the construction of a correct calendar. The Chinese knew the compass — and made no use of it. The Indian Brahmans disfigured their few good insights with fables. The Greeks, benefiting from a society where relatively free men could exchange the beginnings of knowledge, spoiled it by not checking their imagination. Plato, their greatest philosopher, became an unintelligible poet. Voltaire, seeking to counteract the derogatory opinions of his contemporaries, defended the Arabs as fairly enlightened cultivators and transmitters of the best in oriental and classical knowledge. Their university at Cordoba was a ray of light in the darkness of Europe's Middle Ages. But like the Chinese and Indians, they furnished no more than a "holding action" by failing to advance beyond a

---

[104] *Dictionnaire*, in *O.C.*, XVIII, 586.
[105] *Essai*, in *O.C.*, XII, 2.

minimum of good sense. Except for Job, the Jews never had a sensible idea. And, the Christians, their successors as the chosen people, lived for centuries in priest-ridden "savage ignorance." Only at the courts of Alfred and Charlemagne was a ray of light from the remembered classical world permitted. In the thirteenth century, Europeans passed from this "savage ignorance" to the absurdities of "scholastic ignorance" perpetrated by "the Great, the Subtle, the Angelic, the Irrefragable, the Solemn, the Illumined, the Universal, and the Profound Doctors."[106] The discovery of the "true system of the world" had to await the genius of Copernicus, Bacon, Galileo, Kepler, and the great Newton. Meanwhile mankind lived with the ideas which an enlightened man might expect of the Hottentots.[107]

The fruit of a sane philosophy, a decent moral life, was too often marred by religious superstition. As Voltaire moved through the ages, judging the merits of societies, he noticed the same distortion everywhere: the natural deism and simple morality of a few wise men were disfigured by popular superstition. Genuine atheism and immorality were rare. Voltaire's high opinion of China derived in part from his belief that Confucius, and the mandarins trained in his tradition, followed a deistic religion and a simple morality. They built a society on respect for the golden rule, mutual toleration, and the ideal of practical service to the community. The consequences of such a morality were good laws and wise administration by an intelligent ruling class. Yet that elite could not eradicate popular superstition. The excesses of ancestor worship caused a stagnation of cultural life.[108] Voltaire admired the basic convictions of Indian Brahmans. He never shared their ideas of metempsychosis but saw that such ideas might be an ingenious foundation for good moral doctrine. Again,

---

[106] *Ibid.*, XI, 506-7; see also *ibid.*, XI, 225, and XII, 61.

[107] *Ibid.*, XI, 387, and XII, 249.

[108] *Ibid.*, XI, 18, 27, 35, 51, 55, 57, 109, 164-82, 487, XII, 432-33, XIII, 162-68, 181; and *Siècle de Louis XIV*, in *O.H.*, pp. 568, 1101-4; and *Précis*, in *O.H.*, p. 1459.

however, the admiration was overcome by his abhorrence of the incredible popular superstitions of Hinduism and such practices as suttee.[109] Similarly his appraisal of Persian and early near eastern religions was counteracted by misgivings over dualism, the despotic suppression of women, and temple prostitution (which he sometimes discounted as a malicious invention of hostile western historians).[110] Voltaire recognized the evils of classical life: pederasty, slavery, and various out-croppings of polytheistic nonsense. He never shared the humanist's idealization of Greeks and Romans. But skepticism, Stoicism, and Epicureanism were in basic agreement with his own convictions and passed with his approving nod. He liked the general atmosphere of religious toleration and intellectual freedom in classical antiquity, but sadly noted that even then a Socrates was condemned to death.[111] Voltaire rejected the widespread opinion that Islam was a superstition with lax and sensuous ethics. In his opinion, Mohammed taught a pure monotheism and strict though beneficent morality, free from idolatrous ritual. Islam, moreover, was tolerant. The Arabs and Turks were among the world's mildest conquerors. The sultans permit Christian churches in their lands; what Christian ruler tolerates mosques on his soil? But even if Voltaire defended Mohammed and Islam from Christian slander, he was not uncritical of either. Aside from the teaching that Mohammed is the prophet of God, the Koran contains but rewarmed Judaism; it is a tedious book; compared to Confucius, Mohammed was less moral; and more recent sultans had departed from their policy of toleration.[112]

Without any doubt Voltaire was harshest in condemning the foibles of Jews and Christians. The western tradition suf-

---

[109] *Essai*, in *O.C.*, XI, 50–51, 182–89, 194; and *Précis*, in *O.H.*, p. 1467.

[110] *Essai*, in *O.C.*, XI, 28, 34, 196–201, XII, 442–44; and *Charles XII*, in *O.H.*, p. 314.

[111] *Essai*, in *O.C.*, XI, 76–77, 146–48; and *Dictionnaire*, in *O.C.*, XVII, 469, XVIII, 188.

[112] *Essai*, in *O.C.*, XI, 45–46, 212–21, 267, 314, 374, XII, 103, 159, XIII, 176, 179; and *Lettres*, II, 118.

fers from having its roots in the fantasies of Hebrew religion and the immoral teachings of the Jews, who engaged in all crimes save cannibalism. Jesus, a sort of rural Socrates in Galilee, taught better morality, but his followers immediately disfigured his teachings with incredible fables and wild theological speculations. Had Christians at least followed the simple moral rules of their master they might have done good in the world. Instead they obfuscated the morality by doctrinal quarrels. Christianity, meant to be a peaceful, forgiving religion, became instead a proud world power, intolerant and unbearably meddlesome. The papacy, its powers based on untenable claims, was openly involved in the crudest forms of power politics. It prevented kings and emperors from creating order out of feudal anarchy and thereby contributed immeasurably to human misery. It sought protection from human reason behind a shield of obscure doctrine, fortified by secular armies and the Inquisition. Monasteries, havens which had succored men during the barbarism of endless invasions, became oppressive landlords and a refuge for those too lazy to work for society. The Protestant explosion was the natural consequence of priestly tyranny, but the Protestants, engaged in myriad sectional squabbles of their own, soon proved as intolerant. Nowhere in his histories did Voltaire show an understanding of why faithful thousands found happiness in their church; yet in numerous instances his search for evidence of civilized activity led to a kinder judgment of some Christians. The Gregorian chant had some merit; the Pelagians understood the dignity of human nature; at Anagni Boniface VIII stood up with nobility under the disgraceful action of the French king; Alexander III had the courage to declare that men were not meant to be slaves; Leo X at least had taste; Zwingli started as an enlightened reformer; monastic life was usually marked by fewer crimes than secular life; the Jesuits were successful educators who brought civilization to the savages of Paraguay and superior scientific knowledge to the highly civilized Chinese; the Quakers were just colonizers; Gregory XIII reformed the calendar, and both Sixtus V and Paul V adorned Rome.[113] But, on balance, Christian churches had more often defaulted on their many chances to be civilizing agents. Mostly men lived without the comfort of sane philosophy. And superstition had so conquered their minds that even in Voltaire's "enlightened age" the shocking legal murder of Calas could occur.

The historical quest for the accomplishments of taste, that vital component of Voltaire's conception of civilization, involved the poet and *philosophe* in an equally saddening experience. The ages and societies before the *grand siècle* had produced little to please Voltaire's refined demands. Amid the immense crudities of men he found but few things to note. The upper classes in China had cultivated manners; the Persians and Arabs had at least more *politesse* than the people they conquered. But in general the accompaniments of taste — a sensitiveness to order and regularity, refined eloquence, and *délicatesse* in sentiment — were lacking among Orientals, who were rarely free men and "did not admit women into their society."[114] The fertility of oriental imagination was never sufficiently restrained by concerns for composition, formal balance, and regularity of style. Persian and Egyptian architecture (one wonders how Voltaire knew it) was grandiose but lacked taste. Voltaire gave the Chinese more credit for bringing theater into private homes than for the quality of their tragedy and comedy.[115] The Greeks were the most exemplary of the ancients in the development of the arts — but Voltaire said very little about them in his histories. Greek sculpture seemed unsurpassed, though occasionally equaled by modern Europeans. The Greeks were the pioneers in all the arts of eloquence — but for Voltaire they apparently provided no

---

[113] For a kinder judgment on Christian accomplishments see *Essai*, in *O.C.*, XI, 277, 284, 288, 520, XII, 68, 278, 294, 334–37, 419, 424, XIII, 97, 101–10, 167, 177.

[114] *Ibid.*, XII, 62.

[115] *Ibid.*, XIII, 163.

models.[116] One gets the impression that he did not wish to reconsider the relative virtues of ancients and moderns, an issue apparently settled in favor of the moderns. Voltaire was obviously tired of the centuries of humanistic adulation of classical antiquity. The lack of concern for Greek and Roman culture is certainly notable in this first modern historian of civilization. Voltaire either sneered at or was angered and saddened by the crudities of Jews and medieval Christians. Gothic remained synonymous with barbaric. Abelard might almost be considered a *beau esprit*, but after looking at his barbaric language Voltaire turned from him also.[117]

The *philosophe*'s tone changed when he came to fifteenth-century Italy. There a sense for measured style appeared; sculpture approached the level of the Greeks; painting far surpassed the Greeks; Ariosto and Tasso wrote epics superior to Homer; and Saint Peter's, the world's most beautiful edifice, was built. A few circles of society developed refined intercourse and manners in daily life. Yes, refinement was occasionally noticeable even in crimes.[118] When Voltaire approached this age from the direction of the Middle Ages, he was profoundly impressed by the change in the realm of taste and the arts; but he still lamented the fact that real *politesse* was limited to a few narrow circles and that refinement in the arts remained largely restricted to a few Italian cities. When he looked backward at the same age from the *grand siècle*, his judgment sounded less positive. The great mass of European society was barbaric before the time of Louis XIV. Although Spain and England possessed a theater, it was filled with crudities. Therefore the Italians, who alone had some art, were

---

[116] For a brief discussion of this, including references to other discussions, see Sakmann, "Universalgeschichte," p. 39. Cf. also *Lettres*, I, 218, and II, 150.

[117] *Essai*, in *O.C.*, XII, 61; a few pages earlier (p. 58), Voltaire made the reverse remark about Dante, whose language is fine but whose thoughts are "bizarre."

[118] *Ibid.*, XII, 7–8, 53–61, 168, 172, 181, 246–48, XIII, 93–114; and *Siècle de Louis XIV*, in *O.H.*, p. 616.

right in attaching the epithet barbarian to all beyond the mountains.[119]

And then suddenly, after 1650, a new humanity was born in the West which left all the other attempts at *politesse*, manners, the graces of taste and the arts far behind. Within a hundred years there was more progress in these realms of existence than in all the centuries before.[120] All the arts began to flourish after the great poets had pointed the way. Good taste asserted itself in all the minor arts and the adornments of life. France was embellished with beautiful cities, fine buildings, gardens, and statuary, and festivals were celebrated with splendor and taste. The arts of life were cultivated to the highest; the court became a model of good taste and manners; Parisian houses became *écoles de politesse*; and good manners could henceforth be found even in shops and in the provinces. This was indeed *le beau siècle du goût* in which everything seemed to approach perfection.[121] Could it ever be surpassed?

Ultimately civilization must be a shared treasure. Human affairs do not prosper when the individual in his desire for a cultured life withdraws into a private garden.[122] Those agents which disseminate civilization among men were therefore central to Voltaire's historical studies. The civilizing function of the state included both a guarantee of the necessary freedom

---

[119] *Siècle de Louis XIV*, in *O.H.*, pp. 620–35.

[120] *Essai*, in *O.C.*, XI, 56, 65, 215, 354, XII, 375: "Nous pensons, dans l'opulente oisiveté de nos villes, que tout l'univers nous ressemble; et nous ne songeons pas que les hommes ont vécu longtemps comme le reste des animaux."

[121] *Lettres*, II, 128. See also *Siècle de Louis XIV*, in *O.H.*, pp. 616–17, 908, 970, 1021, 1049; *Lettres philosophiques*, in *Mélanges* (ed. Heuvel), p. 97; *Lettres*, I, 284, 295, II, 215, 233, 250, 259–62.

[122] Among indicative statements see: "Le prudent se fait du bien, le vertueux en fait aux hommes" (*Dictionnaire*, in *O.C.*, XX, 573); "Nous vivons en société; il n'y a donc du véritablement bon pour nous que ce qui fait le bien de la société" (*ibid.*, XX, 574); and "L'attention de tous les législateurs fut toujours de rendre les hommes sociables; mais pour l'être ce n'est pas assez d'être rassemblés dan une ville, il faut se communiquer avec politesse: cette communication adoucit partout les amertumes de la vie" (*Russie*, in *O.H.*, p. 431).

for the dispersal of ideas and customs and a benevolent assistance to the full deployment of all civilizing forces.

As a poet and dramatist Voltaire was extraordinarily conscious of the role language played as a civilizing agent as well as an expression of culture. Language required centuries for growing into a refined tool of communication;[123] an understanding of its development presented perhaps the clearest illustration of Voltaire's historical consciousness, of his sense for the historical dimension of human life. When after centuries of polishing, the crude language of the people is elevated to an elegant and sensitive art of expression, a society has acquired a powerful tool for shaping a civilized existence. That galaxy of great poets and writers who perfected the French language made possible the brilliance of the *grand siècle*.[124] The poets taught Frenchmen to think, to feel, and to express themselves; and once these models were given, eloquence could mold a truly civilized community. The treasure of elegant language thereafter must be cultivated with devotion. On his last visit to Paris, where he was destined to die, the very old and ill Voltaire dragged himself from his bed for visits to the sessions of the Académie, which he had persuaded to work for the preservation of Racine's language. The theater, founded on the art of evoking noble sentiments through noble language and imagery, was for Voltaire the most persuasive agency of civilization. The theater is the best *école de moeurs*. It speaks to the whole man, his reason and sentiments. "If the bankers are no longer rude; if courtiers are no longer vain dandies; if the doctors have abjured the robes and hats and Latin consultations; if some pedants have become men, to whom do we owe this? To the theater, only to

---

[123] *Essai*, in *O.C.*, XI, 9, 20, 23, 56, 63, 215, 480–81; "L'usage de transmettre à la posterité toutes les articulations de la langue et toutes les idées de l'esprit, est un des grands raffinements de la société perfectionée, qui ne fut connu que chez quelques nations très-policiées." See also *Russie*, in *O.H.*, p. 376, and *Lettres*, I, 191, 420.
[124] *Siècle de Louis XIV*, in *O.H.*, pp. 1002–18; see also *Essai*, in *O.C.*, XI, 215.

the theater. . . . When the people participate in worthy spectacles [*spectacles honnêtes*], there will be fewer rude and boorish souls. This made Athens a superior nation. . . . [The theater] is the best education we can give to youth, the noblest respite from labor, the best instruction for all the orders of citizens: it is almost the only means for rendering men sociable by bringing them together."[125]

Whereas the theater disseminates good taste, refined sentiment, and polite manners, the academies and learned societies spread sane philosophy and useful inventions. They are the true instruments of enlightenment; for genuine enlightenment is not to be obtained through the socially useless erudition of a few select persons but by making reason and invention available to all who can employ them. The most devoted and most successful of such "republics of learned men" was to Voltaire the group of encyclopedists who compiled and disseminated useful knowledge on the magnificent scale of the *Encyclopédie*. This great work gave mankind a depository of all the sciences, knowledge of all the arts; it was a work so vast that it comprised everything worth knowing.[126]

Knowledge, the arts, good taste, and *politesse* flourish especially when guarded by the presence of women, acting as the gentle guides of men. No nation that excluded women from society could ever attain true refinement. For women are the very embodiment and the grace of society. "It seems, generally speaking, that they were created in order to sweeten and soften [*adoucir*] the conduct of men."[127] As the mediatrix of society, the presence of a refined lady stimulates the growth of more

---

[125] Quoted from that wonderful letter to Capacelli (Dec. 23, 1760), *Lettres*, I, 415–19. See also *Siècle de Louis XIV*, in *O.H.*, pp. 906, 1016; "L'Ingénu," in *Romans et Contes*, p. 273; and *Lettres*, I, 223, 274, II, 235.

[126] *Siècle de Louis XIV*, in *O.H.*, p. 1220. See also *Précis*, in *O.H.*, pp. 1567–70; and "Of the Encyclopedia," in *Candide and Other Writings* (ed. Block), pp. 482–84.

[127] *Dictionnaire*, in *O.C.*, XIX, 98. On the influence of women see also *Lettres*, I, 130, II, 90, and especially 278; *Russie*, in *O.H.*, pp. 360, 431; *Siècle de Louis XIV*, in *O.H.*, pp. 930, 981; and *Essai*, in *O.C.*, XI, 201.

delicate feelings, greater finesse of taste, and propriety of manners.

And, finally, Voltaire admired cities, even though, in his retreat at Ferney, he sometimes spoke of them in derogatory terms. Cities are the visible symbols of civilization. They facilitate the effective exchange of ideas and the rapid dissemination of good taste. They are the centers of cultural activity where all the talents of man can mingle. They are the residence of the "good bourgeois who have already, I do not know why, a glimpse of common sense," [128] a place where reason can more easily displace fanaticism. They provide the most advanced amenities and are the grand emporia of the world's goods. Except for a few courts, the cities were the breeding ground for true *politesse*. Among the few faults Voltaire found with Louis XIV was the king's error in spending lavishly on Versailles instead of adorning Paris so that she might become the world's most magnificent city.[129] While roaming through history in search of evidence of culture, Voltaire was steadily on the lookout for the fate of urban life. A beautiful city, where men sought to cultivate the art of living, meant an oasis for a civilized soul. Civilization itself, much like the city, was a work of art, wrested from a hostile or indifferent environment, by the ceaseless labor and ingenuity of man. "History is a disordered collection of crimes, of follies, and misfortunes amid which we can find some virtues, a few happy moments as one discovers settlements here and there strewn through wild deserts." [130]

Voltaire's composite concept of civilization was made of such balanced blocks as good government, sane philosophy, material welfare, good taste, refined manners, and the agents

---

[128] "Eloge historique de la raison," in *Romans et Contes*, p. 517. On importance of cities see *Essai*, in *O.C.*, XII, 22, 56–61, 68, 128, 168, 219, 486, 513, XIII, 118, 163, 183; *Lettres*, I, 242, II, 23, 70; *Traité sur la tolérance*, in *Mélanges* (ed. Heuvel), p. 570.

[129] *Siècle de Louis XIV*, in *O.H.*, p. 978, and *Essai*, in *O.C.*, XIII, 13: "Versailles . . . un abîme de dépenses."

[130] *Essai*, in *O.C.*, XIII, 177.

of cultural dissemination. Since he had no one comprehensive term for the phenomenon, he resorted to such combinations of terms as *esprit et moeurs*. Civilization is a compound of the spirit and attitude of men, and of the manners which guide their social life and actions. Voltaire did not precisely elaborate these terms, nor did he advance a clear theory of the causal relation between men's spirit and their customs or manners. He did not yet make use of the idea of an *esprit de nation* as the German romantics employed the notion of *Volksgeist* as a causal agent of a characteristic "national" culture. In spite of his occasional admission of the variations in a way of life, he never approached the concept of many civilizations, each complete and justified in its own terms. Thus while he came close to a formulation of the concept of civilization, he did not conceive it in the plural. He did not concentrate on the history of ideas, nor did he, like Condorcet somewhat later, reduce the past to a sketch primarily of the progress of the human mind. And, of course, he was far removed from Hegel's idea of history as a successive, dialectic, concretization of a world spirit. Neither was he contented with a notion of culture emphasizing solely the fine arts, customs, or cultural institutions. Voltaire did not write *Sittengeschichte* in the sense of external manners of man, or *Kulturgeschichte* in the sense chiefly of intellectual and artistic culture. His merit does not lie in a clearly conceived and reasoned theory of civilization, its nature, its causes, and its forms of development. He merely had an instinctive and acquired sense for the attitudes, sentiments, thoughts, and actions whereby man could distinguish himself from a barbarian. With his rich personal awareness of what was involved in a civilized existence he studied the past, breaking ground for a new form of historical investigation but leaving most of the conceptual and theoretical problems to successors.

Voltaire's judgment of societies was conditioned by his commitment to an ideal of life involving many interdependent values. Good government and sane philosophy must supplement each other; material welfare and good taste in social relations are interrelated but are causes as well as effects of good government and morality; the arts and the temper of religion are mutually conditioned; and so forth. In a good society all factors of civilized life are harmoniously balanced. True civilization demands the presence and the fruitful symbiosis of all cultural forces.[131] No society known to Voltaire met such a test. In the *Essai sur les moeurs* the oriental societies were held up as a reproach to the feudal and superstitious anarchy of Europe. A closer look, however, shows that these societies only partially measured up to Voltaire's concept of the good society. China's good government and Confucian morality met with the historian's approval; but Chinese society stagnated because of the prevalence of superstitions, ancestor worship, and the cumbersome Chinese script. China did not perfect the arts and left ingenious inventions unexploited, so that "even" Jesuit missionaries can teach her something when they arrive on the scene.[132] The Arabs served culture well; yet they failed to develop philosophy and science further and proved incapable of resisting the Spaniards, Mongols, and Turks. The Greeks were free men, free thinkers, and great artists; yet they could not break through to true philosophy, they never learned to rule themselves, and they had some deplorable institutions and habits. The Romans knew how to rule and to build, but were borrowing barbarians in the arts.

---

[131] For some examples of Voltaire's concern for a balance of values and cultural forces and accomplishments, see *ibid.*, XII, 62, 66, 71, 134, 172, 179, 219, 247, 250, 300, 302, 358, 366, 444, 507, 550, XIII, 31, 37, 43, 56, 110. The argument is usually: they accomplished this or that, but failed in this or that.

[132] At one point in the *Essai sur les moeurs*, Voltaire contrasted oriental and western society thus: "Tous ces peuples (de l'Asie) étaient autrefois bien supérieurs à nos peuples occidentaux dans tous les arts de l'esprit et de la main. Mais que nous avons regagné le temps perdu! Les pays où le Bramante et Michel-Ange ont bati Saint Pierre de Rome ou Raphaël a peint, où Newton a calculé l'infini, où *Cinna* et *Athalie* ont était écrits, sont devenues les premiers pays de la terre. Les autres peuples ne sont dans les beaux-arts que des barbares ou des enfants malgré leur antiquité, et malgré tout ce que la nature a fait pour eux" (*Essai*, in *O.C.*, XII, 366). See also *ibid.*, XII, 444.

The development of a better life in Europe proceeded spottily with the gradual emergence from feudal anarchy. The Italian cities made great advances in the arts, but their citizens were neither free men nor did they banish superstition. The Germans were first-rate inventors and scientists, but boors in the arts of life. The English discovered the art of government, learned how to enrich themselves by trade, brought forth science and much good philosophy, but knew too little of the refinements of arts and taste cultivated in France. The Anabaptists recognized the rights of men but supported these like wild beasts. Under Henry IV France had more religious toleration than under Louis XIV, and Henry was a greater man than Louis. Still, Sully merely began where Colbert succeeded, and the manners, amusements, and arts of the period were semibarbarous in comparison with the *politesse* of later days. Under Louis XIV society in many fields approached perfection; yet French science was borrowed from foreigners, religious intolerance and sectarian squabbles still hemmed in the full deployment of sane philosophy, and Voltaire concluded his picture of the age with a description of religious quarrels among Europeans at the peaceful court of China.

One by one Voltaire placed whole societies and the actions of groups on his scales and found them wanting. He mostly discerned isolated activities on behalf of a civilized existence, and these were easily swallowed up in the surrounding barbarism. In the Orient he discovered some societies which had, on some levels at least, attained civilization but had then stagnated. Only in very recent times did modes of life develop which warranted the conclusion that his dream of a balanced civilized existence was not mere illusion. The skeptical historian, unwilling to flatter the human race, resigned himself to the fact that the history of civilization was only a small segment embedded in the vast history of "un-civilization," much as gems and veins of precious metal lie embedded in worthless rock. Voltaire's love of mankind prevented him from simply writing off the past as one enormous loss. Instead, he prospected diligently for the isolated veins of precious metal by which men had in part redeemed themselves. "Culture [*police*] and the arts establish themselves with so much difficulty, revolutions so often ruin the construction in process, that one must be amazed that the greatest part of the nations do not live like Tartars."[133]

Voltaire lived in an age when men began to believe in progress. Shortly after him Condorcet preached the new idea of the indefinite perfectibility of man. Because of Voltaire's glorification of the age of Louis XIV and because of the modernity of his idea of civilization, composed largely of recent accomplishments, it might seem that Voltaire was also committed to the idea of progress.[134] The accomplishments of all centuries were less important in his opinion than the startling achievements of the past hundred years. Although much remained imperfect, Voltaire saw around him considerable evidence of enlightenment. He admitted that his contemporaries fought valiant battles for civilization.[135] And yet, was Voltaire a

---

[133] *Russie*, in *O.H.*, p. 376. See also *ibid.*, pp. 323, 335; *Lettres*, II, 170, 187 (building and planting take so long!); *Dictionnaire*, in *O.C.*, XVIII, 157; and *Essai*, in *O.C.*, XI, 162: "Il a fallu partout, non-seulement un espace de temps prodigieux, mais des circonstances heureuses, pour que l'homme s'élevat au-dessus de la vie animale"; and *ibid.*, XIII, 114: "Avec quelle lenteur, avec quelle difficulté le genre humain se civilise et la société se perfectionne!"

[134] See for instance Brumfitt, p. 127: ". . . it is a sense of progress and achievement rather than a feeling of futility which arises from the reading of the *Essai*. This results not from a stated belief in progress, but from the general attitude of the author. . . . This feeling of triumph over the past, which the reader who enters into the spirit of the *Essai* must feel, is far more powerful than the many reminders that cruelty and intolerance are still with us, and will, perhaps, always be with us. For this reason, Voltaire's role in the creation of the *mystique* of progress is no small one."

[135] *Précis*, in *O.H.*, p. 1566. See also *Remarques sur l'histoire*, in *O.H.*, p. 44; *Siècle de Louis XIV*, in *O.H.*, pp. 983, 1022, 1028; *Précis*, in *O.H.*, p. 1557; and *Dictionnaire*, in *O.C.*, XIX, 614–15. In my opinion, the difficulty with Voltaire's idea of progress is contained in the three following points: (*a*) Man is perfectible, or rather, he can perfect, but not indefinitely, certain of his works (". . . l'homme est perfectible; et de là on a conclu qu'il s'est perverti. Mais pourquoi n'en pas conclure qu'il s'est perfectionné jusqu'au point où la nature a marqué les limites de sa perfection?" [*Essai*, in *O.C.*, XI, 20]); Voltaire mostly used the notion *perfectionner* in relation, not to total man, but to such subparts as reason, arts, agriculture, *goût*, and so on. (*b*) Progress in certain realms of

believer in progress? Was he even prepared to place his own age above that of Louis XIV? "Je suis toujours pour le siècle de Louis XIV, malgré tout le mérite du siècle de Louis XV et de Louis XVI." [136] Progress was made in many areas of human endeavor during the eighteenth century, but Voltaire took count of what had been lost as well. Politics had become more *raffinée* than *perfectionnée*.[137] In many ways science had developed further, but the system-builders who founded vast speculative schemes on poor observation were also gaining ground. More than one of these modern philosophers, following the unfortunate example of Descartes, thought to create worlds, like God, simply by uttering a formula.[138] "Wild charlatans" like Rousseau were undermining sound morality and education by voicing "impertinences worthy of an insane asylum."[139] Yet, on balance, it might well be that sane philosophy had been spread more widely by the growing influence of the *Dictionnaire encyclopédique*.

---

human endeavor is usually counteracted by weakness in certain other areas (cf. the discussion, above, on the balance of cultural achievements, and, below, on the weaknesses of the eighteenth century). (c) Voltaire's pessimism about human nature in general and his skepticism about the common man in particular. I have tried to elaborate this in a paper comparing Voltaire's and Condorcet's attitudes toward the feasibility of a "history of the common man," in *Ideas and History: Essays Presented to Louis Gottschalk*, ed. Richard Herr and Harold T. Parker (Durham: Duke University Press, 1965), pp. 39–64.

[136] *Lettres*, II, 176. In the correspondence Voltaire's mood was occasionally very black when comparing his age and the *grand siècle*; "Notre siècle vit sur le crédit du siècle de Louis XIV . . . et c'est dans notre propre langue qu'on dit aujourd'hui dans l'Europe que les Français dégénèrent" (*ibid.*, I, 367); or, "Par moi foi, notre siècle est un pauvre siècle auprès de celui de Louis XIV; mille raisonneurs et pas un seul homme de génie; . . . La France subsistera; mais son bonheur, son ancienne supérieurité . . . qu'est-ce que tout cela deviendra?" (*ibid.*, I, 380); or, "On a voulu tout perfectionner, et tout a dégéneré" (*ibid.*, II, 105); or, "J'ai vu finir le règne de la raison et du goût. Je vais mourir en laissant la France barbare" (*ibid.*, II, 274).

[137] *Précis*, in *O.H.*, p. 1482.

[138] *Ibid.*, p. 1569; see also *Lettres*, II, 37, 113.

[139] *Précis*, in *O.H.*, p. 1569; Voltaire always loved to make fun of Rousseau's idea that man might be better off without civilization; see especially the famous letter of August 30, 1755, to Rousseau upon receipt of the latter's *Discours sur l'inégalité des conditions*, in *Lettres*, I, 336–39.

Voltaire's most serious concern was the deterioration of taste, especially in literature. The superb language fashioned by the great writers of the preceding century had degenerated into a "forced, violent, and unintelligible style."[140] Grammar was largely neglected. Good form, reasoned regularity, and the charm of Racine and Molière were no longer cultivated by generations which adored instead the barbaric crudities of a Shakespeare. The age of genius had been supplanted by feeble imitators and insignificant or tasteless innovators. "Thus genius had but one age, after which it had degenerated."[141] In spite of advances dear to Voltaire's heart, the new age was on balance not superior to the *grand siècle* with its illustrious assemblage of genius. "How did it happen that so many superior men in so many different genres all flourished at the same time? That miracle had occurred three times in the history of the world and perhaps will never again recur."[142] The historian who could not detect a continuous process, who was thoroughly conscious of the unpredictable vicissitudes of human societies, who thought it utterly foolish to predict the future, left no intoxicating vision of humanity moving steadily closer to the gates of some earthly paradise. His mind was not given to illusions. No amount of progress could overcome or lull to sleep Voltaire's skepticism about human nature. He could not explain the presence of so much evil in this world — surely not by simply ascribing it to faulty institutions.[143] He had nearly insurmountable doubts that ordinary human beings could attain the truly refined life

---

[140] *Précis*, in *O.H.*, p. 1570. This is no isolated complaint, see *Lettres*, I, 123, 225, 261, 295, 342, II, 18, 24, 48, 51, 77, 81, 92, 102, 105, 136, 143, 179, 187, 193–95, 218–19, 227, 250–52, 262, and 313.

[141] *Siècle de Louis XIV*, in *O.H.*, p. 1017; see also *Lettres*, II, 179: "Je vois que, chez toutes les nations du monde, les beaux-arts n'ont qu'un temps de perfection; et après le siécle du génie tout dégénère à force d'esprit."

[142] *Défense de Louis XIV*, in *O.H.*, pp. 1285–86.

[143] Among many passages see: ". . . l'origine du mal a toujours été un abîme dont personne n'a pu voir le fond" (*Dictionnaire*, in *O.C.*, XVII, 583), and also the famous poem on the Lisbon earthquake.

of the few select. At best, there is some hope that the enlightened men in power will work to make the hard lot of the masses bearable. Even the few could not expect to live in paradise. Man could not work miracles. By devoted labor and patient resignation to ineradicable imperfections mankind could have a measure of civilization, a cultivated garden amid chaos, never totally secure against a hostile and indifferent world or the resurgence of human barbarism.

Voltaire prepared the ground for future historians of culture. He forcefully drew attention to a new subject matter in the past. He taught historians to ask new questions and thus to discover a fresh dimension of mankind's long existence and varied actions. He himself never resolved many of the queries and difficulties which emerged from this reorientation of historiography.[144] He never clearly defined his central concept: civilization; he did not even have the word. The romantic school of historians — which borrowed much of his general outlook — turned against the "unhistoric" attitude of mind which characterized his judgment. Only rarely could Voltaire judge the men of the past in their own right and by their own values. He did not excel in understanding past forms of life which were profoundly different from the modern life he knew. He was a cultural monist; the idea of civilizations, in the plural, was an alien concept to him. He had one set of norms of civilized existence against which he measured the lives of all men. To the young Herder he probably was the archetype of the historical judge with "toy scales" in his hands on which the dead are weighed and found wanting without a true hearing.[145] But Voltaire weighed with sophistication and as a thoroughly civilized man. His judgment was harshest on crimes against humanity. He made no exaggerated demands

---

[144] Brumfitt, in *Voltaire, Historian*, provides an excellent survey of such difficulties as Voltaire's ideas of causation, determinism, and so on.

[145] The image occurs in Herder's *Auch eine Philosophie der Geschichte zur Bildung der Menschheit: Beitrag zu vielen Beiträgen des Jahrhunderts* (Riga, 1774).

on men; he expected a minimum of decent actions. His sober concern for the most basic human decencies, repeated again and again in his own inimitable fashion, gave a lasting value to his histories. The greatness of his achievement does not silence criticism but surely blunts it. He is still the first classic of cultural history.

2 : Guizot
1787 - 1874

During his very long life, François Pierre Guillaume Guizot alternated between a political and a historical career. History and politics were interlaced in all his activities. As bourgeois and Calvinists, the Guizots had gained greater freedom through the French Revolution. But as a man of law, François's father opposed the Terror and became its victim when the son was seven years old. During the later years of Napoleon's orderly tyranny François started making a name for himself as the author of literary and educational articles and especially with a critically annotated translation of Gibbon. In 1812 Guizot began to teach history at the Sorbonne. It was characteristic of the man that he refused to pay the customary homage to the master of France. After the fall of Napoleon, Guizot entered practical politics and was active politically as long as the principles of constitutional government of the Charter of 1814 prevailed. When these were replaced around 1820 by a return to more autocratic government, Guizot returned to teaching — until the government closed his lectures in 1822. When the ban was lifted in 1827, he gave his most brilliant series of lectures on the civilization of France and Europe before the most enthusiastic audience he ever addressed. The revolution of 1830 placed him once more in the center of political life and ended his professorial career. During the next eighteen years he became the dominant political figure of France. The third revolution in his lifetime, February, 1848, terminated his public career. At his Normandy estate of Val Richer the aging Guizot turned once more to the writing of history and, until his death in 1874, observed the succession of "petites républiques, petit empire." [1]

His two careers, as statesman and as historian, supplemented each other. They were cut from the same cloth. The one explains and justifies the other. Guizot's position in political life was molded by his view of the past. When Guizot worked on his histories of civilization, he was deeply preoccupied with the political problems of contemporary France. Through this life filled with political and historical labor ran a dominant theme: liberty and order. The memorable experiences of his youth had been the Great Revolution, which gained liberty but ended in disorder, and Napoleon, who had strangled freedom by his love of power and disdain for legality, but had been the most urgently needed great man because his horror of disorder had made him put an end to anarchy. [2] With a highly developed sense of duty, a Calvinist background, and majestic self-discipline, Guizot shared the emperor's "profound instincts for government." But neither could Guizot forget his debt to the Revolution. "I belong to those whom the élan of the year 1789 has elevated and who are not at all willing to step down. . . . Born as a bourgeois and a protestant, I am profoundly dedicated to the liberty of conscience, to equality before the law, and all the great conquests of our social order." [3] Guizot was, like his friend Royer-Collard, a member of the *doctrinaires*, men who saw in the Charter of 1814 the best hope for reconciling Revolution and Empire. He devoted his career to the task of making responsible representative government possible in the framework of a constitutional monarchy that would respect the necessary freedom of its subjects. He still defended such a constitution as the best possible fusion of order and liberty

---

[1] Quoted in Ernest Woodward, *Three Studies in European Conservatism*, p. 226.

[2] *Mémoires*, I, 5; and also *Histoire parlementaire*, I, xxxvi-xxxviii.

[3] *Mémoires*, I, 27; see also *Monsieur Guizot in Private Life*, ed. Henriette E. de Witt, p. 26 (hereafter cited as *Letters*).

and believed in its chances of success at a time when most other Frenchmen had long abandoned it.[4] Like the compromisers of the English Restoration who believed in trimming "between the Excess of unbounded Power, and the Extravagance of Liberty not enough restrained,"[5] Guizot relied in political life on that same skill in trimming. The *juste milieu*, this specter of horror and ridicule of his socialist critics, was for him the manifestation of reasoned principle and instinctive sense of balance. He was the arch-bourgeois, serving the bourgeois king Louis Philippe. Yet he saw in the middle class not so much one strictly defined sector of a rigorously structured society as that middle layer of society, neither aristocratic nor plebeian but open in both directions, which was representative of the entire French people and even of mankind.[6] He wanted to build a classless society.[7] Guizot's solution for all problems was education, intelligent discussion, patient submission to duty, and the "persistence of a free government [which] guarantees to a nation far more liberty and progress than a revolution can ever bestow."[8] He called for liberal conservatives.[9] Historians have generally not been very kind in

---

[4] *Mémoires*, I, 156–59, 199–201; and *Letters*, pp. 73, 266, 272–73.

[5] "The Character of a Trimmer," in *The Complete Works of George Saville, First Marquess of Halifax*, ed. Walter Raleigh (Oxford: Clarendon Press, 1912), p. 103.

[6] *Histoire parlementaire*, II, 223 ff.; Rut Keiser, *Guizot als Historiker*, pp. 18–20; and also *Histoire de la civilisation en France* . . . , I, 65 (hereafter cited as *Civ. Fr.*).

[7] *Mémoires*, I, 110–11, 147; *Histoire générale de la civilisation en Europe*, p. 286 (hereafter cited as *Civ. Eur.*).

[8] *Mémoires*, VI, 377–78. See also *ibid.*, p. 244; *Histoire parlementaire*, II, 456; *Letters*, p. 74; and *Civ. Eur.*, p. 420.

[9] *Mémoires*, VIII, 91. George Washington was for Guizot a model of a moderate statesman; he was "of all great men, the happiest and most virtuous" (*Letters*, p. 181). "Washington n'était ni puritain, ni aristocrate, ni encore moins démocrate; il était essentiellement homme d'ordre et gouvernemental, cherchant toujours à combiner et à exploiter de son mieux les éléments souvent discordants et toujours assez faibles avec lesquels il devait combattre l'anarchie et en préserver son pays" (quoted in Benjamin Bardoux, *Guizot*, p. 81); see also *Mémoires*, I, 236.

assessing Guizot's political career. Yet it is interesting that another great admirer of liberty and cultural diversity, John Stuart Mill, despite different political views, praised Guizot's historical treatment of liberty.[10] And Jacob Burckhardt, who shared Guizot's sense of historical continuity, admitted that "the thirties and forties of this century do not only appear to us more pleasant than the present because we were young then, but that they truly and without comparison were more gratifying days. Let us not forget Renan's words on the period of the July monarchy, 'ces dix-huit années, les meilleures qu'aît passées la France et peut-être l'humanité.'"[11]

The statesman's sense of the present and vision of the future were linked to the historian's perspective. "Man lives on a thousand points where he does not dwell, in a thousand moments which are not yet."[12] A sense of open-ended progress into the future and an awareness of the past, living on in the present and driving beyond it, were equally important to Guizot. Civilized life coincided for him with intelligent perception of historical continuity. He demanded "respect for the past without defection from the present and without abandonment of the future."[13] Only the barbarian, the man without imagination, can exist in the pure present without a feeling of responsibility toward the past and future.[14] Separated from his roots, the individual cannot unravel his fate. But integrated into the history of mankind, which may have blanks but is no complete mystery, man can give himself to his task with understanding.[15]

---

[10] John Stuart Mill, "Guizot's Essays and Lectures on History," in *Dissertations and Discussions*, II, 218–82.

[11] Burckhardt to Friedrich von Preen, December 23, 1871, Jacob Burckhardt, *Briefe*, ed. F. Kaphahn (Leipzig: Dieterich, n.d.), p. 359.

[12] *Civ. Fr.*, I, 239.

[13] *Mémoires*, I, 156.

[14] *Civ. Fr.*, III, 234–35.

[15] *Letters*, pp. 116–17: ". . . the history of humanity has for me blanks — large blanks — but no mysteries. . . . His [God's] action on each one of us in particular, His motives in the fate of individuals, are much less plain to me. I

Guizot profoundly distrusted the value of philosophical theory for the understanding of political affairs and guidance in political action. He was committed to the reality of experience. But experience meant to him the "suffrage of the ages"; [16] history, therefore, was the indispensable teacher of the wise statesman. Did Guizot abuse history to justify his political convictions, as some have suggested? [17] "I have never in my life prostituted history in the service of politics. But when history speaks, it is good for politics to listen." [18] As a politician he not merely counted the supporting votes in parliament, but rested his measures on the conviction that "c'est aussi une majorité que celle qui se compte par générations." [19] As a statesman he would not sacrifice his long-range principles to the mood and advantage of the moment. And the politician never ceased to be the professor. His parliamentary speeches were historical lectures and the deputies his captive audience. As a minister he instituted a new educational system for France. For men like him the dividing line between politics and education was very thin. A good government should also be an effective educational institution. To be free, men must

---

do not doubt, but I do not see as clearly: at every step I meet some mystery. I know that one occasionally sees the reasons and the moral results of the trials God inflicts on individuals, and that in other cases one perceives that He has tempered the wind to the shorn lamb. But I also meet with opposite and equally uncontrovertible instances: trials where the sufferer has succumbed morally, and with no apparent good result — miseries which are beyond all power of endurance. . . . when I see these things . . . I cannot understand, I cannot see, I fall back into mystery — terrible mystery."

[16] *Histoire parlementaire*, I, 221. See also *Letters*, p. 141; *Civ. Eur.*, pp. 100–101; Bardoux, p. 174; and *Histoire parlementaire*, III, 153.

[17] Keiser, pp. 3, 142; Woodward, pp. 130 ff.; Sainte-Beuve, *Causeries du Lundi*, 4th ed. (Paris: Garnier, n.d.), I, 312–13; Sister Mary Consolata O'Connor, *The Historical Thought of Francois Guizot*, pp. 22–28; Charles E. Pouthas, *Guizot pendant la Restauration*, pp. 329–34; all address themselves to the question.

[18] Quoted in Keiser, p. 38.

[19] Quoted in Woodward, p. 136. Compare also Guizot's remark in *Méditations*, II, 276: "Il y a un plus profond observateur que Bacon, un plus grand philosophe que Kant; c'est le genre humain."

be informed of their duties. "Liberty is the power of choosing the right." [20]

On the other hand, this first great professor of history in France never divorced his historical labor from his concern with political realities. Seen in the perspective of his entire work, the early notes to Gibbon already suggested Guizot's central concern for understanding the complex pattern of French civilization. Many of the notes showed his interest in the conditions which prevailed at the birth of France when the Roman remnants merged with Christianity and the barbarians.[21] The course of lectures later published as *Essais sur l'histoire de France*[22] proceeded to the more pointed question, Why did England develop representative government so much sooner than France? This theme also ran through the *Histoire des origines du gouvernement représentatif*, which led the government to suspend him from teaching in 1823.[23] Guizot easily made the transition from such topics to his impressive work on English history. When the government forbade him to "breed doctrinaires" through lectures,[24] he used his enforced leisure to study the crisis of English liberty and order, the great revolution of the seventeenth century. "It was at this period that I surrendered myself seriously to a study of England, its institutions and the long struggle which formed them. Passionately preoccupied with the political future of my country, I wanted to know with precision by what verities

[20] *Letters*, p. 212. Cf. also *Letters*, pp. 138, 139, 235; *Mémoires*, I, 156, 302; and Woodward, p. 142.

[21] Guizot read a great number of sources in order to annotate the translation of Gibbon; his disagreements with the English historian centered in particular on the interpretation of the history of Christianity and of the Germanic tribes.

[22] *Essais*, p. ii: "Pourquoi, entre deux peuples si voisins et si mêlés l'un à l'autre, des destinées si diverses? Pourquoi, en Angleterre, le ferme établissement de la liberté politique avec le maintien des éléments essentiels de la vieille société anglaise, et en France le mauvais succès des tentatives de liberté politique avec la destruction à peu près complète de l'ancienne société française?"

[23] This was a series of lectures given between December, 1820, and October, 1822, which were published, without Guizot's consent, in the form of stenographic notes. He brought out a published version in 1851.

[24] Pouthas, *Guizot pendant la Restauration*, p. 304.

and errors, by what persistent efforts and wise conduct, a great people had succeeded in gaining and maintaining a free government."[25] Before resuming lectures in 1828, Guizot had finished that section of the *Histoire de la Révolution d'Angleterre* which covered the reign of Charles I.[26] When permanently retired from public life by the 1848 revolution, Guizot continued to analyze this great English crisis in two volumes on the republic under Cromwell, a study on Monk, and two more volumes on the protectorate of Richard Cromwell and the Stuart restoration. Guizot's persistent preoccupation with the delicate balance of freedom and authority was equally discernible in his *Washington: étude historique* and *Sir Robert Peel: étude d'histoire contemporaine.*[27] Being so strongly guided in his choice of subjects by his overriding political concern, had he prostituted history in the service of politics?

The preface to his *Essais sur l'histoire de France* was consciously addressed to the proper relation of history and politics:

This is not a purely scientific study, it holds for us practical lessons which gain more evident importance with every passing day. . . . whatever people do, they cannot break with their past. . . . amidst their most startling transformations

[25] *Mémoires*, I, 318.

[26] Guizot's major works on seventeenth-century England: *Histoire de la Révolution d'Angleterre depuis l'avènement de Charles Ier jusqu'à la chûte de Jacques II*, Part I (2 vols.; Paris, 1826–27); *Histoire de la République d'Angleterre et de Cromwell 1649–58* (2 vols.; Brussels and Leipzig, 1854); *Histoire de la Révolution d'Angleterre*. Part III, *Le protectorat de Richard Cromwell et le rétablissement des Stuarts, 1658–1660* (2 vols.; Paris, 1856); *Monk; chûte de la république et le rétablissement de la monarchie en Angleterre en 1660; étude historique* (Paris, 1851); and *Discours sur l'histoire de la Révolution d'Angleterre* (Leipzig, 1850).

[27] The study on Washington is an introductory essay to a French edition of Washington's letters which Guizot had been asked to edit (see *Mémoires*, IV, 315 ff.), a task he was forced to leave to others; the essay was included in Cornelis de Witt, *Histoire de Washington* (Paris, 1855). According to Pouthas, *Guizot pendant la Restauration*, p. 328, Guizot had in 1828 promised Lafayette a translation of Washington's letters. The book on Peel appeared in Paris in 1856.

they remain essentially in character and in their destiny what their history has made them. . . . It therefore matters very much, not merely for the satisfaction of the mind, but also for the good conduct of national affairs, that these traditions be well known and well understood. . . . while history enlightens politics, politics, even more, renders the same service to history.[28]

And yet this was not pure "presentism." Rarely did Guizot pursue historical themes down to his own days. He seldom stepped over the threshold of 1789. Most of his books are either on seventeenth-century England or they deal with matters before 1400. He sparingly alluded to current events in historical lectures; and he admonished his students to refrain from applause where they thought they discerned remarks of current relevance. History was a science, and he never tired of trying to inculcate in others his own respect for the "fact." Frequently he warned his students of the perils involved in attributing modern meaning to older terms.[29] He himself gathered enormous collections of documents.[30] As minister he untiringly furthered the work of the Ecole des Chartes with both funds and plans, utilizing such great French scholars as Barante, Michelet, and Sainte-Beuve to gather the hidden source materials in provincial towns and monasteries.[31] His lectures were larded with excerpts from sources. He tried to

---

[28] *Essais*, pp. iv–vi. See also *Mémoires*, I, 296; Bardoux, p. 173; and Guizot's introduction to Gibbon's *Decline and Fall*, I, ix.

[29] *Essais*, p. 289; *Civ. Eur.*, p. 205; *Civ. Fr.*, IV, 260. It is interesting that he spoke in this connection of DuCange as the greatest medievalist (*Civ. Fr.*, IV, 13).

[30] He was actively involved in the compiling and publishing of the *Collection des mémoires relatifs à l'histoire de France* in 31 volumes, and the 25-volume *Collection des mémoires relatifs a la Révolution d'Angleterre*, both begun in 1823 during the period of silence imposed by the French government.

[31] His official papers relating to these enterprises (interesting evidence of the concern for details on the part of a busy minister of state) are collected in France, Comité des Travaux historiques et scientifiques, *Collection des documents inédits sur l'histoire de France publiés par ordre du Roi: Rapports au Roi et pièces* (Paris: Imprimerie Royale, 1835). He also was largely responsible for the founding of the "Société de l'Histoire de France" in 1833.

let the facts speak and he conveyed a deep respect for the right of the men of the past to be understood in their own terms.[32] But the problems he examined, the questions, which like searchlights sought out the relevant facts, retained their close tie to the present. Guizot studied the past so that he might understand the present and orient himself properly toward the future.

It was natural that a man of this kind should devote himself to the investigation and exposition of the history of civilization — as he understood it. Two of his books, the *Histoire de la civilisation en Europe* and the *Histoire de la civilisation en France*, have received continual praise, beginning with such contemporaries as Goethe and John Stuart Mill. Several generations acquired a view of history from these books, which were frequently reprinted and translated.[33] Guizot's reputation as an academic teacher rested primarily on the lectures which make up these five volumes. From April, 1828, students and a large audience of cultured Parisians flocked to the Sorbonne each Saturday morning to absorb and heavily applaud his analysis of European and French civilization.[34] During the first year he presented the outline of European civilization from the fall of Rome to the year 1789. Then he concentrated in greater detail on the development of French civilization. But just as he came to the days of Philip the Fair, those hard times for the bourgeoisie and the medieval communes, the Parisian burghers of 1830 rose up in their July revolution and pulled Guizot back into political life. As it turned out later, this revolution cut short an inspired experiment in cultural history; after 1848 Guizot no longer had his audience, and he never completed the lectures. "The abrupt termination of the *History of Civilization in France* is one of the heaviest

---

[32] For a typical comment see his note in Gibbon, II, 79. See also O'Connor, pp. 16–31.

[33] Before the end of the century more than twenty editions of the lectures on European civilization had appeared in France alone; see O'Connor, p. 85.

[34] "Ce fut un événement politique autant qu'un événement scientifique" (Bardoux, pp. 47–48).

losses which historical science ever sustained, for even in its fragmentary form it stands out as one of the great achievements of the first half of the century."[35]

Through the history of civilization Guizot presented the comprehensive view of the past necessary for his understanding of the present. He presumed that the modern attempt to establish a balance between liberty and order could be understood only when seen as the outcome of a long struggle waged by generations. For a Frenchman this meant a survey of French civilization, in the broader context of the western world, from its cradle to the Restoration. If history was truly an act of orientation whereby men placed themselves meaningfully in the present, the causally linked experiment of a society must be seen as a whole. In addition to the clear view of the total development, analyses of characteristic phases of this civilization could provide comparisons for a deeper understanding of present problems. The historian was thus faced with a complex double task: static pictures of characteristic moments of the civilization had to be welded into the total dynamic lifeline of a nation and of humanity. Only then could Frenchmen understand the current condition of their society and thus, on the basis of sound historical insight into the general course of French life, could they make intelligent decisions for the future. How, therefore, did Guizot conceive of civilization, its development, and its structure? How did he fulfil his task as a historian of civilization?

Civilization is a historical fact — no fiction, no mere concept. As any other historical fact, therefore, it cannot be defined, in Guizot's opinion, but can only be described.[36] Civilization is the most comprehensive and the most general fact. It is the ordered totality of all development, the résumé of life, the complete expression of a people's existence.[37] Civi-

---

[35] G. P. Gooch, *History and Historians in the Nineteenth Century*, 2d ed. (London: Longmans, Green, 1952), p. 181.

[36] *Civ. Eur.*, pp. 5–7, 17–18; *Civ. Fr.*, I, 25.

[37] *Civ. Eur.*, p. 10; *Civ. Fr.*, I, 4, II, 404.

lization is the ocean drawing into itself all the elements and forces of historical life.[38] The history of civilization is, therefore, the most comprehensive history, the only history which provides understanding of the whole through the relatedness of the parts.[39] Guizot saw this historical form as an accomplishment of the eighteenth century, but strangely enough Voltaire figured hardly at all in this estimate, probably because he was so little concerned with development. The real exemplars of this new history were Herder's *Ideen zur Philosophie der Geschichte der Menschheit*, Robertson's introduction to the *History of Charles V*, and Gibbon.[40] Before these, Bossuet and Montesquieu wrote "glorious essays in the history of civilization," but they failed as comprehensive historians because they built on too narrow a base.[41] It seemed to Guizot that the new historical form, the history of civilization, had had to wait for the modern state of civilization.

True civilization is development, not a static fact. Guizot therefore concerned himself exclusively with the civilization of western Europe since the fall of the Roman Empire. He excluded not only primitive societies but also all Asiatic and near eastern peoples who, in his opinion, had stagnated at an early stage of civilized existence. He omitted from consideration those societies which had no open-ended future, because their history consisted only in the realization of one "principle." Such societies, devoted to but one basic civilizing idea, were exhausted after a while and either reverted to the static type or declined altogether. Many promising beginnings fell aside because they got lost in the cul-de-sac of monolithic experiments from which they could not emerge to contribute actively to the modern state of civilization.[42]

---

[38] *Civ. Eur.*, p. 8.

[39] *Civ. Fr.*, II, 400.

[40] Pouthas, *La jeunesse de Guizot*, pp. 136–37; O'Connor, p. 2 n. 10; and Gibbon, I, 47 n.

[41] *Civ. Fr.*, II, 403. Guizot's relation to both authors is worthy of a separate study, too broad for my scope.

[42] Major arguments in *Civ. Eur.*, pp. 11–39.

By restricting civilization to western societies, Guizot sacrificed the breadth of Voltaire's historical vision. For the great *philosophe*, civilized existence could be attained by all men at all times, provided they acted as reasonable men who genuinely desired civilization. He had traversed the ages in search of moments of civilized existence, pursuing any trace of ennobled life. His historical questions had been: Where can man look for examples of civilization? How did this or that moment of life compare with the enlightened standards of the good life? Why did poor mankind find relief from barbarism so seldom? For him civilization had been a state of existence, not a continuous process. Guizot had a different conception of civilization and different questions. He was less interested in asking each age, Why have you failed in reaching a truly civilized level of life? Instead he wanted to know, What has this age contributed to the march of civilization, and why was it necessary in its particular form? [43] For Guizot civilization was less a definitive state of existence than a continuous process. It marches, it moves, it evolves. It is the most comprehensive fact of the historical process and not merely an accidental by-product of certain blessed moments of history. It is a never completed striving for a delicate balance. The true history of man is the steady growth of civilization — in other words, Progress. Guizot did not share Condorcet's conception of man's innate goodness and indefinite perfectibility; but both thought of an open-ended future in which the human condition could continue to improve. [44] Guizot had a profound sense of "life as historical movement" which precluded a vision of utopia inhabited by perfected human beings. He thought of western civilization as a young civilization; [45] he posited no definite end for it and made no claims to knowledge of the future. Ultimately, the Calvinist

---

[43] *Civ. Eur.*, p. 98.
[44] *Ibid.*, p. 28.
[45] *Ibid.*, p. 27.

historian rested his belief in progress on his Christian faith in Providence.

But Guizot differed from such practitioners of providential history as Augustine and Bossuet. Nowhere did he attempt to analyze history in terms derived from Holy Scripture. He wrote no history of a chosen people or a church of the elect. He did not use history as a lengthy justification of the Huguenots. God never intervenes directly as the immediate mover of events. In one sense, man remains the free historical agent. "After all, Messieurs, . . . it is man himself who makes the world; it is ordered and it moves by virtue of man's ideas, sentiments, moral and intellectual disposition." [46] History can be accounted for in terms of human actions and behavior.

And yet the world is God's and history is providential. Behind the complexity lies order and beyond free men are the necessities of historical continuity. As free and intelligent beings, men weave patterns which they did not design.[47] The seventeenth- and eighteenth-century deists had deduced God from the marvelous perfection of the celestial clockwork. But Voltaire, for instance, could not acknowledge a meaningful pattern in history. Guizot could. "The Supreme Mind and Will . . . manifest themselves to me in the history of the world as clearly as in the movement of the stars. God shows himself to me, in the laws which regulate human progress, as evidently — much more evidently, as I think — than in those which direct the rising and setting of the sun." [48] But, like the deist, Guizot deduced the existence of the observable regularity of development from the study of facts. At least

---

[46] *Ibid.*, p. 83. See also Keiser, p. 110: ". . . für den Historiker ist die 'Providence' Deklamation. Es gibt keine Stelle in Guizots gesamter Historiographie, wo er die 'Providence' als einzige Erklärung herangezogen hätte . . .'"; and also Gooch, p. 180: "His philosophy of history is an unshakeable belief in Providence, but the transformations of society are explained on purely secular grounds." In an age of triumphant science and positivism, Guizot wrote a lengthy defense of his religion, contained in *Méditations*. See also O'Connor, p. 71 n. 1.

[47] Qualified statements in *Essais*, p. 405 and *Civ. Eur.*, pp. 301, 315–16.

[48] *Letters*, pp. 115–16.

it seemed to him that he *discovered* Providence within the frame of history: ". . . when my intellectual transformation took place, when my opinions became settled, I turned my thoughts chiefly toward the order of the Universe, the destiny of man, the course, the laws and the aim of his development. It was while considering these subjects that the conviction of Divine intervention flashed upon me, and I recognized, clearly and irresistibly, the Supreme Mind and Will."[49] Guizot never extended his conception of Providence to historical details, just as he admitted ignorance of divine plans for the individual. "In fact, when I think of the design of Providence with regard to each individual, I bow before them with humility, for I feel I am in the dark. When it is a question of the designs of God with regard to the human race, I contemplate and adore, for light pours in upon me from every direction."[50] He did not speak of specific individuals as specially selected instruments of God, or of particular events as divinely willed. He completely reserved his notion of Providence for the grand design and the over-all order. In many ways his treatment of history would not change if the idea of Providence were omitted. For it served him only as the final unifying cause, as the ultimate explanation for the existence of discernible order.

Civilization spans the centuries as a continuous process. It is not a sudden creation; it is no unaccountable flowering of a suddenly enlightened mankind. It is a very slow process of creation resulting from the interplay of multifarious forces and factors.[51] It was lacking wherever a society devoted its existence to a solitary task.[52] A society with external comfort, but lacking freedom of thought, was not a civilized community for Guizot. But where there was freedom without

---

[49] *Ibid.*, p. 115.
[50] *Ibid.*, p. 117.
[51] Among many statements, see esp. *Civ. Eur.*, pp. 14, 17, 65, 218.
[52] *Ibid.*, pp. 11–39, esp. pp. 12, 35, 37, and also 81–82.

order, true civilization was equally absent. A society might in a relatively brief span establish a theocratically ordered life; but having submitted itself to the rule of a single principle of organization, it doomed itself to a fate of stagnation and the loss of equally vital forces of human existence. For this, the Hindus and Egyptians served as examples. The cultural simplicity of the Arabs led to monotony and tyranny. Cultural stagnation and decline can only be avoided by letting life's vital "principles" live. Progress, or continuous creation, which is civilization, can exist only where life's complexity has not been sacrificed to a stifling dominant element.

Only Europe has known such a genuine civilization. Only in its fifteen-hundred-year history could Guizot find a community in harmony with the universe and the plan of Providence.

Let us turn our view on the world in general, on the general course of terrestrial things. What is its character? how does the world move? it moves precisely with that diversity, that variety of elements, prey to that constant struggle observed in European civilization. Evidently it was not intended that a single principle, a particular organization, one idea, or one special force should usurp this world, should model it once and for all, should chase from it every other tendency or should rule there exclusively. Diverse forces, principles, and systems intermingle, limit each other, battle ceaselessly, in turn dominated or dominant, never completely victor or victim. It is the general condition of the world that the diversity of forms, ideas, and principles struggle toward a certain unity, an ideal, perhaps never attained, but toward which the human species moves by liberty and work. European civilization is thus the true image of the world: like the course of things in this world, it is neither narrow, nor exclusive, nor stationary. For the first time, I believe, the character of particularity [*le caractère de la spécialité*] has disappeared from civilization; for the first time it has become as diverse, as rich, as laborious as the theater of the universe. If it is permitted to say this, European civilization has entered into the eternal verity, into the plan of Providence; it moves along God's ways. Therein lies the rational principle of its superiority.[53]

From its cradle it has been complex by virtue of its Roman, Christian, and barbarian component. Its constant theme continues to be the never ending metamorphosis, amalgamation, purification, and rebalancing of its composite riches.

Guizot's glorification of cultural diversity antedated a fear which thoughtful Europeans such as John Stuart Mill, Acton, Ranke, Tocqueville, Macaulay, and Burckhardt expressed, though sometimes with different meaning and intention, later in the nineteenth century: cultural uniformity threatens freedom. As a politician Guizot sought to reconcile opposites, to balance principles and interests, and to leave room for varied expression. "I belong to those who will fight against leveling [*nivellement*] in whatever guise it presents itself."[54] He knew that he could thereby please no one, but "governments were not instituted in order to please,"[55] free government least of all. Representative government is based on never ending mutual sacrifice.[56] As an educator he sought to "multiply capacities." The "manifestation and simultaneous action of all interests, of all rights, of all forces, of all social elements, is the essence of liberty."[57] His entire life expressed loyalty to his concept of civilization. Eternal balancing of complex forces was the rationale of civilization.

Guizot undertook the task of presenting this complex entity called civilization with his customary clear head and vigor. He had to recount a process stretching over fifteen centuries. He had to describe the gradual emergence of a harmonious balance of diverse factors, since he thought of civilization as comprehending all historical reality. And while concentrating on this process, he also needed to portray its crucial phases as

---

[53] *Ibid.*, p. 42.
[54] Quoted in Bardoux, p. 181; see also *Mémoires*, I, 177; *Histoire parlementaire*, II, 133.
[55] Quoted in Bardoux, p. 176.
[56] *Mémoires*, I, 190.
[57] *Civ. Eur.*, p. 401.

intelligible units. In contrast to Voltaire, who concentrated primarily upon the static component of cultural history, leaving the dynamic problem more in the background, Guizot reversed the emphasis, focusing more heavily on the dynamic factor and subordinating the static structural one.

Guizot employed a variety of conceptual devices to simplify these two tasks facing all cultural historians. He divided civilization into external and internal components. The internal facts comprise religion, art, letters, philosophy, sciences; that is, "all those facts which seem to address themselves to man, be it for perfecting or delighting him, and which are concerned with his internal improvement, pleasure, or social condition."[58] The external facts consist of natural surroundings, material factors, and, above all, social relations and institutions. Under optimum conditions these two components are balanced. Though they need not simultaneously develop in exactly the same manner, they should support each other's growth. In an unstunted civilization they are complements, "reflex images of one another."[59] If European civilization is viewed as a whole (but not necessarily in all western countries viewed separately), it appears that the two components developed in close harmony and that the dynamics of European history resulted in part from their effective interplay. But Guizot excluded all other societies exactly because they failed to do justice to both these components, having either sacrificed inner life to the demands of society, or having neglected the external realities through an exclusive concern with internal life.[60] Where the internal facts (the realm of freedom), and the external facts (the realm of order), support each other, the "progress of humanity" combined with the "progress of society" becomes the march of civilization.[61]

Guizot gave further structure to the cultural history on

---

[58] *Ibid.*, p. 9.
[59] *Ibid.*, pp. 21–26, esp. p. 26.
[60] *Ibid.*, pp. 11–21, 35–38.
[61] *Ibid.*, p. 17; *Civ. Fr.*, I, 6, II, 402, III, 22–23. Progress of humanity is equated with internal development, progress of society with the external.

which he worked by subjecting it to his notion of "philosophical history." The "philosophical historian," he thought, had a threefold task: he must concern himself with the past's "anatomy," "physiology," and "physiognomy." [62] "Historical anatomy" involves the study of events qua events, the identification of phenomena which constitute the historical panorama. It permits but a limited view of past reality because it fails to account for the causal interrelation of facts. It remains largely classificatory and descriptive labor. "But facts do not merely subsist, they support one another; they succeed and generate one another through forces governed by laws. There exists, in other words, an organization and a life of societies as of individuals. That organization has also its science, the science of hidden laws presiding over the course of events. It is the physiology of history." [63] But knowledge of the anatomy of events, plus understanding of causal relatedness of facts, does not equal history. Anatomy and physiology must be supplemented by historical physiognomy, the art of historical portraiture, which endows the past with a semblance of life.[64]

Guizot concentrated on the work of the historical physiologist. Certainly in his histories of civilization, he was the historical physiologist par excellence. "Philosophical history" primarily meant to him exposing the hidden cohesive factors of the past. Guizot relentlessly searched out these hidden facts, proceeding on the premise that phenomena hide "principles" which act as the true movers. "What concerns us is the history of civilization; in it we seek the general fact, the hidden one under all the outer facts which envelop it." [65] Like a surgeon Guizot cut through the outer layers until he could place his probing fingers on the inner vital principle. Every segment of history under investigation was reduced to its basic reasons of existence. "La nature des choses" is an ever recurring

---

[62] *Civ. Fr.*, I, 314–17.
[63] *Ibid.*, I, 315.
[64] *Ibid.*, I, 315; *Civ. Eur.*, pp. 236, 341.
[65] *Civ. Eur.*, p. 98.

phrase. Each fact, propelled by the principle it represents, possesses a natural tendency to realize its full potential. Such a tendency would become dominant were it without the opposition from equally strong principles. This, as seen, had been the weakness of most non-western societies. In European civilization, on the other hand, principle clashes with principle, each remaining in a real sense a tendency only, never defeated, never victorious for any length of time. It was for the cultural historian to present this perpetual contest.

Guizot's cultural history thus became one long causal nexus. He presented a completely interdependent development. The accidental had disappeared. "The facts always have their reasons and their laws." [66] As Bossuet, that other great providential historian, had said: the search for understanding leads the historian always up stream toward the headwaters where things reveal their *raison d'être*.[67] This explains Guizot's strong preoccupation with the early formative centuries of European civilization, the period from the fourth to the tenth century. And in the subsequent ages he concentrated upon the "real revolutions," the great crises, those axial points where a new experiment in balancing the tendencies was undertaken. With that austere discipline so characteristic of his life, he restricted himself to essentials, omitting all accidentals. He presented a grand spectacle of the combat of hidden powers by concentrating so strongly on the "study of the progressive organization of the facts." [68] As historical physiologist he traced the causes but neglected the work of physiognomy, the painting of a colorful tableau of civilization.[69] Probably Guizot saw danger in this approach; he

---

[66] *Histoire des origines du gouvernement représentatif*, II, 227. Cf. also *Civ. Fr.*, I, 81, and II, 111.

[67] Bossuet, *Discours sur l'histoire universelle*, in *Oeuvres*, ed. Abbé Velat, Bibliothèque de la Pléiade (Paris: Gallimard, 1961), p. 953. And see also Guizot, *Essais*, p. 57, and *Civ. Eur.*, p. 343.

[68] *Civ. Fr.*, I, 317.

[69] Hippolyte Taine, *Essais de critique et d'histoire*, 6th ed. (Paris: Hachette, 1892), p. 44, puts it this way: ". . . il a diminué la couleur pour préciser le dessin"; Gustave Lanson, *Histoire de la littérature française*, 12th ed. (Paris:

warned that his physiological sketches provided only the barest view of history; he admonished his audience never to forget that the concrete moments of history were lived by human beings with all their human complexity. He expected his students to complement his sketch with extensive reading in sources and secondary works. That he could narrate history colorfully he proved with his *Histoire de France . . . racontée à mes petits-enfants*.[70] He had an appreciative understanding for the narrative art of his friend Barante; but he remained ever suspicious of Michelet's emotional appeal. Mere compilations of facts without theme he abhorred.[71] He saw his own task in mastering the enormous masses of documents and in the systematic ordering of relevant facts. But most readers are likely to share the sentiments which Sainte-Beuve expressed long ago in the *Causeries du Lundi*:

> He was the greatest professor of history we have had [72] . . . more precise than the Germans, a greater generalizer than the English. . . . To take account of all the constitutive elements of history with impartiality . . . to arrange them all and have them march under a law, that was his ambition. Guizot succeeded. But I, in effect, belong to those who doubt that it is given to man to embrace the causes and the sources of his own history in the past with such breadth, such certainty. . . . when I have read some of these high lessons, so sharp and so concisely cut, in the *Histoire de la civilisation*, I quickly open a volume of Retz's *Mémoires* to re-enter the reality of intrigue and human masquerade.[73]

Hachette, 1912), p. 1018, speaks of "ces grandes oeuvres froides"; Sainte-Beuve, *Causeries du Lundi*, I, 321–22, said: ". . . le tout manque d'un certain éclat ou plutôt d'une certaine animation intime. . . . Son style, à lui, est triste et ne rit jamais. . . . Il a l'expression forte, ingénieuse; il ne l'a pas naturellement pittoresque. Son style, aux beaux endroits, a des reflèts de cuivre et comme d'acier, mais des reflèts sous un ciel gris, jamais au soleil."

[70] *L'Histoire de France depuis les temps les plus reculés jusqu'en 1789 racontée à mes petits-enfants* (4 vols.; Paris: Hachette, 1872–75); the last volume was edited by his daughter after his death.

[71] *Civ. Eur.*, p. 236; *Essais*, p. 322; *Letters*, pp. 140, 202.

[72] See also Bardoux, p. 115.

[73] Sainte-Beuve, I, 315–19.

Through his heavy emphasis on the causal structure of history, Guizot reduced the individual human actor, with his personal traits and idiosyncrasies, to a mere instrument of historical forces. He thought of men individually as free moral agents;[74] his personal commitment to freedom was as strong as Tocqueville's or Mill's. But how free was man, in Guizot's conception, to mold the course of history? Guizot felt certain that he himself had affected history;[75] he had seen Napoleon as the master of the continent; history constantly reminded one of the works of great men. Yet, stronger than the strongest of men were the forces of history, the tendencies of an age, the principles struggling with other principles for their realization. The great ordered plan of development was designed by God. A man was free to oppose the movement of history, but greatness could be attained only by voluntarily executing the needs of the time.[76] Man could affect the course of events only by making himself the agent of historical forces. For Guizot great men were the nerve centers of their age through whom were channeled the time's demands and who formulated and executed the necessary actions. Their greatness consisted in their dedication to a task demanded by history, in their skill in assessing trends, in their sense of the possible. Their failures resulted from confusing their idiosyncratic desires and personal inclinations with their historical mission.[77] Guizot therefore concerned himself with the human factor in his analysis of history only in so far as man could be understood to be the manifestation of a historical force or principle in human form. He neglected men as specific, particular beings, each with his own personal complexity. He looked through their individuality as though it were glass

---

[74] See, for example, *Letters*, p. 18; *Histoire de France . . . racontée à mes petits-enfants*, III, 207, and IV, 432; Keiser, p. 131; and O'Connor, pp. 70–81. The work by Guizot listed in O'Connor as *Saint Louis and Calvin* (London: Macmillan, 1869) I have not seen.

[75] *Mémoires*, II, 1.

[76] See, for example, *Essais*, pp. 52–53; *Civ. Fr.*, I, 112, 143, 346.

[77] *Essais*, pp. 229–30; *Civ. Fr.*, II, 85, 113–15, III, 313; *Civ. Eur.*, p. 279.

and sought the inner principle for which they were the human agent. Thus Charlemagne was the executor of the historical demand that the nascent society of the West be protected against the onslaughts of Saracens, Saxons, and Avars; where he sought to implement personal policies (such as providing an administration built on his beloved Roman models), policies not in tune with the tenor of the time, he failed. With a remarkable sense of the possible, Cromwell let the dominant tendencies of his age work for his program, but failed when he did not heed them.[78] Napoleon was a great man only as executor of the "public instinct," but a disturbing force where he sought to impose his private will and ambition.[79] Philip Augustus and Edward I became the expressions of the principle of true royalty in Guizot's pages on medieval Europe, Philip the Fair the expression of the negative despotic one. Gregory VII was the embodiment of the theocratic principle, and Abelard a lonely representative of the principle of free inquiry. Viewed from the lofty position of Guizot's cultural history, all these men's personal lives and individualities were of no consequence. Except as agents and instruments they disappeared in the wider contest of principles. Not even the most powerful individual could break the necessary flow of history for very long. If this is a hard lesson for man, history at least bears this comfort: the times never demand more than the men of a society can fulfil. History never poses an impossible task for mankind.[80]

Guizot had opted for the work of the historical physiologist who placed the main emphasis of his investigation on tracing the hidden forces which made history the same as progress. Even within this simplified framework of his history of civilization, Guizot used a third device to reduce its complexity to manageable proportions. Just as he conceived of certain

---

[78] *Civ. Eur.*, p. 386.

[79] *Ibid.*, p. 274; *Civ. Fr.*, II, 117; *Mémoires*, I, 4.

[80] *Civ. Fr.*, I, 29: ". . . jamais la nature humaine n'a manqué à ce que les circonstances ont exigé d'elle; plus on lui demande, plus elle donne. . . ."

persons as representative instruments of principles, he singled out the progress of civilization in one representative nation in order to clarify his ideas and illustrate them by a concrete example. He could do this because of his conviction that European civilization was a harmonious advance of internal and external components of culture. After he had devoted the lectures of one year to a generalized survey of European culture, he turned to a more detailed analysis of French civilization, which he considered the truest representative of European culture. His great English reviewer found no quarrel with this preference: "A person must indeed need instruction in history very much, who does not know that the history of civilization in France *is* that of civilization in Europe." [81] In a brief survey Guizot rejected one by one the other western societies for failing in the attempt to balance the internal and external component of civilization to the same degree as France had done. In Germany, society advanced erratically; its intellectual development outdistanced social progress; the German people became a people of philosophers, poets, and scientists, with bad manners and no political *savoir-faire*.[82] Italy, at an early stage, developed a brilliant civilized existence in which art and intellect were complemented by a practical sense for external needs; but "the outside world weighed down on Italy and arrested her advance: she is like a beautiful flower, ready to open, but compressed from all sides by a brute cold hand." [83] Spain's isolation had been all too pronounced; she received little from Europe, and gave back even less; great spirits and events have erupted on her historical landscape, but never in related, continuous fashion; so the constitutive characteristic of true civilization was lacking in Spain; there was no progress: "somnolent immobility or vicissitudes without fruits prevail." [84] In this survey

---

[81] Mill, II, 136; italics are Mill's.
[82] *Civ. Fr.*, I, 11–13.
[83] *Ibid.*, I, 14.
[84] *Ibid.*, I, 15–16.

Guizot also rejected the one society to which he personally felt irresistibly drawn during his life. England, the great master in establishing a sound social and political order, had done less than France "for the history of Humanity." Not that England did not develop her inner civilization. But although she labored on the "only system of government which opens to a great people the career of freedom," [85] her inner life adapted itself too markedly to this great task. Consequently her philosophy, her arts, her religion, and her science became predominantly "practical." Common sense rather than speculation, usefulness rather than aesthetic pleasure, sound morality rather than theological thought, characterized the English life. Even the language lacked systematic, regular, rational construction; it did not possess the elegant logic of other tongues; but it was rich, flexible, and sufficed for practical concerns. "Throughout England the principle of utility, or application, is dominant, and is responsible for the physiognomy and strength of her civilization." [86]

Thus France remained the best representative of European civilization. She was the heart and the most typical part of western culture. Guizot did not claim her superiority in all realms of human endeavor. For instance, he did not necessarily value French thought more than the German philosophy he knew.[87] He certainly did not idealize French social and political relations but rather recognized England's superiority in these. Yet he claimed France as the "first-born" of western civilization. Europe's cradle stood in Frankish fields. France

---

[85] *Essais*, p. 430.
[86] *Civ. Fr.*, I, 9–11.
[87] Interesting also is his high regard for the classical literatures, especially since this historian of culture said in general so very little about ancient civilization: "On no account would I abolish, or even diminish, classical studies — the only ones which in boyhood really strengthen and inform the mind. I approve highly of those few years passed in familiar intercourse with antiquity, for if one knows nothing of it, one is never anything but an upstart in knowledge. Greece and Rome are the good society of the human mind; and in the midst of the decline of every other aristocracy, one must endeavor to keep this one standing" (*Letters*, p. 137).

has been the center, the "hearth of civilization."[88] She most completely incorporated the three roots of our civilization. The middle class, in some ways the finest product of western man, was eminently a French institution.[89] French culture was rich in ideas and in sociability, reasonable and rational. Her thinkers were "neither pure logicians, nor mere enthusiasts."[90] But most important: France was the most civilized because the most progressive.[91] For Guizot this meant that her internal and external components lived in ever fruitful contest. Thus her development had been a harmonious progression in which neither the one nor the other component was for too long left behind.[92] Even when the external order of civilization advanced more rapidly (as under Richelieu and Louis XIV), contact was not lost with the development of inner man.[93] French history, therefore, portrayed continuous creativity without serious stagnation.

Since France had a well-balanced culture, her full development would be reflected in either component of civilization. Clearly, the more the external part of civilization was a true reflex image of the internal one, the more it seemed justified to restrict detailed treatment to only one side of civilization.[94] Guizot's treatment of the internal component is negligible compared with the heavy concentration on society. The *Histoire de la civilisation en Europe* was deliberately restricted to the major stages of external development.[95] At the end of this course Guizot announced his intent to treat both components of civilization during the coming years. Yet, of the forty-nine *leçons* of the *Histoire de la civilisation en France*

---

[88] *Civ. Eur.*, pp. 4–5.
[89] *Civ. Fr.*, IV, 216.
[90] *Civ. Eur.*, pp. 5, 101; *Civ. Fr.*, I, 19, 21.
[91] *Civ. Fr.*, I, 5.
[92] *Civ. Eur.*, p. 319; *Civ. Fr.*, I, 5.
[93] *Civ. Eur.*, pp. 406–19.
[94] Guizot never argued this case in detail, but he came close to doing so in *Civ. Eur.*, pp. 26–27. At any rate, he presented his ideas on cultural history by neglecting one, the inner, aspect of civilization.
[95] *Civ. Eur.*, pp. 27, 428.

only nine treated the internal development of man. All nine chapters were among the first thirty *leçons*, so that there was less treatment of the internal aspects as Guizot advanced. The chapters on religion should not be included in this count, since Guizot dealt almost exclusively with the social and political structure of the Christian community and with church-state relations.

Additional limitations were imposed on the treatment of the internal component. Guizot concentrated on the history of thought and literature; the fine arts and music were not discussed. The theme most steadily pursued in the period up to A.D. 900 (and beyond this the treatment of intellectual matters did not extend) was the decline of secular literature and the growing domination of religious thought. The disappearance of secular literature coincided both with the loss of free thought (that basic principle of classical civilization)[96] and with the disappearance of the "classical model of the beautiful" (which was not revived until the fourteenth century). Part of a chapter was given to the Pelagian controversy and the defeat of the free-will position. Another matter which Guizot investigated with interest was the effect of theology on human reason and thought. In classical antiquity

the action, the direct influence of thought on external facts, of pure intelligence on society, was hardly sought by philosophers; essentially they were not reformers; they did not aspire to rule the private conduct of men nor of society in general. . . . With the triumph of Christianity in the Roman world the character of the intellectual development changed; what had been philosophy now became religion. . . . the new form of thought, which was religious, henceforth strove for much more power over the affairs of men; in religion the end of thought is chiefly practical and seeks to rule over the individual and even society. . . . [In the service of religion, solving practical issues and sharing the power to rule society, thought lost its independence.] Reason bought rule [*empire*]

---

[96] *Civ. Fr.*, II, 410.

at the cost of its independence; it no longer developed in its full meaning and according to its inner impulses; but it henceforth affected men and society powerfully and immediately. This is a serious matter, Gentlemen, which influenced the modern history of Europe decisively. . . . The religious form [later] ceased to dominate human thought exclusively; a scientific, rational development began again . . . but reason nowadays still aspires to rule society, to reform it according to its conceptions, to regulate the external world by general principles; thought has again become philosophy, but it has retained its pretensions to rule which it had in religious forms; philosophy aspires to do what religion once did.[97]

Although Guizot, on one level, lamented the enslavement of reason, he also understood that the close relation between thought and social action resulted in the integrated development of Europe's internal and external component. Guizot revealed most of his views on this development in two fine chapters in which he contrasted the theological thought of Hincmar of Rheims and the "free philosophy" of Scotus Erigena. The discussion of the internal development was suspended at that point in the *Histoire de la civilisation en France*. But at three points in the *Histoire de la civilisation en Europe* Guizot had hinted at crucial moments of the general development he sketched in the above quotation: in Abelard "individual reason began to reclaim its heritage . . . and for the first time a serious conflict developed between the clergy and the free thinkers";[98] through the revival of classical thought in quattrocento Italy a new "school of free thinkers" appeared;[99] the Reformation then gave a new élan to freedom, for it was a "great insurrection of man's intelligence" against the abuse of absolute power in the realm of the intellect, but it did not result in the proper conciliation of freedom and tradition;[100] and then during the eighteenth

[97] *Ibid.*, II, 412–14.
[98] *Civ. Eur.*, pp. 194–95.
[99] *Ibid.*, pp. 336–39.
[100] *Ibid.*, pp. 353–56, 362–63.

century the great fusion of thought and social reform proceeded rapidly but in paradoxical fashtion: ". . . notice how the human mind occupied itself with every matter, with ideas which attached themselves to the real interests of life, and which were destined to have immediate and powerful effects; . . . meanwhile the bearers [of such thoughts], the actors of the great debate, remained strangers to all practical activity. . . . A serious fact with prodigious influence on the course of events." [101]

Guizot focused his discussion of the internal part of civilization on the issue of man's freedom to develop his inner life at various moments in history. In so far as he treated cultural details (in the sense of fine arts, spiritual life, taste, and ideas) at all, he viewed them as adjuncts of his much deeper concern with the political, social, and legal structure and development of society. One critic has maintained that Guizot lacked "a sensorium for that which we recognize as culture," [102] and that he therefore remained inferior to Voltaire as a cultural historian. The only artistic interest of which he left a record was his love for literature. In his youth he had once said: "I feel drawn toward literature and poetry by a charm which makes me miserable. But do not fear that I shall yield to it." [103] His first wife, Pauline, was a literary critic of some renown, lauded even by Sainte-Beuve. One of Guizot's literary works, the essays on Shakespearean characters, was written as an introduction to her revised translation of the plays.[104] But one cannot overcome the impression that he liked literature chiefly for its thought and its moral content. Through his discussion of poets and writers in the *Histoire de la civilisation en France* he chiefly tried to answer such questions as: How

[101] *Ibid.*, pp. 423–29.
[102] Keiser, p. 122.
[103] *Letters*, p. 21 (to his mother, who, as a widow, was much concerned that the oldest son learn a practical profession such as the law).
[104] Published separately as *Shakespeare et son temps: étude littéraire* (Paris: Didier, 1852). Madame Guizot revised a translation of the plays begun by Letourneur in 1776 (see *Letters*, p. 61).

did the debate on free will and predestination affect medieval thought? How was philosophical writing first adapted to and then transformed into religious writing? What contributions to the practical objectives of the church were made by sermons, religious poetry, and legends? [105] Only in a few instances did purer aesthetic concerns break through, as, for instance, in the analysis of Mamertius Claudius, in a brief investigation of the style of Saint Caesarius, in a comparison of Saint Avitus' poem on creation and original sin with Milton's treatment of the same theme, and, most impressively, in the discussion of legends as expressions of popular imagination. [106]

It may be impossible to answer the question whether Guizot lacked a sensorium for cultural data, since it is impossible to penetrate to the deeper layers of his personality which might reveal what truly moved him. [107] But the style and tone of his cultural history were in keeping with the part of his character more readily known. This Calvinist impresses readers as a man in whom the force of intellect prevailed over the other facets of the human soul. He presented the development of civilization in clear, sharp outlines which are more those of a steel etching than those of a softly colored portrait. He

---

[105] *Civ. Fr.*, I, 135–36, 137–71, 172–96, II, 1–83.

[106] *Ibid.*, I, 181–93, II, 16–18, 64–77, 28–51.

[107] Bardoux, p. 43, quotes from an interesting letter by Guizot's wife, Pauline, on this issue: "Cher ami . . . quand je lis et relis tes lettres si charmantes, tes expressions d'une tendresse si simple, je pourrais dire si jeunes, et que je pense à l'idée que se font de toi beaucoup de gens: 'cet orgueilleux, cet ambitieux, ce coeur froid, cette tête calculatrice,' cela me présente un contraste si singulier, que je ne puis m'irrite de ces sots jugements; je ris à l'effet que produiraient tes lettres. . . ." And even if Guizot wrote the following words during the dark hours after his wife's death (quoted also in Bardoux, pp. 44–45) in a letter to his close friend Barante, they characterize much of the man who hid his true feelings about many things where one would like to know them: "Ne craignez pas pour moi le découragement, mon cher ami, ce n'est pas mon mal. Je suis comme un homme qui n'a plus de chez lui et qui passera désormais sa vie dans la rue. Je me suis detaché de moi-même, sans personalité intime; j'appartiens tout entier à l'activité. . . . C'est le dedans qui ne subsiste plus. . . . Je ne finirai plus ma journée, je ne rentrerai plus chez moi, je ne retrouverai plus la sympathie dans la vie intime de l'âme, je vivrai toujours au dehors, toujours au travail."

traced the course and the conflict of principles, leaving aside or coldly cutting through those irrational, emotional, confused, but also charming details which are also part of existence. He earned his audience's applause by his cool, brilliant analyses, not by moving their emotions. With his Olympian detachment it came more naturally to him to dissect a law code, or the workings of a legal institution, than to describe with warmth and charm a work of art or the yearnings of a human soul. He shied away from probing the inner life of men and presented but a meager characterization of the internal component of civilization.[108] By following this course, and by implying that the internal component was a reflex image of the external one in a balanced society, he greatly simplified his task and also the structure of his historical work.

Guizot's selection of sources also reflected his preoccupation with the external history of civilization. He was a prodigious consumer of documents and labored extensively on behalf of the systematic gathering of sources. He exhibited an extensive acquaintance with literary, philosophical, and theological texts; but he considered these the less useful sources for the understanding of an age. "Literature is only a pale reflection of life."[109] His real working capital consisted of legal documents. Laws are the precipitate of a society's real interests. Codes are the mirrors of society, the symptomatic expression of its condition, crystallizations of dominant facts.[110] The picture of history culled from the study of laws revealed for Guizot more securely and more clearly the course of develop-

---

[108] Notwithstanding two remarks where he implied that the inner life may be the more weighty causal factor, which he immediately qualified by stating that it may be better to study the outside first and then penetrate to the inside; see *Essais*, p. 73, and especially *Civ. Fr.*, I, 33–35.

[109] *Letters*, p. 135. See also *Civ. Eur.*, pp. 102, 195.

[110] *Essais*, pp. 121, 181, 215; *Civ. Fr.*, I, 286, III, 223, IV, 221, 259. Guizot surely must have known the remark of Gibbon in *Decline and Fall*, IV, 300: "The laws of a nation form the most instructive portion of its history." As so often with Guizot, the influence of Montesquieu seems obvious. As a minister, Guizot "formulated the view that legislation can only register the social condition of the time" (Woodward, p. 133).

ment that other sources merely bear out.[111] Frequent comparisons with other facts of social development could test whether the laws were properly dated and were correctly used as witnesses for conditions prevailing at a specific time. Such comparisons will save the historian from the error of Montesquieu, who in his *Esprit des lois* was frequently guilty of an anachronistic, and therefore historically misleading, use of legal documents.[112] In his study of the Germanic codes, Guizot carefully analyzed the provenience of the different elements of which they consist; he distinguished the remnants of original Germanic customs and institutions from the intrusions that crept in through later contact with the more developed institutions of Rome and Gaul. He was able in this way to illustrate the history of the Germanic migrations from the composition and history of the different codes. On the other hand, he reconstructed the effects of the decline of the Roman municipal system from the Theodosian Code and the so-called Notitia Imperii Romani. The picture he drew of the history of the Christian church was based on careful study of conciliar acts and ecclesiastic legislation. His analysis of the rise of monarchy and the third estate in the Middle Ages rested heavily on royal ordinances and town laws. As it was his habit to intersperse his lectures with extensive quotations from his sources, Guizot read to his audience from these legal documents. Nor did he hesitate to lead them for hours through the maze of feudal terms. It was a triumph of his consummate skill in analysis and presentation that he retained the unabated enthusiasm of his students for a course that sacrificed most of the appealing detail of narrative to the careful study of *coloni, curiales,* Carolingian capitularies, *wehrgeld, antrustiones,* and allodial holdings. John Stuart Mill summed up this effect with his customary perspicacity when he reviewed the lectures in their printed version: "Monsieur Guizot creates in those dry bones a living soul. He not

---

[111] *Civ. Fr.,* II, 259, 279, IV, 295.
[112] *Ibid.,* IV, 37; see also *ibid.,* III, 224.

only inquires what our ancestors were, but what made them so, what gave rise to the peculiar state of society of the Middle Ages, and by what causes this state was progressively transformed into what we see around us." [113]

By using a number of interdependent methodological devices Guizot thus made manageable the complexities of civilization for analysis and presentation. He divided civilization into an external and an internal component. He then concentrated on the most clear and complete expression of the general development of civilization in *one* representative society in which the two basic human concerns had succeeded in establishing a relatively harmonious balance. As a historical "physiologist" he sought out the tendencies and principles which were responsible for the evolution of civilization. In the pursuit of such principles he focused on those sources which could be used as the precipitate of complex social realities. And, finally, since Guizot viewed civilization as a process rather than a permanent state, he could describe it by attending to the critical moments in the metamorphosis of its basic constitutive elements.

If we except the history of the English revolutions and contemporary topics, Guizot dwelled in his historical writings extensively on the period from the fourth to the tenth century. During this age of confusion, in which the process of civilization had just begun to take shape, the basic elements of the future were effectively mixed. Lacking a dominant principle of organization, this age permitted the free growth of diverse forces which subsequently functioned as agencies of civilization.

There were the contributions of the Roman component based on the urban way of life of the old Roman municipal "bourgeoisie," the *curiales*. When the emperors taxed this middle class out of existence, they deprived the realm of its life-giving element. The barbarians therefore conquered a

---

[113] Mill, II, 133.

crippled commonwealth. The "municipal principle" of a cultured, self-governing community was not entirely lost, however, for the church's identification with certain urban nuclei preserved them for later rebirth. Roman law, that formalized crystallization of urban existence, similarly slept until a later time could use it.[114]

The early church was the middleman between the barbarian and the remnants of civilization. Christianity, to Guizot, was originally a moral revolution. Like all religions it was concerned with the private, the "lonely" questions of human life, and so had an asocial component.[115] But it was never completely a personal affair of the lonely soul in search of salvation. From the beginning it was also a form of communal life. The content of its message was subject to increasing systematization. A theology developed, therefore, a coherent system of formalized thought that successfully brought under control the individual's mind and spirit and remained the medium of all intellectual life down to the days of Bacon and Descartes.[116] But more important for Guizot was the formation of a Christian community and its "polarization" into a "religious society" and an "ecclesiastic government." The whole discussion of religion was guided by his emphasis on this split between believers and the highly organized hierarchy. His sympathies were with the "religious society." But he could not avoid paying tribute to the effectiveness of church organization for having preserved this Christian community during those ages of chaos. In the picture he drew, the church emerged as a major civilizing agency: it counteracted secular despotism by protecting man's inner life against imperial and royal encroachment; it provided at least some protection and stability during the Merovingian and feudal disorders; by its

---

[114] *Civ. Fr.*, Vol. I, chap. 9, is entirely given to this subject, including a lengthy discussion of the work of Savigny.

[115] *Ibid.*, I, 151; *Civ. Eur.*, pp. 18, 134–37.

[116] *Civ. Eur.*, pp. 179–80 ("même les sciences mathématiques").

awesome pomp[117] it brought barbarians within the ken of a possible common civilization; and the papal missions to non-Romanized tribes pacified potential troublemakers for the nascent western society. But like all governments, the church had a despotic tendency which, in this instance, was doubly dangerous because of its control over man's inner life. A substantial part of Guizot's discussion concentrated upon those countervailing powers which forestalled complete church domination. Through Pelagius, Scotus Erigena, and Abelard he traced recurrent stirrings of man's inner freedom within the religious community. He saw other checks in the indomitable personality of the barbarians and the persistent assertion of secular interests by the later monarchy. Through the Reformation the religious community partly freed itself from its ecclesiastic overlords; but on the whole this remained an incomplete break and the ideal separation of religious and secular powers was not achieved until the end of the eighteenth century.[118] By greatly oversimplifying Guizot's intricate thought, one might sum up his position in this way: in the ideal model, the polarization of the forces giving expression to the inner life into a religious society and a governing hierarchy is deplorable, but Christianity began its service to civilization in a chaotic age; under these conditions, the crystallization of the structural force of the new religion into restrictive dogma and hierarchical organization was necessary for the survival of the Christian community and for its influence on the emerging culture; with the progress of civilization the religious society could (and was bound to) extricate itself from all tutelage, becoming the most vital active force in the emergence of free western man.

Side by side with Roman remnants and Christian religion, the barbarian presented himself as the third constitutive ele-

---

[117] "Les chroniques prouvent que c'était surtout par ce moyen que l'Eglise agissait sur les barbares; elle les convertissait par de beaux spectacles" (*ibid.*, p. 156).

[118] *Ibid.*, pp. 356, 362.

ment in Guizot's analysis of the formative age of European civilization. The Germanic warrior embodied that unrest and commotion which prevented the sway of theocratic tyranny as well as the establishment of caesaropapist control of life in the eastern fashion. The self-centered strength of these restless adventurers frustrated all attempts to make one central power dominant in society. Their self-assertion provoked the eternal hatred of the subject people because it was so inextricably near and personal. A nakedly egotistic force, the barbarian feudal lord was an oppressive counterweight to any principle of public interest. The one exception, the English feudal nobility, developed a genuine corporate spirit of benefit to the nation's public interest largely through the peculiar circumstances created by the Norman conquest.[119] On the continent, the "Carolingian revolution," though it had consolidated the frontiers, failed to check barbarian prominence. Unable to generate a real society, the feudal "order" dominated several centuries and was not truly eliminated before the French Revolution. Guizot readily acknowledged the positive value of the barbarian factor in the development of European civilization, although the feudal "system," with its reliance on naked force and its insistence upon inequality, was hateful to him. For, from the barbarian conquerors and their indomitable private will, their claims to the right of resistance, and their unrestrained leisure, the modern Eu-

---

[119] This was the great theme of the *Essais*, in which he discussed the various theses of Boulainvilliers, Dubos, and Mably. How far he was influenced by Augustin Thierry is difficult to say; both authors must have worked simultaneously on their respective theses. See Keiser, pp. 124–26; O'Connor, pp. 9–13, 60–63; and Jacques Barzun, "Romantic Historiography as a Political Force in France," *Journal of the History of Ideas*, II (1941), 318–29, and *The French Race: Theories of Its Origins and Their Social and Political Implications prior to the Revolution* (New York: Columbia University Press, 1932). Guizot's belief in the importance of race as a factor in history is most prominent in the early writings: "Du gouvernement représentatif en France" (1816) and "De la situation politique et de l'état des esprits en France (1817), both in *Mélanges politiques et historiques*; I cannot find it a great factor in the *Essais*, written five or six years later, or in the histories of civilization.

ropean derived his sense of personal liberty.[120] "The modern spirit of liberty . . . is the love of individual independence, the claim for freedom of action (with as little interference as is compatible with the necessities of society) from any authority other than the conscience of the individual. It is in fact the self-will of the savage, moderated and limited by the demands of civilized life; and Monsieur Guizot is not mistaken in believing that it came to us, not from ancient civilization, but from the savage element infused into that enervated civilization by its barbarous conquerors."[121] A vital part of Guizot's great story was the "civilizing" of this barbarous "principle" by the counteraction of other European forces.

The two "principles" represented by monarch and burgher were indispensable as the vectors in the process of action and counteraction which produced the first flowering of European civilization in the twelfth century. The western conception of royalty (a composite of the ideas of Roman emperorship, of barbarian leadership, and of religiously sanctioned Judeo-Christian kingship)[122] played a decisive role in the drama sketched by Guizot because the principle of monarchy was gradually identified with the public interest. In a long process of purification, monarchy became the centralizing agent for the effective satisfaction of society's common needs. In the ideal model of the new order it functioned as the depository of public interest, the high judge of the land's peace, and the executor of public opinion and public laws (which are the precipitate of an enduring public interest). Since the best form of government, that based on the federal principle,[123] can be realized only in exceptional cases, the centralized monarchy became the main and the most effective embodiment of the public interest in the course of European history.

---

[120] *Essais*, p. 149; *Civ. Eur.*, pp. 61, 107, 124–26; *Civ. Fr.*, I, 334, III, 379, IV, 75.

[121] Mill, II, 244–45.

[122] *Civ. Eur.*, pp. 272–76; *Civ. Fr.*, III, 311; *Essais*, pp. 251–52.

[123] *Civ. Eur.*, p. 122; *Civ. Fr.*, IV, 281.

Emerging from the contest with the manifold principles, monarchy succeeded in building nations as the shells for the protection of man's internal civilization. The rule of Philip Augustus, Louis IX, Edward I, and Louis XIV were Guizot's main examples through which he illustrated the beneficial role of that monarchic principle. The regimes of Philip the Fair, Philip II of Spain, and also Louis XIV, suggested to him the danger of a stifling despotism inherent in the same principle. So royalty, like every other civilizing principle, could make its contribution to civilization only if checked by countervailing forces.

Out of the unhampered contest of all these civilizing forces a genuine society gradually arose. Such an association, held together by common values and interests, and stretching beyond the narrow limits of locality and corporate spirit, was for Guizot a late cultural phenomenon.[124] It presupposed not only inner self-discipline, to keep the multiplicity of private egotisms under control, but also the free exchange of opinion without which the common interest cannot be formulated. *La grande société* (in contrast to the limited local community), diversified yet coherent, was the finest and the most precious result of the civilizatory process. Without it there was no viable nation, and no enduring civilization.[125] The third estate was for Guizot the symbol and the representative of such a society. It built society piece by piece over long centuries. Until the twelfth century this "principle of society" had no effective spokesmen. Then the towns and the communal movement became its vehicle in the medieval context. In the towns and in the free association of the communal movement those men came together who could not find satisfaction in the stationary life of the rural districts and who were not willing to bow to the assertion of private will by force.

---

[124] *Civ. Eur.*, pp. 83–84, 312, 327; *Civ. Fr.*, II, 233, 240–41, IV, 68–69; *Essais*, p. 158.
[125] *Essais*, pp. 69–71; *Civ. Eur.*, p. 81; *Civ. Fr.*, I, 341, IV, 3; *Histoire parlementaire*, III, 562–63.

These men were, not consistently in practice but in principle, the patient builders interested in historical continuity, legal protection, safety for property, steady non-arbitrary government, freedom of conscience, and freedom of movement. Their long-range interests are always identical with the good society. Guizot was too good a historian to identify his principle of the third estate with any of its historical manifestations such as the communal movement of the Middle Ages. In fact, he devoted some brilliant pages to the clarification of the historically conditioned peculiarities that made the burghers of the medieval towns different from the Roman *curiales* on the one side and the bourgeois of 1789 on the other.[126] But the "reborn social principle" found its first European manifestation in the merchants and artisans of the Middle Ages. The communal movement itself failed during the fourteenth and fifteenth centuries because it was restrictive in scope, choked by particularism and corporate egotism. But in association with a public spirited monarchy the middle class became in the course of time the true representative of French society; it absorbed the professions, the magistrature, and the emancipated peasantry. In 1789 this middle class finally reformulated its relations with its old ally, the crown, and became identical with the nation. From "weak, despised, almost imperceptible beginnings . . . by continuous movement and incessant labor"[127] the middle class had built up modern society. Order and liberty were fruitfully balanced.

For Guizot, neither theology nor philosophy was able to account for the complex social and historical reality as it existed in the nineteenth century. Only the science of history held the key to its understanding because it was the result of a process of historical growth. Only the past could explain the particular constellation within which the nineteenth-century statesman had to find his bearings. The subtle balance of

---

[126] *Civ. Fr.*, Vol. IV, chap. 18 and part of 19.
[127] *Ibid.*, IV, 212.

forces established through centuries of struggle and co-opera-tion was intelligible only as a heritage. Guizot, with his profound sense of historical continuity, was not prepared to let this balance be jeopardized merely to gratify theorists of the right, left, or middle. Guizot partially misjudged the tendencies of his time; he was blind especially to the implica-tions of the social question as it arose in the new industrial order. But his reactionary and his revolutionary opponents on their part failed to reckon with the force of historical reality which he understood so well. Guizot's devotion to his-torical studies developed in him a "slow sense of time" that became a handicap for a statesman in an age of continuing revolution.[128] "Enrich yourself by saving and by labor";[129] he could see no other solution for the problems of his time but that slow, persistent labor and patient adaptation which in the past had proved the decisive force in developing the unique civilization of which he felt himself a part. He found himself opposed to all who wanted to stand still and all who reached for a sudden and miraculous fulfilment of man's justified de-sire for progress and liberty. After he had helped establish the liberties of representative government, the "liberal conserva-tive" consciously sought to conserve the gains of centuries. He knew from his study of civilization that generations had been needed to build this civilized society. He felt obliged to protect it against the dangerous experiments of those who did not see that one also had a duty toward that "majority which is counted by generations."

In Guizot's opinion, the accumulated experience of an entire civilization was, as a guide for action, superior to the abstract theories of philosophy. On the other hand, the "un-philosophical" study of history was bound to leave the scholar and his readers with nothing but an unintelligible mass of

---

[128] "L'Histoire abât les prétentions impatientes et soutient les longues es-pérances" (quoted in Bardoux, p. 124).

[129] Quoted in Bardoux, p. 101 (*Enrichessez-vous par l'épargne et par le travail!*); Guizot's critics usually shortened the remark to *Enrichessez-vous!* See also *Histoire parlementaire*, I, 327.

external facts. The "philosophical history" to which Guizot devoted so much of his life work was the attempt to penetrate through the changing phenomena of the surface of the past to their persistent causes. The historian should not try to extract from the "facts" he establishes a systematic structure of philosophical or sociological laws. History is no mere feeder of facts for the philosopher; it is an independent interpreter of the world. The historian is not less interested in principles than the philosopher is; but instead of formulating them in conceptual terms, he points them out in the context of actual historical events and institutions. When he succeeds in opening a comprehensive view, comprising man's past in one vast sweep, he reveals, at the same time, the forces underlying this historical process and the structure of the process itself — not by condensing historical experience into abstract rules, but by making the interconnections visible in the concrete context of history itself. In this Guizot succeeded, furnishing in the process some "lucid high lessons in cultural history."

3 : Burckhardt

1818 - 1897

In his autobiographical sketch Jacob Burckhardt stated that the death of his mother left him, at the age of twelve, with an indelible sense of the "great caducity and uncertainty of everything terrestrial, despite a temperament given to serenity and probably inherited from his dear mother."[1] According to the old customs of Basel, Burckhardt's personal summation of his life (written in the third person) containing this passage was read at his funeral, where remarks on the transitoriness of human life were in order. But these quoted words have meaning beyond the fleeting moment. The serene acceptance of life's transient and mutable quality speaks from every one of Burckhardt's works. He retained traces of his early fascination for apocalyptic visions, the Dance of Death, and visual representations of last judgments. His students often heard him reiterate the Preacher's *O vanitas vanitatum!* in response to all human pretensions for continuous progress.[2] Burckhardt's language had special warmth whenever he spoke of great endurers, patient and without illusions: the old Oedipus, Heracles, Odysseus, Calderón's Steadfast Prince, and Saint Severin, "who persevered amid the overthrow of everything."[3] He had much sympathy for those who, like Herodotus, Sophocles, or Madame de Sévigny, thought "not-to-have-been-born" the better fate. Among his last recorded statements was the

---

[1] Burckhardt, *Frühe Schriften*, p. vii; see also Werner Kaegi, *Jacob Burckhardt, eine Biographie*, I, 21 and 228 (hereafter cited as *J.B.B.*).

[2] *J.B.B.*, I, 273, 544–45, III, 103, 251, 257, 275.

[3] *J.B.B.*, II, 569, III, 173, 203 300, 385, 535, 537, 631; and *Griechische Kulturgeschichte*, II, 37, 45 (hereafter cited as *G.K.*).

sigh: *Nur nicht noch ein Erdenleben!* — but not another life like that on earth.[4]

It is a serious error, however, to overlook the serenity with which Burckhardt accepted human frailty and death. Burckhardt was one of the truest pessimists of the nineteenth century, and those somber prophecies he hurled at the twentieth may account in part for his current vogue. But he was also a comforter of men. His greatness, refreshing for generations given to pretensions and wishful thinking, rests on his vision of the excellence possible for frail beings. For Burckhardt complemented his unfaltering awareness of human inadequacy with a permeating sense for all that makes life bearable. His distrust of metaphysical solutions, which made it impossible for him to continue the theological studies undertaken in respect for his father's wishes, had a counterpart in the infectious enthusiasm for the concrete values of art, knowledge, and morality. He sometimes spoke of the need to compensate for the inadequacies of the momentary *(Zeitungen)* by concentration upon the lasting *(Ewigungen)*[5]— a not entirely fortunate though haunting play on words. His sense of the caducity of everything terrestrial, so early acquired and so deep-seated, was with him perhaps a cause and fruitful concomitant of life as a historian. "Rarely, I suspect, has a human being of my age had as lively a feeling of the littleness and transitoriness of human affairs, at least in relation to the individuum. . . . But that much more gigantic grows my respect for the universal *[Allgemeine]* and for the breath *[Atem]* of peoples and centuries."[6]

Thus Burckhardt devoted his life to history. "Perish we

---

[4] *Briefe*, pp. clxxv; see also *ibid.*, p. 23, and *J.B.B.*, II, 581, III, 385.

[5] *J.B.B.*, I, 418, III, 257, 548; *G.K.*, I, 331; see also Burckhardt's remark in *Historische Fragmente*, p. 262: "Das Hauptphänomenon unserer Tage ist das Gefühl des Provisorischen."

[6] *Briefe*, p. 105; see also the remark in *Weltgeschichtliche Betrachtungen*, p. 50 (hereafter cited as *W.B.*): "And now we also must remember the size of our obligation toward the past as a spiritual *[geistig]* continuum which forms one of our highest spiritual *[geistig]* possessions."

all may; but I will select for myself the interest for which I shall perish, namely, the culture [*Bildung*] of Old Europe."[7] In a revolutionary age which had erred in wishing to remake society on a man-made *tabula rasa*,[8] Burckhardt saw his task in the tracing of a cultural continuum. He knew what the philistines, punch-drunk with material progress, forgot: that the failure to respect the past was equal to barbarism. *Geschichtslosigkeit ist Barbarei.*[9] He had too highly developed a sense for the economy of human vitality and effort to let the true achievements of men escape from his ken. He understood the price paid by former generations for every piece of true culture and he fought a lifelong battle of preservation. He was painfully aware that only a prodigious amount of channeled energy, with some good fortune thrown in free, had pulled man from barbarism. He feared for civilization's existence in an age intoxicated with the false grandeur of mechanization, pleasurable comfort, superficial virtuosity, a mad lust for power and size, an insatiable *amour du million*, and a taste for cheap effects (*Effekthascherei*). He experienced horror and apprehension of leveling mass-men who severed the ties with past norms and substituted nothing better than the mediocrity of the average man. "I shudder when I see the [leveling] radicalism, smugly sitting in the grass, biting through the neck of a living thing, or tearing off its head merely because it was different. It has no single standard left, and deals with the smallest trifles as if they were the weightiest matters,"[10] and with the weightiest matters as if they were the smallest trifles. Against this specter of a barbaric future, Burckhardt placed a vision of the cultural continuum. Here he sought with undulled senses the great amid the perishables.[11]

---

[7] *Briefe*, p. 139; see also *J.B.B.*, III, 376, where Burckhardt insists on the duty of saving and conserving.

[8] *Briefe*, p. 56; *J.B.B.*, II, 196.

[9] See *W.B.*, p. 50; *G.K.*, I, 15; *Historische Fragmente*, pp. 3, 5.

[10] *Briefe*, pp. 518–19.

[11] See *W.B.*, pp. 126–27; "The greatest gain in this is on the side of the viewer. There exists a marvelous, universal, silent promise to bring an objective

The indiscriminate philistinism and the decline of political values which he had seen in his brief journalistic career left Burckhardt with no desire for a more active civic position. And, as the century progressed, his fears grew stronger that politically and socially Europe would succumb to that leveling mass society symbolized by the large factory, the barracks, and the huge apartment house (*Mietskaserne*).[12] Already on the horizon he saw that crude "caesarism" which would control the otherwise uncontrollable mass democracies and their unpredictable whims by a fearsome display of barbaric power.[13] When immersed in the affairs of the day, he had the oppressive feeling that "the times have been welded tight above us by a lid of lead."[14] Others, with a similar feeling, sailed to America, where life might truly begin anew. But this radical break with the traditions of Old Europe (*Alteuropa*) was out of the question for Burckhardt.[15] His hunger for proven values grew irresistibly whenever he had the impression that a senseless devil was stirring everything with a huge broomstick.[16] "If we are altogether cutting the ties with the great and the eternal, we shall be altogether lost and shall fall under the wheels of our times."[17] So Burckhardt chose that route of escape open to freedom-loving men who cannot bear their oppressive society: the world of contemplation.[18]

By contemplation Burckhardt did not mean that self-

---

interest to everything, to transform the entire past and present world into a spiritual possession."

[12] *W.B.*, p. 23; the image was apparently taken from Michelet.

[13] *Briefe*, pp. 175, 529; *Historische Fragmente*, p. 281.

[14] *Briefe*, p. 162: ". . . sintemal die Zeit oben mit einem bleiernen Deckel zugelötet ist."

[15] *Ibid.*, p. 164; *W.B.*, p. 127.

[16] *Briefe*, pp. 126–27.

[17] *Ibid.*, p. 215.

[18] *W.B.*, p. 52: "However, our contemplation is not merely a right and a duty, but also at the same time a great need; it constitutes our freedom amid the awareness of the enormous general fetters [*Gebundenheit*] and the stream of necessities." With loving care Burckhardt traced the fate of men who turned to contemplation amid a decaying civilization: the early Christian hermits and the "free personality" in the Greek *poleis* during their decline.

centered, introspective private life where one builds a little subjective philosophy. He saw great danger in ceaseless preoccupation with personal moods and feelings (*unsere eigenen Grillen*),[19] fruitless self-indulgence and lack of inner discipline ending in boundless subjectivity. Perpetual staring into the void and chaos never makes us wiser. The objective thing (*die Sache*) outside our limited ego deserves our attention and is our wealth and our cure.[20] Take pleasure in worthwhile things and in intensive labor — that was Burckhardt's prescription. His contemplation was synonymous with the active viewing of the world (if one can thus circumscribe the untranslatable but, for Burckhardt, crucial term *Anschauung*). Through this act of viewing, man gains access to the beauty and value of existence. Burckhardt related himself to a creative continuum transcending the individual limitations (*unser Knirpstum*).[21] Instead of fabricating a personal system of philosophy, which summarizes the rich world poorly, *Anschauung* leads man to the perceptible wealth of things and of men in their context and fullness of life. This theme, which Burckhardt announced even as a student, runs through his entire correspondence and is the key to his life. "My entire study of history, as well as my dabbling in landscape painting [*Landschaftskleckserei*] and preoccupation with art, proceeded from an enormous thirst for *Anschauung* — graphic perception."[22] And in addition to the private contentment gained from such contem-

---

[19] *Briefe*, p. 214.

[20] Kaegi, in *J.B.B.*, III, 541, cites a note by Burckhardt about the danger of wanting to look too deeply in your own self. See also *W.B.*, p. 315, on the dangers of taking oneself too seriously. Burckhardt always had praise for the strong who could take the important matters (*die Sache*) more seriously than themselves. See also *Die Kultur der Renaissance in Italien*, p. 51 (hereafter cited as *K.R.I.*): "Machiavelli was at least capable of forgetting about himself while delving into things," and *G.K.*, II, 160: "Homer's poetry has the greatest objectivity, i.e., the complete surrender of the spirit [*Geist*] to the object without any intrusion of the consciousness of the personal position, relations, and conditions of the subject."

[21] *W.B.*, p. 314.

[22] *Briefe*, p. 57.

plation, Burckhardt found intense satisfaction in opening other eyes to culture. After a highly productive period (*ca.* 1845–60) he published very little; but all he had written was meant for the larger educated public and not for a few specialists. He regularly gave public lectures, which Basel's citizens attended in great numbers. Burckhardt was a teacher and knew the wisdom of Winckelmann's remark, "It is better to write on the hearts of young men than on paper."[23] He gave his strength and rich ability to teaching in his *polis*, turning down offers of the most renowned professorial chairs in Europe. His lectures, elaborately prepared but presented without use of notes, were guided tours through the creations of the human spirit.[24] The man whose life was enriched by continuous viewing shared his riches with that small segment of mankind he knew at Basel. The withdrawn bachelor who, after stormy youthful friendships, revealed his personal feelings to very few, had found in teaching his own manner of serving and aiding his fellow men. ". . . It is best to be thanked for comforting man."[25] His most personal book, perhaps, was the *Cicerone*, that wonderful guide to the art treasures of Italy.[26] During his whole career he was a cicerone to the culture of Old Europe.

A good guide through historical landscapes leads not by rote. In a sense he has no system. He does not merely show the high points, leaving the typical and the details in the

[23] J. J. Winckelmann to H. R. Fuessli, February 18, 1764, quoted in *J.B.B.*, III, 692.

[24] For a more detailed evaluation of Burckhardt's lecture style see *Die Briefe von Adolf Frey und Carl Spitteler*, ed. Lina Frey (Leipzig, 1933), pp. 189–93, or Burckhardt, *Briefe*, p. cl.

[25] . . . Menschen trösten, bringt dir doch den besten Dank," from a poem, "Aussichten aus einem Fenster" in *Briefe*, p. 232; *J.B.B.*, III, 225; see also *J.B.B.*, II, 21, and III, 250. The unostentatious giving of help, the resignation to loneliness which later expressed itself in a search for anonymity, and a strong sense of duty without a trace of moralizing were pronounced character traits of Burckhardt and help to explain his recurring sympathy for the Epicurean philosophers. "Grant to your inner self the innocent and noble Epicureanism, enabling you to be happy by sympathy [*Zuneigung*], and remember that if you do not need others, others may have need of you" (*J.B.B.*, I, 581).

[26] *Der Cicerone* was first published in 1855.

distance; nor does he leave his visitors stranded in the fine sand of detail. He does not limit the vision of others, but neither does he permit eyes to stray indiscriminately. He does not impose a schematized view, and yet does not leave his visitors with unordered impressions of incidentals. He does not deliberately mold his guests, but changes their view by contact with his superior knowledge of the scenery.

Burckhardt asserted often — and not without a tone of pride — that he had no systematic philosophy of history. "As you know, I have never penetrated the temple of real thought, but have steadily delighted myself in the courtyard and the halls of the peribolos where the figurative [das Bildliche] (in the broadest sense of the word) rules."[27] His skeptical mind disliked the great schemes of historical interpretation, especially the attempts to compress the course of history into such a philosophical frame as Hegel's. The complex and often mysterious course of developments must not be fitted into an unhistorically conceived program of cosmic evolution or a theodicy.[28] Burckhardt knew that his students needed a general survey of the course of human history, but he presented the same as a simple narrative and analytical sketch.[29] He

---

[27] *Briefe*, p. 463 (to Friedrich Nietzsche). See also *ibid.*, pp. 56–57, 229 ("philosophieren . . . diese Art von Zeitvertreib . . . dieses alles wiegt doch keinen Gran realer Anschauung und Empfindung auf"), 507; *J.B.B.*, II, 193; *W.B.*, p. 43.

[28] "All chronologically ordered philosophies of history . . . at best degenerate into *Weltkulturgeschichten*" — an ambiguous plural form which leaves unsaid whether they are mere tales; see *W.B.*, p. 45.

[29] The lecture notes which form the *Historische Fragmente* were built from such blocks of material as "The time from 1450 to 1598 and its interpretation in terms of the nineteenth century. England in the late Middle Ages. To Richard III. On the War of the Roses and Scotland. Burgundy. Charles the Bold. France and the idea of unification. Louis XI. The German Empire of Frederick III. The Osman Turks. The Republic of Florence. To the war of 1494," etc. (see table of contents, p. 346). Of course, as with every historical topic Burckhardt handled, the more conventional presentation of this material was frequently interlined with his characteristic observations and concerns: "On the delimitation of culture and barbarism. Why moderns have difficulties understanding antiquity. The suffering and the sacrifices connected with the Crusades. The Reformation and the fate of art. *The Lusiads* of Camoens. Murder as a tool of politics," etc.

taught "world history" only as a propaedeutic subject, since he wanted to provide his students with the indispensable scaffold for their further studies. His highest aim as a teacher was not to train scholarly disciples in the narrow sense but to guide students in such a way that each might learn to establish a very personal relation to the past, and especially to that part of the past which might speak most strongly to him.[30] It is evident from the published fragments of the lecture notes and from the huge biography by Werner Kaegi that Burckhardt himself had formed a personal view of the course of western man. His major books, which deal with three periods only, fit as completed sections into the sketch of the total course of history revealed in the fragmentary notes. But this survey of main events, even though it provided some interpretation of the meaning of developments and explained how the past prepared the present, did not provide a "system." The *Historische Fragmente* are instead "a plastic frieze of figures and pictures." [31] Nor did Burckhardt use his knowledge of the past for a topical systematization of historical forces, causes, patterns, or laws. He did not attempt to reduce historical insights to a comprehensive systematized view of culture or society. He did not devise a "historical phenomenology." The *Weltgeschichtliche Betrachtungen*, deservedly in vogue in our disenchanted century, might at first appear to be Burckhardt's systematic summing-up of historical wisdom.[32] It was his most "theoretical" book, but the theoretical intention must not be overstressed.[33] For it could be argued that the at-

---

[30] *Briefe*, p. 377; see also *J.B.B.*, III, 307.

[31] Werner Kaegi in Introduction to *Historische Fragmente*, p. vii.

[32] Thus Kaegi speaks of this book as "eine Elementarlehre der Weltgeschichte," (*W.B.*, p. 16).

[33] For instance, *W.B.*, pp. 42–43: "The task which we set ourselves for this course consists in tying [*anknüpfen*] a number of historical observations and inquiries to a half-accidental train of thought, at other times tying them to another. . . . we forgo all attempts at systematic formulations; we make no claims to 'world-historic ideas' but are satisfied with perceptions and present only crosscuts through the past, in as many directions as possible; above all, we do not furnish a philosophy of history."

tempted systematization constitutes the book's greatest weakness. These are rather the reflections of a wise historian who saw that his contemporaries' view of historical reality was obstructed by their historical philosophies. Paradoxically, the greatest value of this "theoretical" treatise is its warning against theory.

Yet Burckhardt's reluctance to theorize must not be confused with dislike for generalization or structuring principles, nor should he be compared with the hesitant factual historian who makes a meager virtue of accurate detail at the cost of any larger vision. Burckhardt had a pronounced love for details, but he criticized the busy piling-up of more and more unwanted facts, calling it with little respect *Schutt* and *Quisquilienforschung*.[34] As art historian he sought to rise above the "old cheese of the history of artists" (*der alte Käse der Künstlergeschichte*) by giving the "pure history of styles and forms."[35] His formal analysis of Italian Renaissance architecture, *Die Geschichte der Renaissance in Italien,* was pioneering work for a methodologically independent art history.[36] Burckhardt the cultural historian selected large topics which permitted him to characterize whole epochs or societies, or in other words, styles of life.[37] He preferred to present the "small and single detail as symbol of a whole and

---

[34] *Briefe*, pp. 328, 331, 357, 529; *G.K.*, I, 7; *J.B.B.*, III, 136.

[35] *Briefe*, p. 401; see also *J.B.B.*, II, 168, 463, 464, III, 40, 133, 485.

[36] *Geschichte der Renaissance in Italien*, first published in 1867, dealt with the one form of Renaissance art which Burckhardt later treated separately, after he had decided not to include a discussion of art in the *Kultur der Renaissance in Italien*. See also *J.B.B.*, I, 494, and Wilhelm Waetzold, "Nachwort," in *K.R.I.*, pp. 381–408 (esp. p. 401), this being the article on Burckhardt as art historian in Waetzold's *Deutsche Kunsthistoriker* (2 vols.; Leipzig: Seemann, 1921–24).

[37] *Briefe*, p. 329; *J.B.B.*, II, 158. In *Die Zeit Konstantins des Grossen* and *Kultur der Renaissance* he showed his predilection for periods that lie athwart a watershed between larger ones (for example, the period between antiquity and the Middle Ages, or between the Middle Ages and modern times). Analyzing such periods permitted him a view of an especially vivid and diversified configuration, since it forced him to take account of two major periods at one time.

large view, the biographical detail as symbol of a broader general aspect."[38] Even with a more confined topic, as his *Vorträge* shows, he interlaced the more general concern with the specific. He sought as a historian the same harmony of detail and whole for which the Renaissance architect strove in his buildings. But for this immense task he had no principle of organization or a thought-out methodology. When a friend tried to persuade the young Burckhardt that historical labors need a philosophical position (preferably Hegel's), he was told: "By inclination I cling to the material, to the visible nature and to history. . . . Let me proceed with my humble point of view, let me sense and feel history instead of knowing her by first principles."[39] And the old man simply repeated the point: "We are 'unscientific' [*unwissenschaftlich*] and have no method" — then adding, in his inimitable manner, "at least not that of the others."[40]

The search for structure and order in Burckhardt's treatment of culture leads in two directions. Werner Kaegi, the greatest Burckhardt scholar, has pointed to one of these by drawing attention to an intellectual parallel between Burckhardt and Alexander von Humboldt.[41] The young Swiss very probably met the great naturalist at the home of his most influential teacher, the art historian Franz Kugler, who was a personal friend of Humboldt. At the time when Burckhardt stayed in Kugler's home at Berlin, the old Humboldt had just begun to publish his *Kosmos*.[42] There are statements of

---

[38] *J.B.B.*, III, 290.

[39] *Briefe*, pp. 58–59.

[40] *G.K.*, 1, 8–9. See also *W.B.*, pp. 46–146, 396, and the remark in *K.R.I.*, p. 263: "Colossal events like the Reformation of the sixteenth century elude, in respect to their details, their outbreak, and their development, all the historical-philosophical [*geschichtsphilosophisch*] deductions, even if their necessity in the larger context can be demonstrated."

[41] *J.B.B.*, III, 56, 66–67, 727–28. It is not implied that Burckhardt would not have developed his concern with *Anschauung* had he not known Humboldt and his work. He might very well have got his ideas about *Anschauung* through his reading of Goethe, who probably influenced Humboldt also.

[42] Alexander von Humboldt, *Kosmos: Entwurf einer physischen Weltbeschreibung* (5 vols.; Stuttgart: Cotta, 1845–62).

purpose and method in this comprehensive view of the physical world which anticipate Burckhardt's historical program to an amazing degree. Humboldt strove to integrate the endless variety of natural phenomena into a total vision.[43] He sought this not by subordination of concrete details to abstract natural laws, but by a descriptive mode (*Weltbeschreibung*)[44] which co-ordinated related phenomena in comprehensible tableaux (*Naturgemälde nach leitenden Ideen an einander gereihet*).[45] Far from remaining static, this approach also sought to reveal the metamorphosis of types and the shifting interdependence of phenomena.[46] The integrated conception of the cosmos did not result primarily from clear classification. Humboldt placed more emphasis on learning "to see" and "to visualize" an ordered universe. This involved a constant weighing, juxtaposing, and co-ordinating of phenomena until they formed a unifying vision in which the vital detail was preserved. The aim was *Weltanschauung*, a composite of meaningful (*sinnvoll*) views, a combination of empirical insights integrated by the mind of the viewer.[47] Thus Burckhardt found in the naturalist a companion who demonstrated a versatile art of viewing, of *Anschauung*, in one vast field of human knowledge. And, in addition, the cultural historian noted Humboldt's brilliant chapters on the changing conception of nature and the world through the ages. In his work on the Renaissance and the Greeks, the Swiss historian made similar attempts to trace the experience of nature which both peoples expressed. In a lecture on Sebastian Münster he also voiced his approval of the sixteenth- and seventeen-century cosmographers who, unlike the scientific geographers of mod-

---

[43] *Ibid.*, I, vi, 4–6, 40.
[44] *Ibid.*, pp. vii, 30–32, 60–61.
[45] *Ibid.*, p. 10.
[46] *Ibid.*, pp. 22, 63–64.
[47] *Ibid.*, pp. 16, 63–72. See also Burckhardt's remark in *K.R.I.*, p. 173; "Fortunately the study of man's spiritual [*geistig*] nature began not with subtle inquiries [*Grübeln*] for a theoretic psychology — Aristotle would still have sufficed for that — but with a gift for observation and description."

ern times, presented comprehensible views of the world to their reading public.[48]

The second line of consideration leading to a fuller assessment of Burckhardt's historical "method" involves a discussion of his relations with the fine arts. This in itself constitutes an enormous topic. His contributions to the separate discipline of art history, his wavering over a merger of cultural and art history,[49] and even his writings on art as a feature of cultural history are outside the scope of this chapter. Of primary relevance here are the sense of style, the sense of harmony, and the sense of proportion Burckhardt brought from his encounter with art to his role as cultural historian.

Extensive reading of Burckhardt's writings suggests the central importance of these words: harmony, organic, whole, true measure, and ideal form. His letters attest to the importance which the word "harmony" had for him in a variety of meanings. His desire for harmonious viewing grew in proportion to his anxious awareness of an age which surrendered harmony to fragmentation, specialization, uniformity, boundless subjectivism, dulling luxury, an all-devouring acquisitiveness, and the hustle of metropolitan life. He thirsted for a "refreshing bath" in the contemplation of beauty and harmony when overwhelmed by the "lack of the sweet pensive afternoon hours," or when he saw the "inner vacation" sacrificed to a constant preparedness to telegraph instantaneously for greater profit.[50] And when Burckhardt spoke of such values as harmony and beauty and form, such words as "great" and "eternal" and "divine" also appeared.

---

[48] See *Die Zeit Konstantins des Grossen*, p. 202 (first published in 1853; hereafter cited as *Konstantin*); *K.R.I.*, pp. 160–73, with special reference to Humboldt's work (p. 168) as "das höchste Meisterwerk der Schilderung"; *G.K.*, III, 435–38 and *passim*, the great esteem for Pausanias and Strabo; and *J.B.B.*, III, 533, on Münster.

[49] It seems to be a very complicated issue in what sense Burckhardt meant to combine *Kulturgeschichte* and *Kunstgeschichte*, and in what sense he thought them incompatible; for some remarks see *Briefe*, p. 243, and *J.B.B.*, II, 463, 465, 483, 500, III, 65, 588, 625.

[50] *Briefe*, pp. 202, 340; *J.B.B.*, III, 595.

What did this word "harmony" mean for Burckhardt and what significance did it have for his historical labor? The notion was not limited to the arts, but its fullest meaning emerges there. Harmony, or the organic, can exist only where the manifold diversity is valued, where preoccupation with the whole does not preclude respect for the part, where the total vision is an organic whole composed of many constitutive elements instead of a radical simplification. Art which sacrifices detail to the effect of the whole is boring and lacks greatness. "Just as there once was an abbé Trublet who infuriated Voltaire with a treatise 'On the true causes of boredom in the Henriade,' thus I am studying here [Rome] the true cause of boredom of many, though not all, paintings by the Caracci! But now I know the turning point, especially for Lodovico Caracci: it came when he merely gave the essence [das Allgemeine] of his knowledge and when he no longer fought battles in his soul for the individual figures and their action; when he finally noticed it himself, while working on the colossal Annunciation above the apse of Saint Peter's, he became melancholic and died. . . ."[51] Burckhardt similarly criticized baroque artists who slurred over the details in their quest for an impressive effect.[52] But no better, for him, is the artist who, reveling in detail, suffocates the living whole.[53] The rococo as a play of merely decorative forms was never his favorite style, even if he valued individual expressions such as Poeppelmann's Zwinger at Dresden.[54] Where the viewer must "think

---

[51] *Briefe*, p. 455. See also *Cicerone*, I, 29, and Burckhardt's remark on Buckle, *W.B.*, p. 64: "And then the peril of paralysis if one works for too long on homogeneous matters of limited interest! Buckle got his mental paralysis from the Scottish sermons of the seventeenth and eighteenth centuries."

[52] *Cicerone*, II, 86, 256, 258, 270, 280–81, 293, 298, 477, 832–33; *J.B.B.*, III, 487. In his later years, however, Burckhardt indicated a growing respect for certain accomplishments of the baroque; see *Briefe*, pp. 390, 420, 428, 435, 449, 452.

[53] See, for example, *Konstantin*, p. 193; *Cicerone*, I, 50, II, 579; and *J.B.B.*, II, 530.

[54] *Briefe*, pp. xlii, 429; *J.B.B.*, II, 534, III, 130; *Cicerone*, I, 47; *Konstantin*, p. 189.

away" details to get at the whole, the artist has sinned against objective forms. Thus Burckhardt saw in Flemish painting an artistic product unbalanced by too loving a concern for the partial view.[55] In contrast, great art presents an organic balance where no part can be "thought away" without upsetting the equilibrium. In a Doric temple, such as that of Paestum which Burckhardt knew from his early travels, the supported weights and the supporting structures melt into an organic whole; the slightly tapered columns, enlivened by subtle cannellation, presented for him an ideal form which transformed the mass into a structured totality with the semblance of organic life.[56] No part could be exchanged without destroying the whole. In "the only other strictly organic style," the northern Gothic, the artists accomplished a perfect harmony of external and internal structures and a perfect integration of decorative detail with structural necessities.[57] Similarly the great works of Renaissance architecture display a harmonious blend of structural forms and the love for pictorial (*malerisch*) decoration characteristic of that tradition.[58] In Raphael's painting, "the most comforting subject"[59] for mortal men, "the forms are entirely beautiful, noble, and at the same time animated without harm to the whole. No detail obtrudes or crowds forward; the artist precisely understands the delicate life of his symbolic subjects, and knows how easily the separately interesting [*das Einzel-Interessante*] drowns [*übertönen*] the whole."[60]

But Burckhardt learned more from his encounter with art than merely how to harmonize the detail with the whole. He

---

[55] *J.B.B.*, III, 92–93.

[56] *Cicerone*, I, 2–6; *Geschichte der Renaissance in Italien*, p. 104; and *G.K.*, II, 123–37.

[57] *Geschichte der Renaissance in Italien*, pp. 45, 47, 119; *Cicerone*, II, 24, 71; *J.B.B.*, I, 506, III, 127, 348.

[58] See, for example, *Geschichte der Renaissance in Italien*, pp. 51, 60, 114, 121, 152, 181, 240, and *Cicerone*, II, 88, 118, 144, 145, 165, 224.

[59] *Briefe*, p. 306.

[60] *Cicerone*, II, 701. See also *ibid.*, II, 523 (on Giotto), and *Erinnerungen aus Rubens*, pp. 49, 56 (hereafter cited as *Rubens*).

wrote cultural history with a sure sense, harmonizing his objective and his expression. Harmony in a work of art involved for Burckhardt more than the mere balance of part and whole, of color and composition, of movement and perspective.[61] This harmony depended upon more than the mere balancing of formal aspects. He deemed it necessary, for instance, that the chosen artistic medium be appropriate to the subject matter, that the formal execution of a work be adequate to its purpose, and that both subject matter and form be fused into one.[62] In the great medieval cathedrals the structural forms were perfectly adapted to the functional objective of a ritual in which all eyes were focused on the sacramental acts performed at the altar. Function (or purpose) and form were balanced, as they should be.[63] On the other hand, Burckhardt considered it inappropriate of Bernini to express the momentary floating ecstasy of Saint Theresa's heavenly vision in marble sculpture. He thought that the baroque love for clouds, baldachins, and tricky drapery, all executed in marble, attested to an imbalance of artistic conception and artistic means. Technical skill should be so fused with the artistic intention that neither the one nor the other jars the harmonious blending. Mere formal excellence was never sufficient for a great work of art.

A work of art is not only the fulfilment of aesthetic demands. It should also be an expression of the sublime, a bridge to the realm of values. A good artist unobtrusively communicates his "moral" commitment. This historian similarly strives for more than a merely pleasing aesthetic production; he seeks to contribute to the higher wisdom of man. Burckhardt especially valued the harmony of aesthetic and moral values (*sittliche Werte*), but the word "moral" must be understood correctly. Few things could irritate the young Burck-

---

[61] See especially *Rubens*, pp. 85–96.

[62] See, for example, *Konstantin*, pp. 200, 207, 255; *Cicerone*, I, 109, 183, II, 177, 316–17, 336, 349, 432, 482, 486, 549, 663, 778; and the interesting article "Andeutungen zur Geschichte der christichen Skulptur," pp. 498–506 (esp. p. 502).

[63] *Cicerone*, II 1–3, 6, 13, 35; *J.B.B.*, III, 585, and also p. 166.

hardt more than "art pietists" who claimed that art must serve the higher values of religion and Christian morality.[64] Such artistic moralism presumed the *subordination* of the aesthetic to the moral concerns. A true harmony of all values results instead from the *co-ordination* of all objectives. Burckhardt always had special praise for the artists who fully integrated the good and the beautiful, and harsh words for those who seemed insensitive to anything but their aesthetic tasks.[65] Raphael's "greatness consists in the highest view [*Anschauung*] of the spiritual [*geistig*] nobility of human nature."[66] Of Dutch landscape painters "by far the greatest is Jacob Ruisdael, . . . the painter of the divine in nature."[67] One of Burckhardt's favorites, Claude Lorrain, "a pure-attuned soul [*reingestimmte Seele*], hears in nature the voice which above all was meant to comfort man, and he repeats her words."[68] Great classical art unobtrusively joined the idealized human figure, even the nobility of classical dress,[69] with the moral values of the culture. The famed Laocoön group led Burckhardt to remark: "As soon as one begins to account to oneself for the Why? of all single motives, of the mixture of physical and spiritual suffering, chasms of artistic wisdom open up. But the highest achievement is the struggle against pain, first noted by Winckelmann. . . . The moderation in misery has

---

[64] *J.B.B.*, II, 228–31, 235, 268–70, 276–77, 484, 497.

[65] *Cicerone*, II, 59, 146–47, 213, 230, 248, 349, 433, 491, 527, 551, 555, 716, 731, 750, 766, 779, 791, 803, 833–34; *Rubens*, p. 73; *Konstantin*, p. 196; *G.K.*, II, 299; *J.B.B.*, III, 93, 111, 436–37, 474, 480, 481. See also Kaegi's remark in *J.B.B.*, I, 365: "One stands here in the middle of a classicistic aesthetics which determined Burckhardt's basic views for his entire life. His thirst for graphic concreteness [*Anschauung*], even in this early train of thought, he felt to be a thirsting for the Beautiful and Good, yes, even the Divine."

[66] *J.B.B.*, II, 532; see also II, 505.

[67] *J.B.B.*, II, 512; see also Kaegi, *Europäische Horizonte*, pp. 152–55, where Burckhardt is quoted on Ruisdael, "the greatest figure of the Mennonite religion" and "Ruisdael was a religious man and his art a high ritual for him . . ." and, ". . . landscape painting was a religious service for both" (i.e., Ruisdael and Claude Lorrain).

[68] *Cicerone*, II, 844; see also *J.B.B.*, II, 510–11.

[69] *Cicerone*, I, 110–11, 153, 164; *G.K.*, II, 109, III, 6.

not merely an aesthetic but a moral [*sittlich*] reason."[70] On the other hand, Burckhardt blamed Caravaggio, in spite of his great technical skill, for painting the apostles as a pack of ragamuffins [*Lumpenpack*].[71] In front of Bernini's Saint Theresa "one forgets all mere questions of style over the revolting degradation of the supernatural."[72] And in Rembrandt, who, like Michelangelo, served Burckhardt as a crucial test of art, he mercilessly criticized the use of vulgar human types, of vulgar themes, and the total misuse of art for expressing the base and ugly.[73] "He never denied that Rembrandt was a great painter, but the ability to paint was not the highest of goods for him, not even in painting."[74] Real beauty must be linked to ideal forms and the nobility of the subject, even where this was the demonic and the gruesome.[75]

Great art must represent a composite of values; no single value or concern may dominate; none is sufficient in isolation. The great artist balances "values of equal weight," what Burckhardt called *Aequivalente,* or equi-valents.[76] The meaning of this notion is explained in Burckhardt's description of a painting by Rubens: the representation of the famous scene in which Saint Ambrose refuses to admit the impenitent Emperor Theodosius into his church at Milan.

> Here both groups are weighed out one against the other optically and morally: at the left the energetic imperator with his three adjutants, of whom the one or the other could easily settle the affair by the use of force, but this group has the light behind itself and has been placed in the shadow and two

[70] *Cicerone,* I, 147.

[71] *J.B.B.,* II, 494.

[72] *Cicerone,* II, 491.

[73] *Briefe,* p. 481; *J.B.B.,* II, 508, 544; and especially the lecture on Rembrandt of November 6, 1877, "Rembrandt" in *Vorträge,* pp. 178–97. In *Europäische Horizonte,* pp. 145–48, Kaegi seeks to balance the picture and judgment which Burckhardt had of the great Dutch painter.

[74] *J.B.B.,* II, 505–6.

[75] *Cicerone,* I, 163, 168; *Rubens,* p. 82.

[76] For Burckhardt's most explicit discussion of *"Aequivalente"* see *Rubens,* pp. 85–96; also *G.K.,* II, 96.

steps lower, one of which Theodosius is in process of ascending; on the steps to the right, stands the saint with his calm and mostly elderly companions, materially helpless, but in the full light, in a bright bishop's coat, and with majestic gesture and a most venerable expression.[77]

Burckhardt was aware that the artist's ability to fuse all his equi-valents into a harmonic, organic whole depended on the artist's "moral" attitude. The harmony of creations — whether in art, in a work of history, or even a whole culture — has its origin in the internal harmony of the creators. The crucial virtue for Burckhardt was tact, *sophrosyne*, a virtue as much aesthetic as "moral." It involves the inner sense of measure, balance, and proportion, man's instinctive knowledge of limitation and ability, a sense of the possible, an inner restraint which preserves an inner harmony. It is the "sense of the fitting." Without this virtue the artist oversteps the bounds or laws of his subject matter, of his ability, of his medium, and of his tradition.[78] This problem of the boundless — ultimately the problem of the subjective — was of such immense importance to Burckhardt because he was so strongly committed to the ideal of a harmonious existence. Artistically the issue was exemplified for him in the contrast between Raphael and Michelangelo. Raphael was the "predominantly healthy soul, the normal personality," the artist with "tact" and "conscience," "rich in all simplicity," the "most comforting subject," for whose art Burckhardt had a sense of "religious reverence."[79] By contrast, Michelangelo was the "man of fate," for the arts as well as for modern man in general. "He led the three fine arts to the highest summit and then he himself took them down again."[80] Why? This "titanic, demonic genius" sacrificed his own sense of harmony, and the laws of his artistic

[77] *Rubens*, p. 96.

[78] Among many possible references see *J.B.B.*, II, 466; *Geschichte der Renaissance in Italien*, p. 50; *Cicerone*, I, 15, 28, 30, 56, 60, 93, 95, 107, 131; *G.K.*, II, 92, 123, 147–48, 285, 308.

[79] *Cicerone*, II, 683–95; *J.B.B.*, II, 490–93; *Briefe*, p. 306.

[80] *J.B.B.*, II, 489.

forms, to his desperate struggle "for ever greater creative freedom."[81] In his later years, Michelangelo could not consider himself bound to any rules, to any tradition.[82] Beyond such released subjectivity lay the realm of arbitrariness (a word which poorly expresses Burckhardt's use of *Willkür*) which would undermine art and modern life.

The fusion of all equi-valents into a harmonious whole culminated for Burckhardt in the problem of style. His conception of style is a difficult subject. For excellent reasons he used it sparingly. Yet it is a crucial term which could serve to pull his many ideas together. In its most important sense style is that unity of factors which constitutes a specific harmony. In that sense, man can give style to his life by integrating the diverse components of his existence into a related whole which preserves his many-sidedness. "Thus even the beggars have honor and style."[83] The ideal which Burckhardt held up to modern man, who was in process of losing a clear sense of style and harmony, was not by accident that of the Renaissance man, who had no philosophy but a style of life, and the example of classical man, who had once aimed at the harmoniously formed human being (*der gleichmässig ausgebildete Mensch als Lebenszweck*).[84] If one looks further into this problem, it appears that styles of life, like styles of art, involve

---

[81] *Cicerone*, II, 455; see also *ibid.*, p. 464. Cf. *Geschichte der Renaissance in Italien*, p. 44; "[Michelangelo] befreite die Kunst mehr als gut war."

[82] *Cicerone*, II, 676.

[83] *J.B.B.*, III, 297. For some examples of Burckhardt's use of the term "style" (in a broader sense than just style of architecture, etc.) see *Historische Fragmente*, p. 243 ("Stile des Lebens"); *J.B.B.*, II, 370 (". . . es lebte eine Judenschaft, im ganz alten Sinn, mit Styl . . ."); *K.R.I.*, pp. 225 and 262, where harmony as a way of life approaches the notion of style of life closely; or *G.K.*, III, 65, where the Greek ideal of *kalokagathia* has all the qualities of an existence with its own style; and *G.K.*, II, 104, where Burckhardt speaks of a Greek "Stil des bösen Mundwerks." It is my conviction, obviously, that there exists a very close relation between Burckhardt's ideal of a harmonious existence and the idea of a style of life; and, moreover, that Burckhardt deliberately placed his vision of two such styles of life (Greek and Renaissance) against the nineteenth-century idea that man lives by a "philosophy."

[84] *Cicerone*, I, 85.

the acceptance of a tradition. The "normal personality" (as Burckhardt occasionally expressed it), therefore, will find the means for personal expression within the traditional forms of proven quality. The "titan," who breaks loose from all inheritance and seeks to create a unique existence out of nothing but his own inner resources, rarely is great enough to give a harmonious style to either his life or his art. Burckhardt illustrated this point again clearly in his thinking about art. The "basic trait of all classic artistic activity [*Kunsttreiben*]" was "the repetition of the acknowledged excellence."[85] The Greeks did not demand from their artists originality in the modern sense, that is, they did not expect from them constant innovation in the forms of expression or in the themes expressed; when a subject had once found its highest expression, this remained the norm for centuries.[86] In addition, the classical artist, like the medieval one, possessed an established stock of mythological and religious forms.[87] Such artists did not need to invent their subject, but could truly re-experience its tested significance and thus endow it once more with that measure of personal life which it acquires from a sensitive personal experience (*nicht erfunden, sondern empfunden*).[88] For Burckhardt, it was again Michelangelo who exemplified the fatal break with tradition and who, stepping into the realm of *Willkür*, or subjective arbitrariness,[89] sought all content

---

[85] *Ibid.*, p. 193. See also *ibid.*, pp. 68, 87; *G.K.*, II, 83–95.

[86] *Cicerone*, I, 64.

[87] See, for example, *Cicerone*, II, 335, 526; *W.B.*, pp. 175, 177, 202, 320; *Briefe*, p. 398; *Geschichte der Renaissance in Italien*, pp. 36, 104, 160, 161, 210; *G.K.*, I, 35, 467, II, 84, 88, 147–48, 204, 292, III, 424; *J.B.B.*, II, 473, III, 73, 490, 494, 500.

[88] *G.K.*, II, 111; *Rubens*, p. 36. Burckhardt associated the decline of an artistic style with mere repetition, which was not active re-experience by the artists; see *Konstantin*, p. 192, and *Cicerone*, II, 503, 595, 668.

[89] See, for instance, the remark in *W.B.*, pp. 203–4: "The true result of free spiritual exchange [*geistiger Austausch*] is the clarity of all expression and the certainty of purpose, the abandoning of arbitrariness [*Willkür*] and of the miraculous, the acquisition of a standard and a style, the effect of art and science on one another. Whether the creations of any period came into existence under such conditions can be clearly detected. The less expressive form [*geringere Ausprägung*] is the conventional, the nobler one the classic."

and form within his own turbulent soul. "No time-honored myth guards and limits his fantasy."[90] Raphael and Rubens, on the other hand, worked within a tradition and invested their great artistic talent in the reinterpretation, reformulation, and renewed expression of the society's rich stock of themes and myths. Both artists raised painting to new heights — but they stayed within the bounds of proven aesthetic canons. In back of all these arguments stands Burckhardt's deep conviction that man, divorced from tradition, is too weak and too poor a creature to create greatness out of himself.[91] Instead, Burckhardt saw man's real chance for a decent life in the attempt to build upon the accumulated wealth of generations, to add to this by constant effort guided by proven norms, and thus slowly to transform the inheritance. So the argument has run full circle: without his past, man is a barbarian. And life is bearable only when related to a cultural continuum.

In the *Erinnerungen aus Rubens*, the last book published during his life, Burckhardt once more surveyed a great favorite at work. Perhaps the old historian also read his own way of composing a book into Rubens' art. Throughout, the reader is tempted to draw parallels between Burckhardt's image of Rubens and Burckhardt's own life: the early death of the mother, the search for harmony in life, the sense of proportion, the serene joy in landscapes, the quiet helpfulness toward others, and so forth. But the main parallel for us is the relevance of the painter's "method" to that of the cultural historian. After Rubens, on his Italian journey, had learned to see with Titian's eyes,[92] he gradually found his own manner

---

[90] *Cicerone*, II, 458.

[91] According to Burckhardt, Michelangelo had in many of his works attained genuine greatness; in others he overstepped the bounds of the possible. Much of Burckhardt's criticism of Michelangelo rested on the opinion that Michelangelo had "misled" lesser artists by his example, especially by his disregard of norm and tradition; see *Cicerone*, II, 460, 463, 464, 667, 668, 677, 683.

[92] *Rubens*, p. 16; earlier, Burckhardt attributed the influence to Veronese; see *J.B.B.*, II, 171.

for "glorifying man in all his capacities."[93] His cultural milieu still was a coherent unity. Rubens found the subjects of his art in the immense stock of biblical, legendary, mythological, allegorical, and historical figures in which the imaginative spirit of western man had summed up its rich experience. Rubens' "enormous inventive powers were used essentially to experience these given matters anew and then to render them afresh."[94] All individual parts of his subject were for him, to a high degree, components and expressive means of a highly vivid whole.[95] From an early moment Rubens felt called upon to act as the "guardian of a higher harmony of presentation."[96] "In painting he combined the most extensive symmetric handling of the different but 'similarly valuable,' the equi-valents, with the most vivid, even the most vehement action, achieving thus that kind of successful effect which enchants the external view and the inner senses simultaneously. . . . These equi-valents do not appear separately but interpenetrate." Masses and colors, lines and forms and facial expressions are balanced, "and above all, he counterpoises optical values and ideal ones. The moving is balanced by the resting . . . and accents of the most differing types and dignity are brought together in one painting." "Only through the combination of such ability and such a will"— held together by a self-imposed discipline — "with the moving, actually the very vigorously moving and rich narrative, the amazing works are created which can only be explained by an inner process peculiar to Rubens."[97] In a total vision the artist simultaneously balances all the equi-valents, perceiving (as in a flash of the moment) all components in their proper relation. He became the master of moving scenes through this ability to solve the most momentous tasks of organization by an internal vision

---

[93] *Rubens,* p. 34.
[94] *Ibid.,* pp. 35–36; see also *W.B.,* p. 328.
[95] *Rubens,* p. 49.
[96] *Ibid.,* p. 13.
[97] *Ibid.,* pp. 86–87.

before he even began to draw.[98] Rubens and Homer were thus the greatest narrators of mankind.[99]

Burckhardt was correct in saying he had no "method," if method meant to organize historical data by means of the systematic use of logical tools. He was right to add "at least not the method of others," if the less conceptualized ordering of manifold impressions by the visual artist constitutes a method. Burckhardt had learned to see, to view contemplatively, and to form his views into larger visions. He had developed a sureness of judgment without relying on clearly reasoned principles of judgment. The consistent and subtle judgments on the whole realm of Italian art in a "fat, little book of a thousand pages," the *Cicerone*, is an astounding testimony of his highly developed "art of viewing." He applied this technique of viewing, the "gathering of the world as an external image," to the less immediate world of the past.[100] Thus his historical work is rich in those expressions which reveal him as the viewing historian. He desired the most replete view of the past, "the nature of the European spirit wants to be touched at a thousand ends at once." [101] But within this diversity he sought also the typical, the lasting, the European continuum. Burckhardt never lost sight of his chosen center, "the suffering, striving, and acting human being as it is, always has been, and will be." [102] He searched for the changing human spirit (*der*

---

[98] *Ibid.*, p. 88; see also *G.K.*, II, 117, on Greek artists: "Man sieht in ein Kunstvermögen hinein, das keine Grenzen hat und oft das Trefflichste mit dem ersten Griff trifft."

[99] *Rubens*, 193.

[100] See, for example, *Briefe*, p. 57 (". . . die Geschichte . . . ist mir eine Reihe der schönsten malerischen Kompositionen"), and p. 282 (". . . die Welt zugleich als äusseres Bild fassen"), and p. 559 ("Bilder zusammenstellen"); *J.B.B.*, II, 305, III, 327, 646, 664, 674, 682, 691, 742; *G.K.*, II, 463–68, where Burckhardt expressed his admiration for Herodotus' "Gabe der unmittelbaren Beobachtung"; and also his remark on Taine in *Briefe*, p. 423: "Autor hat zwei grosse Eigenschaften: er sieht die geistigen Konturen und Farben überaus deutlich and schreibt merkwürdig einfach schön."

[101] *J.B.B.*, III, 290.

[102] *W.B.*, p. 45; *J.B.B.*, III, 554.

wandelbare Menschengeist), and for the changing qualities of the universal or the common (*das wandelbar Allgemeine*), and the continuum.[103]

Burckhardt developed his idea of *Kulturgeschichte* to answer the need for a historical view of the general, the typical, that which gives meaning to the purely momentary. In one lecture he answered his own question, What is *Kulturgeschichte?* thus: ". . . *Kulturgeschichte* is the history of the world in its general conditions [*die Geschichte der Welt in ihren Zuständen*], while history commonly means the development of events and their connections. . . . For us the standard holds: what moves the world, and what is of penetrating influence." [104] Moved by the startling events of the Franco-Prussian War, he confided to his friend Friedrich von Preen: "For me as a teacher of history a strange phenomenon has become clear: the sudden devaluation of all mere events of the past. Henceforth my courses will only bring out the *Kulturgeschichtliche*, restricting the external frame to the indispensable." [105] He meant by no means to exclude events and development. But he saw the more vital task in presenting that description of the general condition without which man is delivered captive to the vicissitudes of events.[106] While Burckhardt's view of the past was affected by his general evaluation of the contemporary world, his choice of cultural history left him free to pass over the merely sensational events

---

[103] *W.B.*, p. 61; *K.R.I.*, p. 49. Especially the remark in *W.B.*, p. 61: "Every single perception of facts possesses . . . in addition to its specific value as knowledge or idea of a particular concern, also a universal or historical value as knowledge of a specific epoch of the mutable [*wandelbar*] human spirit and, if put in the right context, furnishes simultaneous testimony of continuity and immutability [*Unvergänglichkeit*] of this spirit."

[104] *J.B.B.*, III, 693–94. See also *ibid.*, II, 50, 53, 75, 117, 563, III, 396; *G.K.*, I, 4 (". . . wir dagegen haben Gesichtspunkte für die Ereignisse aufzustellen"); *Briefe*, p. 559 (". . . so etwas Zusammenhängendes . . . so etwas Kulturgeschichtliches . . ."), and p. xxxvii (". . . der Hintergrund ist mir die Hauptsache, und ihn bietet die Kulturgeschichte").

[105] *Briefe*, p. 350, and also p. 328.

[106] *Ibid.*, p. 355; *W.B.*, pp. 54–55.

of the moment. *Kulturgeschichte* could preserve a sense of the true proportions and of the true relations without magnifying facts of current interest.[107] It aimed at the compound view.

As a cultural historian Burckhardt accepted the difficult task of describing culture as a composite reality. His objective was the presentation of all the characteristic manifestations produced by men of a specific outlook, the traceable expressions of an underlying *Denkweise* and *Lebensauffassung*.[108] But such a history of many interlinked aspects could not be composed by following the philosopher's way of *subordinating* various matters according to principles; it could only be done, in Burckhardt's opinion, by *co-ordinating* the various elements in a composite view. In this sense, history could not be history of art, or history of institutions, or history of thought. Nor was Burckhardt's *Kulturgeschichte* the history of *Kultur* in the narrower sense in which he sometimes used this word.[109] Those segments of history which Burckhardt described could not be compressed in keeping with such themes as the "clash of Principles" (*à la* Guizot), or, the translation of a basic psychic condition into external forms of culture (*à la* Lamprecht). He expressed his awareness of the basic problem in one simple sentence in the *Kultur der Renaissance in Italien*: "The Renaissance would not have been the high necessity of world history [*die hohe weltgeschichtliche Notwendigkeit*], which it was, if one could so easily abstract the Renaissance."[110] Great artists presented lifelike wholes by preserving all the equi-valents, all the elements which demanded each other's presence for their peculiar balance. Ideally, cultural history was also an image, for: "We deal with an enormous continuum which should most correctly be formed as a pic-

---

[107] *G.K.*, I, 7.

[108] See esp. *G.K.*, I, 3–10, of the introduction to the *Griechische Kulturgeschichte* where the program is most clearly stated.

[109] This touches on one of the most difficult issues in the discussion of Burckhardt; he himself contributed little to its clarification. For further discussion of this issue see the appendix at the end of this chapter.

[110] *K.R.I.*, p. 98.

ture. . . ." [111] Practical limitations were set by the "successive course of speech, narrating gradually, while things actually were a largely simultaneous, great One." [112] The ideal of the image-like composition thus determined the historian's ordering process, but the use of words restricted him. While Rubens had solved the problem on canvas, Homer, that other great narrator, had shown the possibility of "linear composition," at least in the *Iliad*.[113] The basic problems of composition are shared by artists and historians; and high among these ranks the handling of equi-valents. Although Burckhardt never discussed details of his working habits — and may never have consciously followed a scheme or method — he co-ordinated equi-valents of thought, art, religion, festivals, state, myths, poetry, and all the other expressions of the spirit of a culture, into balanced parts of one whole.

But as Burckhardt had clearly seen with Rubens: co-ordination of equi-valents was not the result of careful calculation and deliberate placement.[114] It demanded a vision which related the parts to the whole. How does the historian acquire this? Burckhardt emphasized the hard work of learning to see. As cicerone to Italy's art treasures, he admonished the reader to keep his eyes open for this, to train his view on that, to visit this hall of the Vatican between three and four when the light is best, to take in this aspect of the work before approaching it with another interest, and "to keep the power of the eye unimpaired for the frescoes." [115] One of his favored methods of training was the constant "parallelizing of facts." [116] Compare and contrast, look for similarities, learn to

---

[111] *G.K.*, I, 8. See also *K.R.I.*, p. 1; *Konstantin*, pp. 361–62.

[112] *G.K.*, I, 8.

[113] *G.K.*, II, 156–72, supplemented by pp. 113–14, contains an analysis of the structure of Homer's *Iliad*, which is a miniature of the more extensive analysis of Rubens' way of telling a story; characteristic, for instance, is Burckhardt's description of Homer's "langreliefartige Kompositionsweise" on p. 161.

[114] *Rubens*, pp. 27, 33.

[115] *Cicerone*, II, 655.

[116] *W.B.*, pp. 27, 67, 118, 147; *Briefe*, p. 58; *J.B.B.*, I, 243, 513, III, 74, 294, 375, 395; *Cicerone*, I, i; and cf. *Konstantin*, pp. 39, 84–85, 234; *K.R.I.*, pp. 9, 142, 143, 195, 247; *G.K.*, I, 69, 540, II, 228, 443, II, 59.

see differences, trace the common amid the different. His *Weltgeschichliche Betrachtungen* should perhaps be looked upon as a training manual through which the historian, though more the political than the cultural historian, acquires adeptness in moving freely, but responsibly, through a broad range of historical data, testing a view here by comparison, widening a sight there through an analogy. Burckhardt underlined his emphasis on the visual, *das Anschauliche*, through the advice to avoid the inherently opaque, the origins hidden in impenetrable fog, all the subjects which never will take on clarity. We "must concentrate on the active races and among these on the peoples whose history permits us cultural tableaux [*Kulturbilder*] of sufficient and undisputed clarity." [117] And as he learns to discern suitable subjects, Burckhardt's historian trains his eyes to peruse sources. Burckhardt, a student of Ranke's seminar, retained a deep respect for genuine sources, even concentrating upon them to such an extent that other professionals accused him finally of neglecting secondhand scholarship. To imagine his life, one should think of a prodigious worker using his time to view treasures of sources, as he used his travels to view galleries and landscapes.[118] In his introduction to the *Griechische Kulturgeschichte* he gave pages of advice on how to train the historical view by reading the right sources. The best advice any professor ever gave his students: learn to see with your own eyes; "that thousands before us have done the work does not save us the labor"; read sources, leave the rubble (*Schutt*) aside; and find your own focused view of the past — or history means nothing. "Slowly the eyes grow sharper and we learn how to obtain some secrets of the past by questioning." [119] That was the "method" Burckhardt taught; he knew from his study of the arts that the rest was in the lap of the gods. Great visions were rare, and man must treasure them. For the same reason

---

[117] *W.B.*, p. 46. See also *W.B.*, p. 149; *G.K.*, I, 10; *Historische Fragmente*, p. 1.
[118] See the interesting discussion on sources in *W.B.*, pp. 63–66.
[119] *G.K.*, I, 11. See also *K.R.I.*, p. 79, on the "sehr geschärfter kulturhistorischer Blick."

historians have revered and will continue to revere Burckhardt's own work: he was a genius in the art of viewing.

Burckhardt's cultural histories are integrated visions of whole periods. During his early days he had planned to survey the whole of western culture through a connected series of monographs on the great ages of European history.[120] But he lost interest in publishing, and only three cornerstones of this projected survey reached the public; as the lecture notes show, only his students received the wider survey. *Die Zeit Constantins des Grossen, Die Kultur der Renaissance in Italien,* and the *Griechische Kulturgeschichte* still give evidence of the original plan. They were crucial segments of the plan to which he restricted himself — and certainly they dealt with fateful moments for the understanding of the modern predicament. All three themes are made relevant to moderns by Burckhardt's "parallelizing of facts": the coming of the *Gewaltmenschen,* the men of brute force who impose order, the imperiled existence and breakup of a harmonious, balanced life, the flight of the best into the contemplative life, the wonder of creatively free men, and the dissipating dangers of subjectivism. It is difficult to summarize Burckhardt's subtle and complex compositions in a few brief generalizations. At best one can extract some themes and indicate elements of structure. Generalizations of his work tend to sound false. The following is a hazardous and tentative effort to hint at the structural "method" of a historian who, more than most others, deserves to be read and reread because there is no way of summarizing his vision.

The *Kultur der Renaissance in Italien* and the *Griechische Kulturgeschichte* focus on Burckhardt's vision of peoples who gave expression to life as a harmonious whole. As such the central point of the books is already composite. Life as harmony is life as style; it is a balancing of components, each of which may be in tension with another. In the Renaissance work Burckhardt was concerned with the factors which permitted

---

[120] *J.B.B.,* II, 561, III, 169–70 especially, and 287.

a style of life in quattrocento Italy and with the forms used to express this co-ordinated diversity. It is very much the *Zustandsschilderung*, the fresco of general conditions, which the cultural historian sought, with little concern for developmental features (although there are suggestions where these are to be found). The presentation was held to the plane of *typical* manifestations of the Renaissance, and it only hints at a culmination of the "golden age" in Leonardo, more so in Raphael, and the fateful turning point in Michelangelo.[121] Although the work was not a crippled version of the intention to integrate *Kunstgeschichte* and *Kulturgeschichte*, Burckhardt spoke of it as *ein Schmerzenskind*,[122] a child of sorrow. It is a rounded vision and yet an incomplete essay. The *Griechische Kulturgeschichte* shares this double quality, but in a different sense. It is the more comprehensive vision of the entire course of a culture but has the disadvantage of being only a half-finished book. The second half of the book was not rewritten by Burckhardt for publication but was posthumously edited from lecture notes. It provides as much *Zustandsschilderung* as the Renaissance work but also describes the gradual formation of a harmonious life and its disintegration. The older Burckhardt became, the more he felt an inner compulsion to lecture on this culture, the base of all European civilization, partially alien to the modern man born with the Renaissance and yet fundamental to that man and to that age.[123] Through the Greeks the European found his basic view of the world, his models of excellence as citizen and artist, his sense of measure and harmony. How basic these forms were for European culture, Burckhardt expressed in one sentence: "The hour when our culture will no longer find beauty in the

---

[121] Perhaps the most revealing aspect of Burckhardt's procedure here is his passage on the *huomo universale* where he describes Alberti at length and then leads with one sentence to the highest expression of the type: "And Leonardo da Vinci was to Alberti as the finisher to the beginner, as the master to the dilettante" (*K.R.I.*, p. 82).

[122] *Briefe*, p. 255.

[123] *Ibid.*, p. 367; *G.K.*, I, 52.

great Greek types of gods will be the beginning of barbarism."[124] As long as the West has a culture (and it was Burckhardt's chosen task to preserve this continuum), "we will remain the admirers of the Greeks' creation and ability, and their debtors in knowledge of the world."[125] We see with their eyes and speak in their forms. Here the Swiss historian depicted the supreme attempt of western man to create a balanced whole out of a diverse life, and at the same time he wove into this presentation the dramatic, even tragic, view of self-inflicted destruction. The structural problem created by this dual intent in a more complex and comprehensive work should be considered with the problem of composition in the more static description of conditions of the *Kultur der Renaissance in Italien.* Although the latter may be the more accomplished work of art, the *Griechische Kulturgeschichte* has a wider vision and broader task.

Each of Burckhardt's total visions of a cultural age was a composite of a number of partial views. What were these subviews and how did they give the impression of a whole? The three great factors, *die Potenzen*, of state-religion-*Kultur*, whose interrelations Burckhardt described in the *Weltgeschichtliche Betrachtungen*, are recognizable building blocks in Renaissance and Greek culture. In the *Kultur der Renaissance* the state "as a work of art" (i.e., as a skilfully constructed and manipulated mechanism) is the powerful structural element which opens the work; a description of religion and morality concludes the book. Between these two blocks lie four sections on the development of the individuum, the revival of antiquity, the discovery of the world and of man, and conviviality and festivals. These middle sections color the content of the first and final sections, so that it is not possible to say that the chapter on the state is a purely political intro-

---

[124] Quoted by Felix Staehelin in Introduction to Vol. XIII of *Gesamtausgabe* (1934), p. 14. See also *G.K.*, III, 172–73, on the Hellenistic age as a vital link in the continuity of European culture.

[125] *G.K.*, I, 15, and II, 451 (on the Greeks as "das Auge der Welt").

duction. The *Potenz Staat* is clearly related to "cultural" factors, partially as the cause of the particular cultural development, but partially also as a concomitant feature of the culture. Morality and religion are not given as the final products of the cultural condition but emerge as attendant aspects of the culture. The unity is therefore more than a loosely connected sequence of three separate factors (state-culture-religion); it is the unity of a tableau in which the subviews communicate their meaning only by being part of a whole. In a way the end of the book rejoins the beginning, for the short passage on the *Weltanschauung* of Lorenzo il Magnifico contrasts strikingly with the ruthless political mentality of the great prototypes of tyranny, Frederick II and Ezzelino. The strongest theme of the book emerges from the second section: the individuum free to contemplate this world objectively, capable of a rich life but yet in danger of capsizing as an unrestrained subjective creature (the fate of the humanists in section three). This theme has already been introduced with the tyrants of the first section and still appears in the last pages, on those who found an inner hold in religious and moral norms. In the third section Burckhardt traces the revival of classical antiquity, not as the causal factor responsible for this age, but as a concomitant feature of an indigenous development which could supplement the awakening individuum, but could also act as a seductively misleading (*irreführrend*)[126] element. And again, this theme appears in the chapter on tyrants and city-states, and is woven into the final passages where Burckhardt describes both aspects of the theme, the beneficial assimilation of classical morality and its harmfully misleading influence. The fourth and fifth sections are almost adumbrations of the previous themes: a description of the forms man used to view the world objectively and to express these insights in literary and in social forms.

---

[126] *K.R.I.*, pp. 154–55; cf. also Burckhardt's conception of Alexandria as the melting pot in which contact among cultures could lead away from a style (*Konstantin*, pp. 91, 195).

But the objective viewing of political and military reality is part of the first section, and objective viewing is still a vital factor at the end in the description of man's search for metaphysical and moral certainties. The fifth section, on conviviality and festivals, surely an astounding exercise in social-cultural history, is related to the preceding sections in such matters as the equalization of classes and the sexes, the physical appearance of individuals, the norms of social conduct, and the festivals as works of art which require as a common social link the new forms of education (if that, in any sense, approaches Burckhardt's term *Bildung*). The transition to the final chapter on moral conduct and norms is an obvious one.

These subviews of the whole are so much a part of the whole, and the whole depends so much on all the parts, that analytical abstraction becomes falsification. The sections are so balanced as "equi-valents" that no one of them can be said to be central, revealing the gist of the whole. More than one falsification of Burckhardt's intention has resulted from the desire to extract a quintessence from the complex work. The graphic (*anschaulich*) quality of Burckhardt's vision makes a conceptual reformulation impossible. Could a logically arranged argument fully convey the Rubens view of Theodosius before Saint Ambrose? But more about this later.

A table of contents of the *Griechische Kulturgeschichte* suggests, but at first sight only, a less ordered work than the Renaissance book. First section: the Greeks and their myth; second: state and nation; third: religion and cult; fourth: exploration of the future; fifth: the total balance sheet of Greek life; sixth: the fine arts; seventh: poetry and music; eighth: philosophy, science, and rhetoric; and ninth: Hellenic man in his chronological development. Some of these (sections one, four, and five) amount to no more than 30–80 pages each, while another (section nine) constitutes a book of 480 pages. And yet the brief sections are not overshadowed by the lengthier ones. The fifth section with its summary title seems strangely placed in the middle; the first and fourth sections look like asides that fit nowhere; and the lengthy last part looks like a separate treatise patched onto the whole as an afterthought. This organization appears more astounding when related to the following line of thought which runs through the work like the red thread through the cables of the British navy. The Greeks, early in their development, created a harmonious existence which blended the varied expressions of their spirit admirably; but then they proved incapable of restraining the divisive and dissociative forces of their political institutions; thus their political life developed its own direction and ultimately the states were subjugated by Rome, while the individual, detached from political activity, took flight into contemplation and private fulfilment. In this process the increased reliance on rationality corroded the earlier common elements of culture and the base of harmonious existence. Given such a theme, it may seem unlikely that the chosen organization can hold everything together. Yet it does. As one takes in the topography of a landscape cumulatively by walking through it, Burckhardt's presentation of Greek civilization takes on its form by our gradual movement through it. The whole was one vision in which the parts are integrated equi-valents.

The first section, a mere thirty-three pages, in a sense frames the whole work, for it introduces the myths as the cohesive factor of Greek civilization. This basic expression of the Greek spirit pervades, like the "Oceanus of that world," all other sections, and as one progresses deeper into the work the feeling grows ever stronger that the very existence of the Greek style of life depended on its ability or inability to preserve the life-giving quality of these myths. As one approaches the eighth section (with its subpart, the break with the myth), this feeling has assumed the quality of dramatic suspense. The almost predestined result is the break with the myths and the emergence of the "free personality." Yet this sense of suspense is sustained in spite of the fact that each separate section takes its own subject down to Roman times. The theme of former harmony is present in the reader's awareness even when Burckhardt deals with its disintegration and transformation. The three big sections on the state, religion, and the arts are related through the myths as well as by the fact that they are at first mutually interdependent *Potenzen*, which only gradually go their own way (in so far as they ever really separate). The suspense factor *and* the sense for the interdependent harmony *and* the sense for the delicate balance of the basic elements are all supported by the two short chapters (sections four and five) which at first seemed mere irrelevant intrusions. The chapter on the Greek concern with a prognosis of the future ties the treatment of the state and the treatment of religion to each other and at the same time underlines the sense of uncertainty prevailing in Greek life. The transition to the "balance sheet of Greek life" (section five) is natural since this chapter deals essentially with the pessimism which pervaded Greek civilization. Its position, before the sections on art and philosophical as well as scientific thought, is eminently fitting because for Burckhardt the Greek accomplishments in these realms were the values which outlasted the perishable reality of harmonious life[127] and comforted men forced to find a refuge outside a collapsed world. Then the sections on art and thought serve first as mirrors of the prevailing harmony and subsequently as projections of an idealized world which no longer exists but still exercises its power over the imagination. And finally, what about the last long section on Hellenic man in his chronological development?

Der Mensch in seiner Wandlung — man in his variations and sameness — was really Burckhardt's historical center.[128] He treated it differently in his three main historical works. In the book on Constantine's age, the image of "aging classical man" was put primarily in the central sections in which Burckhardt described the theocrasy (the amalgamation of deities), the hope for an answer in the mystery cults, the petri-

---

[127] See *W.B.*, pp. 118, 321.
[128] *W.B.*, pp. 45, 48, 61; *Historische Fragments*, p. 3.

fication of the older cultural forms.[129] The reader almost always can perceive the outlines of such a generalized classical "man-in-crisis," but he cannot really extricate him as a clear separable figure from the context. In the *Kultur der Renaissance*, Renaissance man in his varied expressions becomes almost a portrait; and yet he is not really set apart from the context. The early drafts of plans for the book, however, had culminated in an intended section on *der Mensch der Renaissance*.[130] Burckhardt then dropped this section, as he also eliminated the treatment of art which originally had been intended as a major component of the whole. His fine architectonic sense must have persuaded him that such a weighty section on Renaissance man might easily have unbalanced the delicate structure of the book and would have forced upon him a conceptualization he hated. But in the more comprehensive *Griechische Kulturgeschichte* the weighty section on Hellenic man through the ages served a wonderful architectonic purpose. Here Burckhardt treated a subject which stretched over a long span of time and which permitted him to attend to the problem of cultural *development* in addition to the description of cultural conditions. The first eight sections of the *Griechische Kulturgeschichte* presented the complex tableau of cultural conditions. Against this total view of Greek civilization, Burckhardt placed in the last, the ninth, section the typical Hellene in his temporal variations as Heroic Man, Colonial Man, Agonistic Man, Man of the Fifth Century, Man of the Fourth Century, and as Hellenistic Man. This involved the author in repetition; but it was the enriching repetition which compares with the shift in vantage point for getting another view of the same complex scene. The total effect of the architectonic balance of the whole does not depend upon the length of the chapters but on the manner in

---

[129] And there is also the emergence of the new man, analogous to the "free personality" in Greece during its decline, the man with the ascetic ideal who flees from the old culture; see *Konstantin*, pp. 277–87.

[130] *J.B.B.*, III, 668–69, 734.

which these, as building blocks of equal weight, have been fitted together while yet remaining meaningful parts in their own right.

The feeling that these subviews are equi-valents, in the sense in which Burckhardt himself spoke of Rubens' equi-valents of composition, is enhanced by a number of observations. These are compositional blocks of like weight, balancing one another even when they at first look uneven. The second section on "the development of the individuum" in the *Kultur der Renaissance* is only one-fourth and one-third as long as the contiguous sections before and after. And what are its internal building blocks? The first three of the twenty pages deal with the role of the individuum in political life. But these few pages have a reinforcement outside this section in the eighty pages on the state as a work of art. After these three pages comes a three-page discussion of the many-sided man which, despite its brevity and despite the fact that the most amazing universal genius is not discussed, impresses most readers as one of the most striking passages of the whole book. Then follow six pages on the importance of glory, dealing largely with an "apparently" minor issue of the cult of birth-places and graves of great men.[131] The remaining nine pages, almost half of the entire section, are given to the "apparently" even more subordinate issue of forms of mockery and wit and the art of slander. Taken separately, these small sectors seem uneven and only partially relevant to a common theme — like interesting asides. But welded together they are balanced parts of a larger block which, for all its briefness, is a vitally significant section of the book. In fact, this shortest section, with its peculiar sub-blocks, is a key chapter which could not be taken out without causing the collapse of the whole work. Subject any other sections of Burckhardt's cultural visions to the same experiment, and you will get the same impression of their

---

[131] A parallel discussion of this phenomenon is in *Geschichte der Renaissance in Italien*, pp. 290–97.

intrinsic balance and irreversibility. The picture-like composition of these equi-valents is further borne out by a strange test which gives specific meaning to the notion of irreversibility. One can read these works by taking chapters in arbitrary order; as long as all chapters are read, the effect of a balanced and ordered whole will still communicate itself — just as it is possible to obtain the total impression of a picture without an arrow which tells the viewer: start here and then proceed as follows. "In the presentation, as in one's study, one asks oneself anxiously: where to start? The answer will have to be: just somewhere. . . . Since the matters touch each other everywhere, some repetition is unavoidable."[132] Yet, the reader still gets the impression, as does the viewer of the painting, that the whole is focused and has a center. Unlike books dependent upon sequential order of logical arguments, Burckhardt's compositions depended on the "inexplicable gift of vision" which he attributed to Rubens, that other great narrator.

The visual-pictorial quality of Burckhardt's cultural histories emerges even more strongly as one realizes that he told his story by means of pictures and not through abstract arguments. Of course, all narrative historians rely on the story built from scene-like sequences; but this is not the "visual tool" which Burckhardt employed. He presented knowledge of conditions as well as his historical "arguments" in visual form. The theses which he advanced about certain cultural epochs are communicated more through concrete "pictures" than through generalized statements. The crop of summary statements to be reaped from his works is a fairly meager one. Although they seem weighty in his excellent formulations, these general statements are nonetheless subordinate parts, almost asides. It is always tempting to take these fine general formulations as the core of Burck-

---

[132] *G.K.*, I, 8.

hardt's position. But there is danger in doing so, and many useless arguments over his theses have resulted from too heavy dependence on summary statements about individualism, irreligiosity, and the like. The real meaning of the theses rests in the concrete examples, usually descriptions of a *representative* phenomenon of the period. Burckhardt did not employ images of detail merely as illustrations of his generalized summaries. They were the indispensable building blocks of his sections. The conception of the "free personality," which plays such an important role in the *Griechische Kulturgeschichte*, is communicated through a skilfully arranged group portrait of biographical sketches, not through a definition. In the Renaissance section on the development of the individuum there are some summary statements on the appearance of the many-sided man (*die Vielseitigen*), but the crucial case of the all-sided (*die Allseitigen*) is presented, without such general remarks, completely through a concrete description of the appearance and activities of Alberti. The section on the aging classical culture in *Die Zeit Konstantins des Grossen* is almost completely "argued" in terms of concrete examples, of precise visual quality, describing physical appearance, barbarian influence on dress, the look of the cities, the new use of art forms and rhetoric. Again and again it is the summation of picture-like episodes which carries Burckhardt's interpretation and "argument," while the generalized statement merely underscores them.[133] The proof of his view should be tested in his composite of images.

---

[133] See also the following two comments on this point: Erwin Rohde in a letter to Friedrich Nietzsche (quoted by R. Marx in "Nachwort" to *G.K.*, III, 504); "Um Deine Kollegien bei Burckhardt beneide ich Dich: wenn es einen ganz specifisch historischen Geist gibt, so ist er es. Gerade die hohe Kunst, keinen 'Grundgedanken' hinein zu dozieren, aber in Anschauungen denkend, das Wesen und Tun vergangener Zeit so zu erkennen . . . das ist die hohe Kunst des Historikers." Werner Kaegi on section two of the *Kultur der Renaissance in Italien*, in *J.B.B.*, III, 713: 'Einen Kommentar gibt Burckhardt selbst durch den Text des ganzen Abschnittes. Hier aber liegt die Schwierigkeit.

Burckhardt could not use the concrete images as mere *illustrative* material because his conception of cultural history aimed at describing the most general conditions. He could not rest his case on a mere compilation of colorful details, selected for their value as ornament and picturesqueness. Neither could he construct his visions from the most spectacular impressions and examples. The truly exceptional, the outstanding figure or event, is either missing from his picture or appears very briefly among a vaster array of lesser persons and actions. This kind of cultural history depended altogether on the historian's ability to recognize the "typical" as such, as that which could be called representative of a style of life. The selected visual parts had to be representative; the general (*Allgemeine*) had to speak through the singular (*Einzelne*), which therefore must be the typical.[134] As Burckhardt told his students: only long and intensive exercises in viewing, the constant parallelizing of facts, the laborious steeping in the best sources, can develop the all-important sense of style and the awareness of the typical.[135] He himself developed such a sense into an astonishingly sensitive and accurate instrument. Thus he could permit himself to sketch the Greek *tyrannis* with a series of short image-like scenes which portray the

---

Burckhardt erläutert seine theoretischen Aussagen nie begrifflich, sondern mit Bildern und Vorgängen. Auch dieser Abschnitt vermittelt vor allem Anschauung. Und gerade dies ist Burckhardts Grösse. Das Erstaunliche an ihm liegt nicht in seinen abstrakten Thesen, sondern in der Fülle der Erscheinungen, die sein Blick umfasst."

[134] *K.R.I.*, pp. 2, 49, 170, 191 (some of these on Aeneas Silvius as a "Normalmensch"); *G.K.*, I, 6 (". . . Wert durch das *Typische* der Darstellung"; italics are Burckhardt's). See also *J.B.B.*, III, 290, where Kaegi quotes Burckhardt's promise to his audience to present "das Kleine und Einzelne als Symbol eines Ganzen und Grossen, das Biographische als Symbol eines Allgültigen."

[135] *W.B.*, pp. 63–64: ". . . one also learns to guess at the whole through a part, but risks overlooking the important half-page among all the paltry stuff [*Wust*] if a happy ability to surmise does not accidentally (at least that is what some believe) lead the eye to it." See also *J.B.B.*, III, 640: "It is understood that only the hundredth part of the content will be of value to you, but the work in itself, which consists in peeling out this one-hundredth, is the educational part [*das Bildende*]. Does the miner work differently?"

phenomenon in its typical aspects, its variations of the typical, its strength and appeal, its weakness and tenuous existence. And is not the description of the Renaissance tyrant presented through a gallery of specific portraits, none of which the reader could ignore, and none of which falls outside the frame of the typical?[136] Burckhardt was not averse to using the mere anecdote if it could help to catch a mood, a mode of thinking, a sentiment of a former age. Often a single descriptive incident could save pages of general remarks and observations.[137] The feud among the Baglioni of Perugia and the "bloody wedding of 1500" tells more of the age than pages of abstract analysis.[138] Giovanni Maria Visconti's order to Milan's priests to substitute *tranquillitatem* for the word *pacem* in the traditional invocation *dona nobis pacem* in order to contain popular discontent over a lengthy war[139] — who can forget this so specific, yet so typical, description of these autocrats? One page on the sonnet form as a beneficial restraint for the "free" Renaissance artist[140] deals effectively with one of the age's greatest problems: the relation of creative freedom to subjectivity and artistic norms. When Diocletian let the defeated caesar Galerius run for a mile alongside the emperor's chariot, dressed in purple and in plain view of the troops, before he would permit Galerius to report — this told Burckhardt more about the Diocletian system than pages of constitutional analysis.[141] It is unlikely that anything compares as a hauntingly

---

[136] The same is true of the short portraits of third-century Roman emperors in the *Konstantin*.

[137] See, for example, *Konstantin*, p. 354; *K.R.I.*, pp. 49, 247, 313; *G.K.*, I, 77, III, 41; and especially the discussion of Greek historians in *G.K.*, II, 456: "If we, through our training, depend on the exact and see no virtue [*Heil*] beyond it, the Greeks perceived types instead, and the expression of the type is the anecdote which is altogether true and yet has not been true at any specific time." See also *Cicerone*, I, 151, II, 687.

[138] *K.R.I.*, pp. 16–19.

[139] *K.R.I.*, p. 8.

[140] *K.R.I.*, pp. 175–76.

[141] *Konstantin*, p. 82. Other striking examples: *K.R.I.*, p. 105, on the rediscovered corpse of a Roman girl as a characteristic illustration of rediscovery of

effective image of Greece's decline with the passage compiled by Burckhardt from Pausanias' description of desolated *poleis* and landscapes.[142] No general statement, no abstract summing-up could equal this presentation of the end of a rich civilization in the form of visual impressions.

A hundred illustrations of Burckhardt's skill in selecting the characteristic incident could be supplemented by a hundred samples of the descriptive style which marks his works. Burckhardt was a master of ecphrasis, the art of describing the visual in words.[143] He could translate his graphic perceptions (or *Anschauungen*) into words which again evoke the image in the reader. He was expert at coining words and short phrases of descriptive excellence. He could teach art history, and lecture on painting and architecture, when projectors and other "visual aids" were still largely unavailable. He could, in asides, express views and judgments which would take others paragraphs. He is one of the most quotable historians, but also perhaps the least translatable. Without his literary skill, his fine visions would have remained locked in his mind. And the skill in expressive language was accompanied by a marvelous sense of proportion. Burckhardt never overloaded his images, he never used an unnecessary passage, he instinctively stopped just in time. He preferred to give less rather than risk giving too much. We never "have to think things away" — as he often had to do in studying certain artists — in order to get at his thought and form.

Burckhardt knew he had no science, only personal knowl-

---

antiquity; p. 94, on Aretino ("ein Blick auf sein Wesen erspart uns die Beschäftigung mit manchen Geringeren seiner Gattung"); and as an example of a simple symbolic act which communicates a complicated sequence of events in a brief "anschaulich" sketch, see *G.K.*, III, 265, on Alexander the Great and the consequences of his conquests: ". . . clearly symbolic is the fact that he places a manuscript of the *Iliad* in the magnificent little treasure chest which became his booty with Darius' splendid tent; thus it happened literally: Hellenic spirit was to be framed in oriental riches."

[142] *G.K.*, III, 377–81, which also includes passages from Strabo.
[143] *J.B.B.*, II, 472, and III, 68.

edge. "Ich gebe nicht mehr als ich kann, und ich sage nicht mehr als ich weiss" — I give no more than I can and say no more than I know.[144] He viewed his master work on the Renaissance as merely an "essay," an attempt. He called the *Griechische Kulturgeschichte* also an essay *(ein Probestück)*.[145] These were not merely exercises in modesty; they must be taken seriously. They proceeded from his profound awareness that his art of viewing, his "method" of *Anschauung*, depended upon personal factors. "From the same studies on which we built these lectures arbitrarily [*eigenmächtig*], by adjusting our subjective procedure to the relative significance of phenomena in regard to the whole [*proportionale Wichtigkeit*], another would have made a different selection and arrangement, and would often have attained even different results."[146] Or, as he explained in the brief introduction to the Renaissance book:

> To each eye perhaps, the outlines of a cultural period [*die geistigen Umrisse einer Kulturepoche*] present a differing picture; and in treating of a civilization which is the nearest mother[147] to our own, and whose influence is still at work among us, subjective judgment and experience [*Erlebnis*] interferes constantly with both author [*Darsteller*] and reader. In the wide ocean upon which we venture are many possible ways and directions; and the same studies which served this work could in different hands receive different use and treatment, and, moreover, could lead to other results. . . . It is the most essential difficulty of cultural history that it must break down a great spiritual [*geistig*] continuum into separate and partially arbitrary categories in order to present it to

---

[144] *J.B.B.*, III, 290, and also III, 371.

[145] *G.K.*, I, 3.

[146] *G.K.*, I, 9; see also *Konstantin*, p. 361.

[147] The phrase "nearest mother," strange as it may sound, must be taken seriously, for it shows that Burckhardt thought of the Renaissance as *one*, though the most important, of the periods which shaped the life of modern man.

the reader [*um es nur irgendwie zur Darstellung zu bringen*].[148]

Yet, Burckhardt's reservations about his personal procedure and his lack of a teachable scientific method, omits one crucial consideration. When a gifted "viewing artist" communicates in truly descriptive terms a vision of an age which has been based on an intensive and sensitive acquaintance with the major sources — how then can the lesser artists extensively alter this vision? True, further refinement on specific points may take place (which by no means need improve the total vision). True, new historical experience may open new vistas, in the same way in which the nineteenth century seen from Basel affected Burckhardt's own view. He himself admonished his students: "Each age looks at the more distant past anew and differently; it could be, for instance, that Thucydides reported a fact of first significance which will be recognized only a hundred years from now."[149] According to Burckhardt, others can draw a completely new picture; they can write another "essay." Yet, his composite views of three ages — Greek civilization, the age of Constantine, and the Italian Renaissance — have stood the test of time exceedingly well.[150]

---

[148] *K.R.I.*, p. 1. See also the remark in the *W.B.*, pp. 362–63; "Wir sehen zwischen Tannen des hohen Juras hindurch in weiter Ferne einen beruehmten Gipfel mit ewigem Schnee; er wird freilich zugleich von vielen anderen Orten aus in anderer Art gesehen . . . er ist und bleibt aber der selbe Montblanc."

[149] *G.K.*, I, 11, and *W.B.*, p. 66.

[150] On Burckhardt's conception of the Renaissance, see Wallace K. Ferguson, *The Renaissance in Historical Thought*, p. x: "No other generally accepted interpretation arose to take its place." Perhaps the finest verdict of its lasting quality came from Burckhardt's friend, the poet Paul Heyse; see *J.B.B.*, III, 746. *Die Zeit Konstantins des Grossen* has remained one of the basic interpretations of the Constantine problem and one of the finest cultural histories of the age. The *Griechische Kulturgeschichte* was condemned by the philologists, for insufficient attention to the most recent philological scholarship. For many years Burckhardt himself had qualms about publishing it, and it retains an unfinished quality. For what such a personal conviction may be worth, I am convinced that the book will remain fundamental to the understanding of Greek civilization.

This man, who claimed no profound scholarly methods, found an astonishingly successful way for ordering and constructing the complex data of culture while retaining its diversity. His "way," his "method," is not readily available in capsule form; the success which he had with it may have depended upon a fortunate combination of personal factors; it may never be equaled, but one can learn from it. He sought no system, but he found an integrated view of western culture. He had no philosophy, but lived by his *Weltanschauung*. He saw that man's greatest accomplishment was the art of forging a harmonious style of life out of life's disharmonies; he found his own style. By patiently training his eyes and his judgment, he learned to discern the comforting realities of human existence. Voltaire and Guizot were filled with the wonders of their own age; each, in his own way, sought to teach men respect for culture by relating themselves meaningfully to the past. Burckhardt was out of tune with his age; but thereby, perhaps, he gained a more balanced and a wiser view of human inadequacy and potential greatness. He, with his early sense of the mutability and transitoriness of life, became a great guardian of western culture. It was only fitting that such a conservator of culture should become the most eminent cultural historian.

APPENDIX

Although Burckhardt did not elaborate the problem it is perhaps important to ask the question: What was the relation between his conception of *Kultur* and *Kulturgeschichte*? Occasionally one finds discussions of his cultural history based on his "definition" of *Kultur* in the *Weltgeschichtliche Betrachtungen*. In its famous chapter on the three great *Potenzen* — the forces of state, religion, and *Kultur* — Burckhardt undertook to relate three highly significant segments of life found in all larger historical constellations. The virtue of these chapters is that they provide numerous occasions for asking necessary questions about the intricate interrelations of the basic activities and institutions of man.

How do religious convictions condition political life or poetry (and vice versa)? What effects can scientific ideas exert on religious life (or vice versa)? What happens to *Kultur* when it becomes subservient to state or religion? Or what happens to the state when it is subservient to *Kultur* or religion? And so forth. Not enough emphasis can be placed on the fact that Burckhardt sought to perceive the varied manners in which such interrelations have existed. It is, however, dangerous to take too seriously the "systematic" intent of these reflections. They originated in Burckhardt's desire to awaken in his students a sensitive, questioning attitude toward the complexity of historical reality; they fulfil this function magnificently. They were distinctly not meant to be another philosophy of history, another *Historik*, or a systematization of Burckhardt's thought (see *W.B.*, pp. 42, 43, 46, 61, 74–75, 146–48, and *J.B.B.*, III, 370). Probably, though one cannot prove this conclusively, it is therefore mistaken to base Burckhardt's ideas of *Kulturgeschichte* on the use of the term *Kultur* found in pages of the *W.B.* where he tried to distinguish *Kultur* from the other *Potenzen*. He there sought to differentiate the two "stable factors," state and religion, from *Kultur* "als das spontan zustande gekommene" (pp. 42, 74, 113). *Kultur* in that sense is primarily the specific realm of society, the constantly modifying and decomposing factor. As its separate components Burckhardt discussed especially language, arts, sciences, and in an odd way also morality (*Sittlichkeit*) and trade (as if they did not quite belong and yet had something to do with it; see pp. 121–26). The *real* subject of the *Griechische Kulturgeschichte* — *Lebensauffassungen, Denkweisen*, etc. — is missing in this circumscription of *Kultur* given in the *W.B.*; *Kultur* in the *G.K.* is not a *factor*, but the substratum of the whole. Occasionally Burckhardt was conscious of this limitation when he referred to the arts, etc., as "Kultur im engeren Sinn des Wortes" (see *G.K.*, III, 416; *W.B.*, p. 74). In my opinion Burckhardt did not equate cultural history with a narrow conception of culture, such as the arts. As a matter of fact, he had doubts about the merger of these two historical forms (see n. 49). In the Renaissance book he excluded art altogether (but for extraneous reasons) and yet wrote cultural history. His conception of cultural history was much broader than the circumscription of *Kultur* in the *W.B.* would warrant (although it may be well to keep this circumscription in mind as one reads the histories). Most basic, perhaps, was his early idea that the cultural historian describes the *Zustände*, the general conditions, a way of life, in terms of which events take on their true meaning (see n. 104). This included the total configuration, therefore, of all three *Potenzen*. In his latest cultural history, the *Griechische Kulturgeschichte*, Burckhardt introduced his intention to study "die Lebensauffassungen der Griechen," "die Geschichte der griechischen Denkweisen und Auffassungen," "die Erkenntnis der lebendigen Kräfte, der aufbauenden und zerstörenden" (which preserves the notion of the spontaneous aspect of *Kultur*), "die Geschichte des griechischen Geistes." And especially see the sentence: "Kulturgeschichte . . . geht auf das Innere der vergangenen Menschheit und verkündet wie diese *war, wollte, dachte, schaute*, und *vermochte*" (*G.K.*, I, 6, all italics are Burckhardt's). In that introduction, Burckhardt expressed his own awareness of the fact that he was free to formulate his own conception of cultural history: "So können wir uns frei bewegen. Glücklicherweise schwankt nicht nur der *Begriff* Kulturgeschichte, sondern es schwankt auch die akademische Praxis (und noch einiges andere)" (*G.K.*, I, 5).

4 : Lamprecht
1856 - 1915

Voltaire labored for cultural history in the hope that this historiographic form would make men conscious of their real achievements. Guizot studied the historical evolution of civilization so that he might better orient himself in the present. Burckhardt, horrified by the barbarization of modern life, wrote cultural history to preserve a cultural continuum. But in Karl Lamprecht, long a professor of history at the University of Leipzig, we encounter a professional fighting a professional cause.[1] Only incidentally did he ask questions such as: Is civilization a value? Is historical understanding of civilization necessary for the welfare of society? More emphatically than his predecessors, Lamprecht argued the case for cultural history within the context of disciplinary problems. At the same time, Lamprecht was a great popularizer who wrote his main work, the *Deutsche Geschichte*, for the general public. Despite this fact, it is thoroughly characteristic that his struggle for a new historiographic form and program was marked by his long involvement in as typical a professional matter as a methodological dispute.

When Lamprecht, during the last quarter of the nineteenth century, left his student years behind him, the historical discipline was faced with problems largely resulting from an

---

[1] The most significant dates of Lamprecht's life are the following: born at Jessen (Saxony) in 1856; attended famed Schulpforta Gymnasium, 1866–74; attended universities of Göttingen, Leipzig, Munich, 1874–79; habilitated at Bonn, 1881, extraordinarius at Bonn, 1885–90; professor at Marburg, 1890–91; professor at Leipzig, 1891–1915; died 1915. In 1904 he was in the United States as a lecturer in connection with the St. Louis Exhibition and the sesquicentennial at Columbia University.

astounding productivity over the last hundred years. Historians had gathered great quantities of source materials, thus permitting ever more detailed views of the past. More systematic university training had greatly increased the number of professional historians who, in conjunction with a still sizable group of non-academic writers, pushed historical investigations into previously neglected areas. At the same time, the questions and findings of archaeologists, economists, sociologists, ethnologists, art historians, and literary historians enriched the historical discipline by subject matter and methods. Herder, Hegel, Comte, Marx, and Darwin had raised broad issues historians could not avoid. The discipline had become enormously rich and complex. Men inside and outside the profession felt the need for a more systematic and comprehensive view of all new knowledge and diversified concerns. None fought more vehemently for a fresh orientation than Lamprecht, who had received training in political and economic and art history.

Three movements in particular met in the career of Lamprecht: the concerns of Condorcet, Comte, Buckle, and Spencer for a historical view of progress and for history as a "genetic" science; the Romantic tradition with its notions of *Volk* and *Volksgeist*; and a concern for biological, especially psychological, development. Running through these main lines were concerns with specific historiographic trends: the "idealism" of Ranke's school, the historical materialism of Marx, and various recent experiments in cultural history by Burckhardt, Karl Wilhelm Nitzsch, and Gustav Freytag.[2]

---

[2] For a lengthier discussion of the various influences in Lamprecht's historical thought see Annie M. Popper, "Karl Gotthard Lamprecht," in *Some Historians of Modern Europe*, ed. Bernadotte Schmitt, pp. 217–39; Gustav Schmoller, "Zur Würdigung von Karl Lamprecht," *Schmoller's Jahrbuch*, XL (1916), Part 3, pp. 27–54; Walter Goetz, "Karl Lamprecht's Stellung in der Geschichtswissenschaft," in *Historiker in meiner Zeit*, pp. 309–13; Heinrich Ritter von Srbik, *Geist und Geschichte*, Vol. II; Franz Eulenburg, "Neuere Geschichtsphilosophie; kritische Analysen," *Archiv für Sozialwissenschaft und Sozialpolitik*, N.F., XXV (1907), 283–337; Adolf Kuhnert, *Der Streit um die geschichtswissenschaftlichen*

Lamprecht did not address himself to these movements and trends separately. But in his efforts at a new synthesis, he became involved in a host of problems, as well as solutions, related to the work of these particular predecessors. To translate these problems into the form of questions, it appears that the following were of predominant importance to Lamprecht's activities. What exactly was the historian's proper subject matter: individual or collective phenomena? How could the total development of mankind be studied? Specifically, what was the relation between the history of separate peoples and the history of mankind? How could the history of the many diverse activities of man be brought together in one unified form and intelligible structure? Could the intricate details of a long development be presented as a coherent structure and an orderly process by attending to some specific causal factors?

Lamprecht was fundamentally convinced that the "new history" must be collective history.[3] The historian, especially the German historian, must break with the "individualistic school" which Lamprecht thought to be that of Ranke's followers.[4] As long as historians assumed that the individually unique was the historian's proper subject matter, they were, in Lamprecht's opinion, the captives of biography. History, in that form, amounted to little more than an account of great men, and largely those prominent in wars and political life.[5]

Theorien Karl Lamprechts; Emil J. Spiess, *Die Geschichtsphilosophie von Karl Lamprecht*; and Herbert Schoenebaum, "Karl Lamprecht," *Archiv für Kulturgeschichte*, XXXVII (1955), 269–305.

[3] Lamprecht's most significant theoretical pronunciamentos are: *Alte und neue Richtungen in der Geschichtswissenschaft* (hereafter cited as *A.N.*); *Die kulturhistorische Methode* (hereafter cited as *K.M.*); *Moderne Geschichtswissenschaft*; and *Einführung in das historische Denken* (hereafter cited as *Einf.*).

[4] Ranke (who had lauded the young scholar for his *Deutsches Wirtschaftsleben im Mittelalter* during a personal meeting which took place shortly before Ranke's death) remained in many ways Lamprecht's touchstone on which he tested his own thought. See *A.N.*, pp. 24–48, 71; *K.M.*, pp. 22–25, 32–35; *Einf.*, pp. 13–14, 32–42; and *Deutsche Geschichte*, X, 328–32, XI, 178–80, Erg. Bd. I, 383, 454–63 (hereafter cited as *D.G.*).

[5] *D.G.*, X, 235–36, and Erg. Bd., I, 461.

"Political history is at its core the history of persons [*Person-engeschichte*]."[6] It was no longer justifiable to assume that individuals, even great individuals, were the prime movers of history. "What, today, are for us the names of a Pericles or an Augustus? Names; no more! Labels for great times!"[7] At most, the individual was a representative of his times, an expression of a collective life. Thus, the individual could not be understood in isolation but only in the context of the special world of which he was an integral part and product. The fascination with the individually unique (of which historians of certain schools made such a fetish) could result in little more than description, without explanation of causes.[8] By its nature such historical investigation might lead to an artistic *Anschauung* (graphic perception); it could not serve to make history a science. For, "working scientifically means to determine not what is singular but what is general, not to ascertain in things what separates them but what connects them. . . ."[9] An individual phenomenon derives its meaning from the general context in which it occurs; it cannot even be understood as a unique existence except by contrasting it with the prevailing mode of life. The historian's task, therefore, was to understand the broader collective phenomena which, in turn, might throw light upon individual phenomena — if one wished to investigate these. Before Lamprecht, Auguste Comte had called for a "history without names," and, even earlier, Condorcet had begun to consider the history of the common man.[10] The German professor wrote neither a his-

---

[6] *A.N.*, p. 19.

[7] "Über den Begriff der Geschichte," *Annalen der Naturphilosophie*, II (1903), 267.

[8] *D.G.*, IV, 134, Erg. Bd., I, 141, 436–37, 463, Erg. Bd. II, Pt. 1, p. 4; *K.M.*, pp. 5–9, 24, 29–30; *A.N.*, pp. 7–10; Srbik, II, 231.

[9] Quoted in Popper, p. 223.

[10] Lamprecht's relation to positivism has been debated inconclusively: E. Bernheim, *Lehrbuch der historischen Methode und der Geschichtsphilosophie*, pp. 710–18; Kuhnert, pp. 34–35; Schmoller, p. 33; Otto Hintze, "Über individualistische und kollektivistische Geschichtsauffassung," *Historische Zeitschrift*, LXXVII (1897), 60–67; Eulenburg, *passim*; Srbik, II, 227–29. Lam-

tory bared of individuals and their contributions, nor did any "universal-average-man" stand in the center of his investigations. There are many individual names in his works, but they appear always as illustrations of a collective phenomenon, as representative types, not as individually fascinating subjects. Lamprecht aimed at a historical form in which the individuals would be totally embedded in the broadest collective context.

Theoretically this demand for a broad collective history could have resulted in plans for a universal history. Indeed, Lamprecht felt strongly attracted to the ideal of describing the course of all human history. The most inclusive view, the broadest view of human development — *der Blick für das Grosse*[11] — was desirable and necessary for modern man. But Lamprecht was convinced that a scientific form of universal history, of *Menschheitsgeschichte*, was unattainable during the prevailing methodological confusion.[12] *Menschheitsgeschichte* in the older style of Iselin and Herder seemed untenable to Lamprecht because it was based on the intuitive and speculative idea that the history of mankind entailed different functions for different human groups, that each people made its own specific contribution, and that the sequence of such concrete realizations of divine objectives constituted the whole of history — but a history seen from a transhuman viewpoint.[13] Nor was Lamprecht willing to admit that universal history could be built on geographical theories as Karl Ritter, Friedrich Ratzel and Hans Helmolt had recently tried to do.[14] A geographical scale (*Massstab*) cannot be used to integrate the accomplishments of peoples into a single

---

precht denied the influence (see *K.M.*, p. 33) and once wanted to publish all the notes of his student years in order to refute the persistent speculations. Surely any publisher must have thought this too high a price for establishing Lamprecht's claim to originality.

[11] *K.M.*, p. 43.

[12] *K.M.*, pp. 19–21, 27, 30, 39 46; *D.G.*, Erg. Bd. I, 383, and II, Pt. 2, p. 25.

[13] *K.M.*, pp. 19, 41.

[14] *K.M.*, pp. 20–21, 42–46.

process "for geographical conditions, although they are strong causal factors, are not the core of the history of peoples." [15] A scientific treatment of universal history had to await the results of a new, highly necessary, task: a comparative study of the process by which peoples are formed. "The true scale must be found in the moments common to the development of all human communities, repeated in the fate of each people (*Völkerschicksal*): the general type of development of peoples must be found (*der Typ des Völkerwerdens*)." [16] The essential task consisted in discovering the developmental stages common to all peoples. So that this great work might be accomplished, Lamprecht organized his favorite creation, the Institut für Kultur- und Universalgeschichte [17] in Leipzig. Leaving universal history to future historians,[18] he occupied himself with analyzing the development of one people, the German *Volk*.

The *Volk* was for Lamprecht the human group best suited for historical study. This German notion, so difficult to translate into English (the mid-nineteenth-century English usage of "race" perhaps comes closest), denoted for him the fundamental form of collective life which, as a substratum, underlay the common experience of a group having both a common origin and a common destiny. A *Volk* is that which has truly "developed" and is "developing" (*das Gewordene und das Werdende*).[19] It is a group of human beings whose characteris-

---

[15] *K.M.*, p. 44.

[16] *K.M.*, p. 44.

[17] He founded the Institut in 1909, invited many guest lecturers (among whom Pirenne was prominent), and arranged programs of study which varied from such topics as Greek vase-painting, English economic thought around 1800, the *Shi-King*, the French novel, Byzantine theology, Japanese ornamental art, to intensive research in children's paintings (the latter being of great importance to Lamprecht's conception of stages in psychological development). Walter Goetz, who became director of the Institut in 1915, sought to focus its activities more on problems in Geistesgeschichte. The Institut with its first-rate library resources suffered seriously when the inflation of the years 1922–23 wiped out its endowment.

[18] Lamprecht, however, acted for many years as editor for a revised edition of the large Heeren-Uckert series, *Geschichte der europäischen Staaten*.

[19] *D.G.*, Erg. Bd. II, Pt. 2, p. 44.

tic "life of the soul" (*Seelenleben*) passes through stages of development, fulfilling ever more of the potential which it originally possessed in raw, uncultivated form. In a rather brilliant sketch, which Lamprecht later placed at the very beginning of his *Deutsche Geschichte*, he elucidated those forms of collective consciousness experienced by the German *Volk* at different stages of its development as a cohesive society.[20] From a community of kinship groups (*Geschlechtergemeinschaft*) grew, especially through the experience of the migrations, a community of *Völkerschaften* (i.e., loosely federated tribal groups with a strong consciousness of common destiny and experience); when these settled, they formed larger and more cohesive groups of tribes, the so-called *Stämme*, which coalesced, over many centuries of certain common experiences and through the appearance of territorial states which partly cut across them and partly coincided with them, into the modern *Volk*, the nation.

A group, at various stages of its development, is a genuine community only when its members are held together by a characteristic and common "psychic" state. The *Seelenleben*, the psychic life, psychic activity, psychic state — all these connotations are applicable, depending on the context in which Lamprecht used the word — constitutes the cohesive factor of a *Volk*.[21] Here was Lamprecht's key term for the understanding of history. He adhered to the position that the condition and the activities of the soul, or psyche, mold all human life. Psychic realities, especially as they are consciously manifested, constitute the substratum for all men's works, activi-

---

[20] "Geschichte der Formen des Nationalbewusstseins," *D.G.*, I, 3–55. See also *D.G.*, Erg. Bd. II, Pt. 2, pp. 204–5, 463; and *K.M.*, p. 44 (*"der Typ des Völkerwerdens muss entwickelt werden"*). A major component of Lamprecht's treatment of German history was his concern with Swiss, Dutch, and Austrian history and the life of Germans in the overseas areas such as the United States and Brazil.

[21] See for example *D.G.*, II, 71, III, 62, V, 11, VI, 3, 6, 28, 98, 163–64, VII, 164, 399, VIII, 250, 355, 591, 669–70, IX, 3, X, 248 (esp.), XI, 705, Erg. Bd. I, 81, 234, 425–27, 455, 461, II, Pt. 1, pp. 11–12, 66–68, and II, Pt. 2, p. 4 (*Geschichte ist Seelenleben in statu nascenti*).

ties, and attitudes.[22] Lamprecht assumed that individual psychic life (hardly knowable to science as yet, in his opinion) closely reflected the psychic life of others with common origin, common basic experiences, common traditions. First, individuals of a cohesive group, such as a *Volk*, find themselves at the same level of psychic development. Second, their individual consciousness depends largely on the general consciousness, or *Geist*, as it has expressed itself concretely in the cultural forms and institutions developed by previous generations of the group. For *Geist* is essentially that aspect of psychic life which has found expression in the world (*das in der Welt ausgewirkte Seelenleben*).[23] The individual psyche (the integration, or *Zusammenhang*, of all psychic experiences, or *Erlebnisse*, of the individual consciousness) is directly related to the social psyche (*Volksseele*, the form of the general spirit, or *Gesamtgeist*, which is the total reality of all psychic events occurring in a specific community through the interaction of all separate psychic energies).[24] The total social *Seelenleben* is, moreover, characterized by certain dominant psychic conditions which give it coherence and unity. The total psychic activity is a harmony of all activities, much as consonant musical tones may constitute a harmony known as "diapason." Lamprecht was enchanted with this word and often alluded to the unified substratum of the social psychic condition as the diapason of a particular phase in the life of a *Volk*.[25]

Lamprecht's conception of a state of culture rested on his

---

[22] Lamprecht "defined" consciousness as follows: "Bewusstsein aber heisst nichts als jeweilig zu klarer Vorstellung gelangte Summe psychischer Potenzen, jeweilige psychische Kapazität eines bestimmten Zeitalters. Mit der jeweiligen Qualität seelischen Bewusstseins ist also die Qualität der Anschauungen . . . gegeben" (*D.G.*, Erg. Bd. I, 426–27).

[23] *D.G.*, Erg. Bd. I, 455.

[24] This summary is almost a verbatim statement of Lamprecht in *D.G.*, X, 248; but see also *Einf.*, pp. 65–72.

[25] For instances see *K.M.*, pp. 3, 26; *D.G.*, VIII, 65, 67, 356, 550, Erg. Bd. II, Pt. 1, p. 286, Erg. Bd. II, Pt. 2, pp. 19, 203.

idea of the *Seelenleben*. At any given time men can express only the particular psychic condition which prevails then. And all their expressions will reflect that particular condition of the soul. A specific *Seelenleben* permits but a specific sense of religiosity, a specific artistic mode of expression, a specific sense of justice, a specific kind of awareness of the external world, a specific sense of language, a specific sense of morality. All external works of men can only express an internal state. Social relations, the political state, the economic institutions, arts and literature, science and philosophy, are no more than external forms of the *Seelenleben*. Culture, which subsumes all external expressions of the soul, is therefore the total manifestation of a *Volksseele*, or social psyche.[26] It consists of a unity of creative and expressive efforts in as much as it results from a people's *Seelenleben* harmonized by a prevailing dominant. All cultural phenomena derive their character and their meaning from a psychic substratum. They are intelligible only as expressions of that substratum. Ultimately science, politics, art, religion, and all such phenomena, are meaningful only when related to the *Seelenleben* which produced them. Consequently only cultural history can provide true historical understanding.[27]

Culture, as Lamprecht used the term, is therefore not a specifically circumscribed part of the life of a *Volk*, not merely the valuable portion of human creation within an otherwise uncultured existence. It is not, as with Voltaire, an "artifice," a world of noble life separated from man's natural existence.[28]

---

[26] *K.M.*, p. 29.

[27] *A.N.*, pp. 12, 54–70; *K.M.*, pp. 11, 38; *Einf.*, pp. 6, 37–38; *D.G.*, VII, 399, VIII, 250, 590, XI, 706.

[28] Indicative, to me, is the relation of both men to the theater. For Voltaire, the theater was a symbol of the creative order of civilization and a major "civilizing" factor. That the theater represented an artifice made it that much more important for Voltaire as a characteristic expression of the act whereby men create a civilization, which also is an artifice. Lamprecht disliked the theatrical type of life (*der Theatertyp*). It was almost a cultural lie for him, since it deviated from the expression natural to a social psyche at a given moment. The theater was of value for him only in so far as it correctly reflected

It is instead the totality of life to which a people gives expression. It is, therefore, not a reality which men can decline or accept, or which they can cultivate with special effort. It is the contingent necessity of an internal condition and activity. Where there is a collective *Seelenleben*, there is a corresponding cultural form.

But Lamprecht did not believe in a static soul or in culture as an unchanging reality.[29] The life of the soul — and Lamprecht was speaking of the *Volksseele*, a collective reality — is growth. All activities of the soul result in its continuous modification. The psychic realities of a *Volk* in its early stages of development are thus different from those in later stages. And the history of a people is the history of the growth of its soul. This growth, however, was seen by Lamprecht as "phased development." The total knowable *Seelenleben* of a *Volk* (i.e., its history) revealed to him continuous growth which was clearly subdivided into stages of growth. Each stage or phase of development (*Kulturzeitalter*) is characterized by the gradual assertion of a "psychic" dominant which gives structure to the life of the soul for a while and then weakens. As this dominant begins to weaken, a dissociative process begins in which those psychic forces, previously held together by a dominant, each grow according to its own inner necessity. These are the moments of apparent chaos and crisis of the *Seelenleben*. Actually it is the moment when a new dominant

---

the peoples' *Seelenleben*. He was much more fascinated by the consciousness of fate (*Schicksalsbewusstsein*) as it appeared in the drama of the German *Volk's* different phases of development; see, for example, *D.G.*, VIII, 45, XI, 211–12.

[29] Lamprecht's commitment to "developmental history" (*Entwicklungsgeschichte*) was so strong that he at times impatiently brushed aside matters which might be of interest for a more adequate description of a *state*, a moment of cultural life. "Only the always new, the progressive addition, is the truly historical [*das im höchsten Grade Geschichtliche*]" (*D.G.*, VIII, 487); or: "But for the historian it will ever be a supreme rule to pay less attention to phenomena of decay if they are not typical events of human development; for only the 'creative forward' [*das schöpferische Vorwärts*] is the soul of man's evolution" (*D.G.*, IX, 148).

(necessitated by the fulfilment of the preceding one) is latently at work to organize a newly constituted unity of psychic activity—which, when it emerges into dominance, lasts for a while, fulfils its function, and then weakens in turn. Each of these phases contributes to a progressive differentiation of the *Seelenleben*. The history of a *Volk* is the history of the gradual enrichment of its psyche, the fulfilment of its psychic capacities, the multiplication of its psychic activities and sensitivities, the differentiation of its consciousness.[30]

The *Seelenleben* was characterized, for Lamprecht, by two basic forms of existence: the "fettered," or "bound" mode, and the free or "unbound" mode. He subdivided the first of these into three phases of development; the second into two.[31] In the fettered *(gebunden)* state of the soul, man is relatively undifferentiated from his environment, from his social context, in his work, and his basic life processes. He has no inner distance from the surrounding reality but feels immersed in it; he has no awareness of himself as a separate individual. During one subphase of this "bound" age, the "symbolic" age, man relates himself to the world around him, and the world inside him, by activities and attitudes which have a predominantly symbolic character. Then, stimulated by an expanding experience, by his own creations, and at times by the impact of outside events, this particular psychic disposi-

---

[30] *K.M.*, p. 28; Eulenburg, p. 331; Schmoller, p. 36. See also *D.G.*, Erg. Bd. I, 455, on Lamprecht's notion of a *historical* sociology.

[31] The "fettered" age of the German *Volk* lasted essentially from the *Urzeit* to about A.D. 1500. It was subdivided by Lamprecht into the following *Kulturzeitalter: Zeitalter des Symbolismus*, which lasted until the times of the great migrations; *Zeitalter des Typismus*, which lasted from the migrations until the early twelfth century; and *Zeitalter des Konventionalismus*, lasting from the twelfth century until about 1500. Then the German *Seelenleben* entered its free stage of development, which Lamprecht subdivided into a *Zeitalter des Individualismus*, which characterized the time from the early sixteenth century until the middle of the eighteenth, and a *Zeitalter des Subjectivismus*, which began around 1750. His own times Lamprecht often called *eine Zeit der Reizsamkeit*, but it is not entirely clear whether this is the beginning of a new phase or a late stage of the "subjectivistic" age.

tion becomes more complex and differentiated. The symbols subdivide into types and man enters the "typical" age. He classifies his experiences into types of experience, types of cognition, types of activities — each of which constitutes a refinement, a differentiation of a symbolic experience, symbolic relation, and so on. In turn, this dominant mode of relating himself to the world, and to himself, by reference to types gives way to a further differentiated mode of *Seelenleben*, the "conventional," which brings with it the "conventional" age. Conventions, in this sense, were for Lamprecht a further refinement, a greater variegation of types. Man has extricated himself a little further from the binding external context; he has gained a more stratified and detailed consciousness of himself, his social relations, and the world around him. The next step of development displaces the conventions by an individualistic mode of *Seelenleben*. And with this "individualistic" age man enters the free, the unfettered, stage of psychic existence. Man now reverses his relation to the internal and external reality. Where he had been held captive through his psychic inability to cope fully with conditions, the individual begins to impose himself on realities, molding them by his visions and works. Since man now experiences himself as an individual and subsequently as a subjective reality, Lamprecht divided the "unbound" state into two phases: the "individualistic" and the "subjectivistic" age. When Lamprecht in his treatment of German history reached his own times, a late phase of the "subjectivistic" age, he described a *Seelenleben* characterized by a striking sensitivity — even irritability (*Reizsamkeit*) — to stimuli from outside and from within subjective beings, a great awareness of details, and a pronounced consciousness of self. What had once been essentially the unvariegated soul of primitive Germanic kinship groups had become a highly differentiated German *Volksseele* with complex external cultural expressions.

On the basis of these psychological theories Lamprecht built an entire historical program. In his opinion, history should be concerned with the largest intelligible entity. Ultimately this might be a universal history of mankind, but, until the process of development was better understood, he preferred to study such an entity as the German *Volk*. In turn, the history of such an entity had to be studied as a whole. This meant, for Lamprecht, a history of all its expressions, that is to say, a history of culture. No other single branch of the historical discipline, such as political, economic, or intellectual history, could accomplish such a task.[32] And Lamprecht held that no such separate, specialized historical investigation as economic or art history could fully and meaningfully comprehend the specific subject matter unless it was brought into relation with the entire cultural context to which it belonged.[33] In addition, cultural history had to be developmental or genetic history. The past must be understood as a necessary, a causally linked process. But the historian must find the right causes; on the one hand, he should not resort to such external or transcendent movers as God's will, the "ideas" of some mysterious world spirit, or, on the other hand, to such secondary forces as economic realities which are but manifestations of

---

[32] *A.N.*, pp. 12, 54–70; *K.M.*, pp. 11, 38; *Einf.*, pp. 37–38; *D.G.*, VII, 399, VIII, 250, 590.

[33] See, for instance, *A.N.*, pp. 7–9; *Einf.*, p. 18; and *D.G.*, VIII, 355, XI, 718. The most illustrative incident is perhaps Lamprecht's attack on Wilhelm Windelband's attempt to derive Spinoza's pantheism from unresolved problems in Descartes's philosophy. He admitted that this approach had a certain validity, but lamented its limitation and its failure to understand Spinoza's thought in terms of his own background and historical setting; the passage is almost untranslatable: "Gewiss kann man den Gottesbegriff Spinozas auch aus Descartes ableiten. . . . Gleichwohl war as schwerlich diese logische Ableitung, der Spinoza seinen Gottesbegriff verdankte, sondern vielmehr das Wesen seiner eigenen Persönlichkeit. In der Geschichte der Philosophie ist es möglich, fast alle aufeinanderfolgenden Systeme aus den Gedankenreihen der jeweils vorhergehenden durch logischen Schluss abzuleiten, aber diese logischen Ableitungen, die in sehr verschiedenen Kombinationen und Permutationen der Endsumme ihrer Schlüsse gedacht werden können, sind nicht immer die historischen, unter denen man ebenfalls wieder die gelegentlich recht zufälligen Beweisableitungen der einzelnen Philosophen und die tieferen historischen Zusammenhänge, die in ihnen als allgemeine Motive wirken, unterscheiden kann" (*D.G.*, VI, 196).

deeper and more fundamental causes.[34] Freed from any metaphysical ties, proceeding merely (as he thought) through careful analysis of his proper subject,[35] the modern scientific historian had to identify the fundamental causes *within* his subject. Immanent realism had to supersede the transcendent idealism which had bedeviled the historical discipline during the nineteenth century.[36] The varied cultural manifestations of a people, as they formed a unity during certain cultural phases *(Kulturzeitalter)*, and as they were transformed into new configurations, had to be seen and understood as the necessary consequence of the psychogenetic process whereby a *Volk* gradually moves toward realization of itself.

Lamprecht elaborated his theories in more than sixty methodological articles. He put his ideas into practice in the form of the nineteen-volume *Deutsche Geschichte*. As a student he had prepared himself for this future task by seeking training in economic and art history as a supplement to his medieval studies. While still a student, he had asked himself, in an interesting paper, whether the Middle Ages could be said to have produced and understood individuality.[37] His

---

[34] *K.M.*, p. 19. Lamprecht thought of Marx as a man with transcendent ideas, scientifically outdated *(schon längst überholt)*, who had, however, correctly foreseen the importance of the *Arbeiterstand*; see *D.G.*, X, 336–38, XI, 65, 300–304, 712, Erg. Bd. II, Pt. 2, pp. 20–21, 139–44, 148–52, and 164–65.

[35] Lamprecht later on always maintained that purely empirical study, not a priori metaphysics, had provided him with his basic insights and basic concepts; see *A.N.*, p. 78; *K.M.*, pp. 13–14, 26–27, 33; Bernheim, p. 761; and Paul Barth, *Die Philosophie der Geschichte*, p. 505.

[36] *A.N.*, pp. 24–48; *K.M.*, pp. 13, 24, 33. Much of the argument was directed against Ranke and his followers; see *A.N.*, pp. 27–30, 71; *K.M.*, pp. 22–25.

[37] "Über Individualität und Verständnis für dieselbe im deutschen Mittelalter," written in the summer of 1878 and reprinted in *D.G.*, XII, 3–48. The importance of Lamprecht's reading of Burckhardt (whom he does not mention in the context) seems self-evident. Later on, Lamprecht placed Burckhardt against Ranke *(als Hauptvertreter des anderen Systems)*; see *K.M.*, pp. 29–32. In his opinion Burckhardt had seen both the importance of cultural ages as such and the need to approach history without metaphysical preconceptions. But he objected that Burckhardt had not developed his insights into a system and had not provided a developmental history of cultural ages in succession.

early publications were focused on economic and artistic aspects of medieval culture.[38] Then he sat down to produce his life work. By 1894, after five volumes of the *Deutsche Geschichte* had appeared in fairly rapid order, Lamprecht interrupted the chronological treatment of German history and prepared three volumes on the development of German culture since 1870.[39] Moreover, he began to answer the critics of the first five volumes and became involved in a polemic which lasted in intensive and tempestuous form until about 1905, but never really subsided until his death in 1915. He became a central figure in a controversial debate, the so-called *Methodenstreit*, which involved, however, many more and much broader issues of the historical discipline — its methods, its relations to other disciplines, its particularities — than those raised by Lamprecht and his immediate critics.[40] Through this involvement in the *Methodenstreit* Lamprecht clarified his conceptions of collective and scientific history, historical causality and laws, the primacy of psychogenetic understanding of development, and his conception of *Kultur* and *Kulturzeitalter*. He became a *cause célèbre*, but the polemic became so acrimonious that he found it difficult to find good academic positions for his students. After a while, hardly any publisher or editor was willing to lend his facilities

Mention of Lamprecht's relation to Burckhardt is also made in Srbik, II, 228; Kuhnert, pp. 23, 35; and Schmoller, p. 36.

[38] *Beiträge zur Geschichte des französischen Wirtschaftslebens im 11. Jahrhundert; Die Initialornamentik des 8.–13. Jahrhunderts*; and *Deutsches Wirtschaftsleben im Mittelalter*, which no less a critic than Gustav Schmoller thought worthy of comparison with the work of Maurer, Nitzsch, and Inama-Sternegg.

[39] The first five volumes appeared between 1891 and 1894; then Lamprecht brought out three huge volumes, *Zur jüngsten deutschen Vergangenheit*, which appeared in 1901–3 and were treated subsequently as Ergänzungsbände I and II of the *Deutsche Geschichte*. Volumes VI–XII appeared between 1904 and 1909, but Lamprecht revised some volumes as late as 1911.

[40] A fair summary of Lamprecht's participation can be found in Popper; Kuhnert; Spiess; Bernheim, esp. pp. 717–18; and the list of Lamprecht's own publications by Koetzschke. A complete history of the *Methodenstreit* still needs to be written.

for the continuation of the bitter pen warfare. Lamprecht meanwhile went for a visit to America to spread his historical program, and after his return to Leipzig founded the Institut für Kultur- and Universalgeschichte. Above all, he took up his *Deutsche Geschichte* where it had been interrupted in 1894 and finally completed it in 1911.

The *Deutsche Geschichte* remains his great work. But today it is rarely read. *Mega biblion, mega kakon* — a big book is a great evil. Nineteen volumes would be too much, even were each of the eight thousand pages brilliant. Nor did Lamprecht, like Toynbee, find a D. C. Somervell to digest his volumes. The work is uneven, the later volumes, where he steered a more clearly charted course, perhaps being the better. Despite his intention, Lamprecht filled large sections with plain historical narrative. Much of this is rephrased material borrowed from the works of others — a fact gleefully pointed out by his opponents. Lamprecht admitted this and justified the borrowing. Even though the accusation that there are as many mistakes as sentences is little more than an unethical attempt to ruin a troublesome fellow professional, still the text abounds in errors.[41] Lamprecht sought to justify himself by the haunting pressure of the task before him. "I must rush ahead, otherwise I shall not succeed in producing this German history from one mold."[42] Obsessed with factual accuracy, and averse to daring speculation, many historians have written him off totally. And yet there is a richness of conception and detail, a profusion of images, a vast erudition, and a wealth of suggestive cross-weaving of cultural phenomena in Lamprecht's huge work. Even though it occasions skepticism, and at times even aversion, it opens views on history closed to the less daring. One looks differently at the past after having read the *Deutsche Geschichte*.

A detailed summary of all these volumes can hardly be our task. Two interrelated aims of his work deserve more detailed

---

[41] Below, "Die neue historische Methode," p. 252; Goetz, p. 303; *A.N.*, p. iii.

[42] Schmoller, p. 38; see also *D.G.*, VII, Pt. 2, "Vorwort," and Erg. Bd. I, ix, xi.

treatment in the present context: the use of a key concept (1) for gaining insight into the intricate structure of a cultural period, and (2) for analyzing the causal connection between two successive cultural epochs. The best illustration of his "principles-in-action" can perhaps be given by providing a brief characterization of Lamprecht's view of a specific *Kulturzeitalter* and a brief investigation of the dynamic factors whereby such an age is linked to another.

In but four of the nineteen volumes Lamprecht worked out his conception of the *gebundene Zeitalter*, the early and "middle" ages when the German psyche was "fettered or bound" in its form of life.[43] The expert medievalist therefore allotted a disproportionately small part to the treatment of the first three cultural epochs. Perhaps this imbalance was dictated by a lack of appropriate sources; it also resulted from the fact that Lamprecht progressively discovered more interrelations among cultural data. He subdivided the "bound" stage of German development into three ages: the "symbolic," to about A.D. 800, the "typic," from about 800 to 1150, and the "conventional," ending in the fifteenth and sixteenth centuries. In his treatment of this last period Lamprecht provided the fullest characterization of a cultural age during the "bound" stage of development. So I shall single out this age for special consideration. How does it relate to the preceding "symbolic" and "typic" ones, and what is its characteristic structure?

German culture before the fundamental transformation of the late fifteenth century is marked by a *Seelenleben* in which men's actions and reactions are kept within a tightly guarded range by internal limitations and external collective ties. Men are not sufficiently differentiated as yet to relate themselves in an autonomous manner to others and to the surrounding world. They reveal no mental and emotional distance from the situation in which they find themselves. In

---

[43] *D.G.*, Vol. I–IV; but parts of the later volumes return to medieval subjects at times.

these less differentiated phases men relate themselves to the worlds of their inner and outer experience first by "symbols," then by use of "types," and ultimately by "conventions." During the earliest stages, experience, as immediately given, is neither ordered by reflection nor interpreted by conscious intellectual action. Life is more action than meditation.[44] Abstraction plays a subordinate and only gradually noticeable role, while the direct, the unconceptualized grasping of reality (*Anschauung*) is the predominant form of cognition.[45] The sense of space derives from the measurements of the body and physical activities, for men measure by feet, ells, and the day's labor. Their sense of time is established only by the change of the seasons and the sequence of generations. Historical consciousness grows slowly and expresses itself first in myth and hero songs; yesterday's events may seem eons removed and the events of a hoary past appear like the happenings of yesterday.[46] The inability to comprehend large numbers aptly characterizes a state of mind that tends to rest with the immediate impressions and feels uncomfortable with reflective abstraction.[47] But the experiences of their eyes, ears, and other senses lead to secondary, derived experiences which take the form of "symbols," "types," and "conventions."[48]

In their early phases of the "fettered" *Seelenleben* the Germans lived immersed in nature, and their gods were natural forces conceived in human shape. The early Germans were essentially unprepared to accept Christianity in the form given to it by the patristic age.[49] They adopted from this alien world only what corresponded with the state of their *Seelenleben*: a rich cult of saints which fitted their polytheistic and pandemoniac outlook; a Christ seen as a *Heliand* hero, a fighter for God; the warrior's fascination with the efficacy of

---

[44] *D.G.*, I, 203, 373.
[45] *D.G.*, I, 7, 361–62, II, 188.
[46] *D.G.*, III, 6.
[47] *D.G.*, II, 189, IV, 255, VI, 93.
[48] *D.G.*, I, 202, 361, II, 199.
[49] *D.G.*, I, 225, 374–94.

asceticism as a preparation for the saint's battle; a eudaemonistic conception of a sensual heaven and hell; and all the visual and audible ritual to which the "symbolic" and "typic" existence is attuned.[50] But a moral attitude, imposing on man a conscious choice of good and evil, is as yet impossible.[51] A rational understanding of doctrine is rare. The imaginative processes (*Phantasietätigkeiten*) are given external expression through a strictly limited stock of repetitive patterns of art. Alliteration, the same limited number of images, rhymes, and themes appear in the literary forms, among which the adage (*Sinnspruch*), the anecdote, the fairy tale, and the heroic epic prevail.[52] The graphic genius of the nation expresses itself most readily in the form of ornament. The dynamic geometric patterns, often intricately intertwined, dominate in the "symbolic age" and betray the Germanic predisposition for action in motion. It merges in the "typic" age with plant and animal ornaments. Yet, this more elaborate effort to represent a richer experience of the outside world is expressed only in "types." The leaf is more discernible as a generalized leaf than a specific oak, birch, or chestnut leaf. The animals appear more readily as quadrupeds and birds, than clearly as horse, rabbit, or dog, swan, nightingale, or eagle. By the end of the "typic" age, the entire experience of nature is too undifferentiated for a naturalistic rendition.[53]

During the "symbolic" and "typic" epochs the same "fettered" *Seelenleben* is mirrored in the social and economic conditions. Society held every single man and woman firmly. As congenerous members of their sibs (*Geschlechter*) all are absorbed in a collectively bound existence. Even the breakup of the sibs into smaller family groups, which occurred in the "typic" age, does not yet set the individual free.[54] Lamprecht

---

[50] *D.G.*, I, 218–25, 374–80, 388–94, II, 199–214, 303.
[51] *D.G.*, I, 213, II, 183, 186.
[52] *D.G.*, I, 203–7, 370–71; II, 195–98.
[53] *D.G.*, I, 14, 25–26, 209, 362–66, II, 46, 77–80, 192–95; and *Einf.*, pp. 76–86.
[54] *D.G.*, I, 108, 113, 190, 194, 348, II, 179–81. One aspect of the lack of individuality is the inability to understand foreigners; see *D.G.*, II, 190, III, 218.

even spoke of a homogeneity of appearance which accompanied this psychic and social congruity.[55] In the early phases, the German evinced his absorption in the basic blood groups through his behavior and morality. The institution of the blood feud was possible only where the actual killer was not aware of a personal responsibility. The oath retained its collective character even longer and public law concepts developed very slowly.[56] Where man has no sense of an existence separate from that of large and powerful "natural" groups, the public force, the state — as different from society — can only slowly gain a foothold. Only gradually do kinship and family relations give way to the new realities of the *Völkerschaftsstaat,* the *Stämmestaat,* and eventually the territorially based state. Only as the hero can a human being break the moral ties *(gebundene Sittlichkeit)* and transcend the mass. Only in such exceptional men, Lamprecht thought, could the personal will break through to a life unchecked by communal norms and void of any sense of moderation; for, outside the bounds of socially imposed morality, the barbarian soul throws off all standards of action other than its own arbitrary and capricious will.[57] In economic relations this leads to theft and conquest — brief and spasmodic escapes from the collective economic pattern — but the undifferentiated psyche permits only vague notions of personal property; it does not allow for any individualistic form of enterprise and has room only for a rudimentary division of labor. Collective needs are satisfied, without rational planning, by immediate work according to traditional patterns. Even when personal holdings become more widespread in the later "typic" age, the needs and traditions of the village communities restrict the freedom of personal action.[58]

---

[55] *D.G.,* I, 200.

[56] *D.G.,* I, 179, 187, 193, 338.

[57] In this form, a late insight; see *Einf.,* p. 10. In *D.G.,* II, 187–88, however, Lamprecht came close to expressing the same idea.

[58] *D.G.,* II, 179, Erg. Bd. II, Pt. 2, pp. 18–19. In the later volumes Lamprecht considers the relation between *Wirtschaftsbedürfnis* and *Wirtschaftsbefriedi-*

The "conventional" cultural epoch was for Lamprecht the last stage in which the German people existed in its "bound" state. It is therefore the most differentiated stage of the "bound" soul, the age which prepares the emergence of the individual from the collective context.[59] Neither its beginning nor its end is demarcated by sharp chronological breaks, but during the thirteenth and fourteenth centuries the "conventional" *Seelenleben* existed in its purest form.

The concept of this age implies that the Germans now are experiencing their inner and outer life in the form of "conventions." The meaning of this term, as of all five names which Lamprecht gave to his *Kulturzeitalter*, is nowhere defined by him but emerges from his description of the five forms of culture. The "conventional" German is not yet prepared to experience his existence as an individual.[60] He is not yet differentiated enough to approach reality independently but remains tied to the ready formulas of the collective. Yet, the "conventional" is a refinement of the "typic." The once unvariegated community is now subdivided into groups with experiences somewhat different from those of others. The "conventional" German is aware of more detail and he classes his experiences in more varied categories. The "conventional" age reflects this more diversified experience in its arts, language, religion, morality, economy, and social life.

It is obvious from an analysis of the two volumes in which Lamprecht described this "conventional" epoch that the designation "conventional" suggested itself to him through the study of morality and manners. In the lives of the knights

---

gung the most fundamental issue of economic history; see *D.G.*, Erg. Bd. II, Pt. 1, pp. 16, 47, 35–36, 50, 58–59, 65.

[59] *D.G.*, III, 13, 25, 27, 57, 74, IV, 243–46.

[60] *D.G.*, III, 27, 216, 239–40, IV, 260, 351. It may be worth noting that Burckhardt used the term "conventional" also in connection with medieval art: "Allein diese Perlen liegen zerstreut in einem Meere des Konventionellen und Künstlichen. . . . Inhalt und Gedankengang sogar ist der konventionell höfische" (*Die Kultur der Renaissance in Italien* [Vienna: Phaidon Verlag, n.d.], p. 174).

and the burghers, the two pillars of "conventional" society, he finds a formalized behavior which correctly reveals their inner condition: still "bound" and yet more free. It is of more than passing interest that the first of these groups includes those "heroes" who in the earlier, the still barbarian, society had been most likely to break through the ties of kinship and tribe. Now, in a more refined age, the knight is the hero whose will has been bound through a code, half imposed on or, better, drilled into him and half agreed to. This motivation of his action, half-free, half-bound, correctly reflects the middle position of the "conventional" age between a stage in which morality and manners are entirely imposed by the collective existence and the subsequent stage when the individual discovers for himself the principle that determines his moral actions. With the burghers the situation is slightly different, according to Lamprecht. As a "newborn" layer of society, the townspeople are, on the one hand, still strongly dependent upon the cohesive power of their communities; and, on the other hand, they are so much differentiated by their professional activities that they require a code of behavior which leaves each member more freedom of action. Like the knights (*Rittertum*),[61] the burghers live by a code of externally imposed rules of conduct which, more than before, are upheld by a conscious inner acceptance.

The moral life of the "conventional" German is marked by a greater tension between personal will and social obligation than was true in the "typic" or "symbolic" age. The characteristic feature of the "conventional" code is, therefore, the stress on self-restraint and the careful observation of detailed rules of decorum (*das Masshalten als Kern des Sittlich-Schicklichen*).[62] Morality thus coincides with good manners. Etiquette rules behavior. The true sin is an offense against decorum, punishable by derision and shameful exposure.

---

[61] *D.G.*, IV, 249, 252, 298.
[62] *D.G.*, III, 201, 215.

Education becomes good breeding; a man is judged by his mastery of the forms of conduct. Personal excellence is attained by a sense for good forms, by the active life that moves within carefully circumscribed rules, by skilful execution of pleasing and noble deeds. It was a way of life which put more stock in propriety, skill, and a sense for aesthetically pleasing conduct than in knowledge.[63] It contained what Lamprecht called an idealistic strain, since it posited a normative model of behavior.[64] In its secular aspect it was marked by the codes of chivalry as well as the rules and conventions which bound townsmen along corporate lines.[65] In the religious field this morality demanded, on the one hand, observation of a highly formulated ritual; on the other hand, it consisted in the imitation of idealized figures who devoted their life to altruistic service. Parsifal and Saint Francis seemed to Lamprecht comparable expressions of the age.[66]

As the Germans lived with such codes of decorum, these became ever more refined until they deteriorated into the minutiae of petrifying ceremonial. The harmony of morality and manners (which the German word *Sitte* so satisfactorily connotes) broke down and there developed that tension between more observation of rules of external action and the gradual appearance of a new, deeply felt, moral commitment which subsequently led to the Protestant revolt. Fashionable fads, the remnants of ever more speedily disintegrating conventions, characterized the last, the dissociative, phase of the age.[67]

Lamprecht found analogous phenomena in the imaginative processes and the intellectual life of these "conventional"

---

[63] *D.G.*, II, 204.

[64] Lamprecht was concerned with idealism as a factor in the development of other cultural ages as well; see *D.G.*, II, 367, V, 127, VIII, 381–82, 488, Erg. Bd. I, 84, 274, 317, 353, 410, Erg. Bd. II, Pt. 2, pp. 37, 406.

[65] *D.G.*, IV, 249–52.

[66] *D.G.*, IV, 247, 268; also *Einf.*, p. 98.

[67] *D.G.*, III, 209.

Germans. The simpler forms of cognition, by which earlier Germans had classed their experiences in the form of types, were both inadequate for and disproportionate to the subtler manner by which the "conventional" age ordered its enriched experience. Even now the power for abstraction was still largely undeveloped. Only in theology, where deductions could be drawn with relative ease from given verities, did it have a function. In most other mental processes, thought and actual sense experience were still insufficiently distinguished.[68] Few men even among administrators, and especially merchants, had a sense for figures, or something one could call a "statistical sense."[69] The typical mode of reasoning was still by analogy (der Analogieschluss). Generalizations were not yet reached through abstractions from many single cases. Instead a single case, which had the appearance of more general features, was elevated to the status of truth. "It is evident that this is the treatment of the poet; here poetry becomes the form of thought."[70] As in the two earlier ages, belief in miracles was still the product of analogous reasoning based on too few observations, and faith in authority was an act of submission to thought inherited from another, a more developed, civilization.[71] Such were the complementary forms of thought of the "conventional" German. Though not originally German in formulation, the allegory of the sun and the moon, as the expression of the papal-imperial relation, is one example of the need felt by these people for graphic ideas and the simplification of difficult notions through the use of similes.

Thus the aesthetic attitude toward life, which Lamprecht noted in the adherence to formal conventions of social intercourse, found its complement in the German mental world. It was a visually conceived world. The observed external forms were translated into a code of images. A language, rich in com-

---

[68] D.G., III, 213, IV, 257, VI, 80–84.
[69] D.G., IV, 255.
[70] D.G., III, 213.
[71] D.G., VI, 81–84.

mon images, formed the medium of thought. The poets' formulas were accepted as reality.[72]

> Everyone believed in the existence of the Knights of the Round Table, in the historicity of Aeneas' adventures and the possibilities of Ovid's metamorphoses; any skepticism would have been viewed as a social offense. . . . Men were still far removed from entrusting their hand to the guidance of science; art claimed all attention. It dominated the world of thought and the external existence; it gave poetic form to knowledge and turned poetry into truth, and it transformed the everyday life into "Courtoisie," into "hövescheit," into aesthetically cultivated existence.[73]

Through its content, art formulated and reinforced manners and morality. The poet rarely emerges as an idiosyncratic individual outside the social context.[74] His themes and images express variations of the common life. Thus the use of a fairly fixed stock of themes and images preserves the meaningful conventions. No literary product breaks through the conventional style. Not until a later age do the variations and adumbrations of the same theme become so stylized and complicated that the epic forms die of petrification. The characteristic concern for measured restraint (*das Masshalten*) appears in the poets' denunciation of violent emotions and crude behavior. The emphasis in the poetry is on the external features of stylized behavior which are described by the poet as an onlooker. The drama, which thrives on reflective insights into human motivation and makes the actors themselves express their moods and thoughts, did not suit his age. Lamprecht finds the greatness of this literary epoch in its gift for plastic description, free from reflection on nature and soul, but excelling in vivid simplicity. He was struck later by a comparison of this early simplicity with the verbal "mood-

---

[72] *D.G.*, III, 213, 216, IV, 271.

[73] *D.G.*, III, 214.

[74] *D.G.*, III, 216, 239–40; only Wolfram von Eschenbach is a distinct personality; see *D.G.*, III, 247.

painting" of the "subjectivist" poet Klopstock, who presented
Satan steeped in thought:

Wie auf hohen unwirtlichen Bergen, drohende Wetter
Langsam und verweilend sich lagern: so sass er und dachte.

To which Lamprecht added:

Who will not recollect in contrast the plastic art of Walter
von der Vogelweide, as he draws himself pensively:

Ich sass uf eime Steine
Und dachte Bein mit Beine
Daruf fast ich den Ellenbogen
Ich hat in mine Hand gesmogen
Das Kinn und ein min Wange.[75]

Painting and sculpture, Lamprecht's favored cultural ba-
rometers,[76] reflect that psychic disposition which still is bound
to conventional forms of cognition but already tends toward
a more individual form of perception. (Architecture can never
mirror the state of the soul as immediately because it is more
dependent upon structural and material conditions.) In the
representational art of the "conventional" age Lamprecht
detects the first major attempt of the Germans to portray an
idealized human figure. He attributed human figures in
earlier German art to relatively crude copying of classical
models.[77] In the sense that German artists made "autonomous" efforts to reproduce a Germanic artistic conception of
the human figure, the "conventional" age had developed beyond the prevailing plant and animal art of the "symbolic"
and "typic" ages. Just as the literary arts gradually resorted to
a description of man's appearance and behavior, so the fine
arts began to be seriously concerned with man's outward
semblance. In the evolution of an ever greater consciousness
which constitutes German history, the "conventional" age

---

[75] D.G., VIII, 428.
[76] ". . . die besten Gradmesser" (ibid., VIII, 13, 591, X, 86, 318).
[77] Einf., p. 86.

presents that stage when men have a vague foreboding of their individuality, when they slowly distinguish themselves in and from their natural and social context.[78] Their imaginative processes hesitatingly produce a form of the outward man. The naked human being appears rarely in the early stages of this age; the only inescapable exceptions are Adam and Eve. The anatomical sense is poorly developed, and emphasis on nudity runs counter to the strict conventions of this age.

The stylization of life is mirrored in the human figures drawn and sculptured by these artists: neglect of anatomy goes hand in hand with careful rendering of all external appurtenances. Decorously flowing dress, with skilfully produced folds and pleats, and meticulously presented status symbols, covers a body whose limbs can neither move nor support a man's weight. The etiquette of the gown parallels the decorum of life. The refined manners reveal themselves in a refined appearance, devoid of offensive crudities. Facial features tend to be smooth and even, often with the delicate charm and inexplicable smile of "archaic art."[79] More labor is bestowed on flowing hair and beards than on facial expression. Where there are efforts to portray specific persons, the distinguishing quality lies in the outward symbol of a king, an archangel, a knight, or a specific apostle.[80] Thus, the attempt at portraiture is fitting to this age of awakening individualism, but the art of the painter and sculptor still relies essentially on external means for expressing the peculiarity of a person of whom the artist is already dimly aware.[81]

A constantly increasing interest in the observation and imitation of nature also points to the "middle position" of the age. The highly typified plant and animal forms of earlier

---

[78] D.G., IV, 276–93.
[79] D.G., III, 219, 255.
[80] D.G., IV, 257–58.
[81] "Im allgemeinen bleiben die Bildnisse wie die geschichtlichen Charakteristiken und Selbstbiographien in der Wiedergabe des Berufmässigen, des nicht eigenartig Persönlichen stecken" (D.G., IV, 258).

German art become increasingly varied and more naturalistic. One now recognizes specific plants; capitals and bases of columns, for instance, are decked with flowers and leaves whose models can be distinguished in forest and garden. The animals clearly now become dogs, horses, doves, and so on. Whereas the earlier artists used color primarily for decorative value, now the artist's palette can render the natural colors of the external objects.[82] The same will to observe and to follow nature leads to a decreasing use of heavy contours and to the more successful attempt to place figures and inanimate objects into proper space relation to each other and to a more realistically conceived background. To be sure, this art remains standardized. Bushes, trees, rocks, and mountains still do not show true and full individuality, nor do the human beings, castles, and towns.[83] It remained for artists of the next age to portray *this* individual man, *this* specific landscape, *this* particular rabbit or meadow (Dürer), or to capture *one* moment in its characteristic mood. "Man is not yet in control of nature, either materially or spiritually [*geistig*]; generations had to pass before he faced his surroundings as a totality, ages before he masters it through 'thinking, imagining, and creating' [*denkend, dichtend, und bildend*]."[84]

It is a necessary consequence of Lamprecht's theory that he finds the truest mirror of man's inner condition, of the state of his "soul," in his more or less unreflected, direct reactions to experience. The products of man's imagination (*Phantasietätigkeiten*), his sense of piety (*Frömmigkeitssinn*), his sense of justice (*Rechtssinn*), reveal his internal life with a minimum of distortion.[85] Social, economic, and political relations — and occasionally religious life as well — may present much less revealing expressions of the cultural diapason. For

---

[82] *Einf.*, pp. 86–95.

[83] *D.G.*, III, 222.

[84] *D.G.*, III, 222; for a parallel development in music, see *D.G.*, VI, 206 ff.

[85] *D.G.*, I, 202, VI, 3, 28, 98, VIII, 591, 669, X, 188–91, Erg. Bd. I, 3, 338, Erg. Bd. II, Pt. 2, pp. 87, 407; and Eulenburg, p. 326.

here man can express himself only in the framework of institutions which have their own life, and whose slowly changing forms may no longer be the best vehicle for the expression of men's inner mood. Thus the more fixed sectors of society cause a cultural lag or drag. Lamprecht sees and states this, but he cannot always hide a certain embarrassment when he tries to explain the economic or social structure of an age in the terms he has chosen for characterizing the general mood of the age. For instance, what is "symbolic" about a natural economy with a communistic mode of production? Why should a feudal landholding system be characterized as "typic," or a guild as "conventional"? But since these terms are not derived from the economic or social aspects of life, it is unfair to expect a close correspondence between them and the traditional nomenclature of social and economic history. At all times, however, Lamprecht, conscious of this problem,[86] sought to show how particular structures of economic, social, and political life were adequate, fitting, and necessary expressions of the prevailing *Seelenleben*. Here more than in other sections, his analysis becomes burdened with those lengthy stretches of narrative which make his work appear loosely structured. In his later volumes he had learned to handle this problem with greater adroitness.

Both the social and economic aspects of the "conventional" age are rather complex. Here, as in the last phase of the "bound" stage, the differentiation within this system reaches its peak. The older German had been submerged in a relatively unstratified society; the "conventional" man still remains an integral part of one or more collective units which, however, are vastly different from one another. This more stratified society resulted, on the one side, from the enormous territorial expansion of the German people in its colonization beyond its eastern frontiers, and, on the other side, from the differentiating activities of a town-centered money economy

---

[86] *Einf.*, pp. 103–5.

with the concomitant increase in trade and productivity, and the division of labor. The nearly homogeneous experience to which each man was exposed in the older society was now replaced by a composite of widely variegated group experiences. The contrast between landowners and tenants, that most far-reaching socioeconomic differentiation of the "typic" age which had split the kinship society, lasts throughout the "conventional" age.[87] But some of the large landholdings (*Grossgrundbesitz*) now take on the character of centrally controlled baronies, often comprised of contiguous holdings, which soon will become the nuclei of territorial states. This territorial consolidation diminishes the chances of many members of the old nobility to have an estate of their own; consequently the class of knights, who had been the chief representatives of a higher form of life, is absorbed into the administrative apparatus of the magnates who eventually emerge as territorial princes. The *Markgenossenschaft*, the association of all landholders of a region, in which peasant and lord met on an equal footing, loses much of its autonomy by a changed relation to the landlord and yet retains many collectivist features governing village relations. The peasantry, as a matter of fact, does not keep pace with the general development of the "nation" and is fully reabsorbed only during the much later "subjectivistic" age.[88] This cultural lag worried Lamprecht, since there were obvious difficulties for his thesis when a large social group could stand outside the collective psychic diapason.

The spread of separate professions was, for Lamprecht, the main driving force behind the diversification of Germany's social structure during the "conventional" age.[89] The side-by-side existence of the magnate, the peasant, the knight, the cleric, the merchant, the artisan, the lawyer, and the administrator created social subdivisions in the once unstratified peo-

---

[87] *D.G.*, III, 52–83, 100–106, 181–88, 363–71.
[88] *D.G.*, III, 180, IV, 176, V, 90, IX, 4, 221, 281.
[89] *D.G.*, III, 5, 87–88, 91, IV, 203–4, 247.

ple. It seemed to Lamprecht that it was the special function of the "conventional" age — in its middle position between a *Seelenleben* marked by a tightly cohesive collective experience and a *Seelenleben* marked by the emergence of the individual — that it should prepare the transition from the tight collective to the individual. Viewed from the totality of German history, the formation of these professions (*Berufsbildung*) is a vital step in the psychogenetic process that finally leads to the emergence of a differentiated individual. Yet while the all-absorbing collective of the "typic" age is broken up, the human being within each group during the "conventional" age still receives the support of a collective way of life.

None of the new social groups can so dominate the life of the nation that it could form the sovereign center of national existence.[90] For a while it had appeared as if the *Rittertum*, the class of knights, could assume such a position; but its chances were over at the end of this period and it was reduced to an administrative class of the magnates.[91] At one point it had appeared as if the *Bürgertum*, the burgher class, might make Germany a republic of cities; but it also missed its hour, and, as Lamprecht says, it became obvious that the nation's political future was meant to be monarchical (princely).[92] For centuries this did not mean, however, that one prince would become the effective ruler of the whole nation. Just as the burgher and the nation were not yet prepared for the higher burgher culture of the "subjectivist" age, so the nation was not yet prepared for centralized power.[93] The empire had never been the most characteristic German political institution. Its real center was Italy. The Interregnum following the Hohenstaufen collapse was therefore, in Lamprecht's opinion, not a catastrophic end of a strong German state. Even a strong kingship over German lands only, no longer aspiring to rule

---

[90] *D.G.*, IV, 175.
[91] *D.G.*, III, 288.
[92] *D.G.*, IV, 471.
[93] *D.G.*, III, 106, 119, IV, 171.

over Italy, was now impossible. The stronger princes, electors, archbishops, towns, and town-leagues became fairly independent powers, united only by a loose electoral system of empire. Certain dynasties, with a large *Hausmacht* of their own, like the Hapsburgs and Luxemburgers, could occasionally assert more power. But in general "the nation stood no longer behind the king but behind the Estates [*Stände*] of the realm."[94] This was fitting for a people too differentiated for a homogeneous nation-state, yet not sufficiently differentiated to permit a centralized empire at the same time that it still needed the smaller groups for the full development of its characteristic *Seelenleben*.[95] The social "interregnum," when no group could dominate, was therefore the natural companion of the political situation in which no single power could maintain effective centralized rule for any length of time.

Yet Lamprecht concentrated his discussion upon the one group which set the tone during most years of the "conventional" age. The way of life, initially formulated by the knights, is ultimately sustained by the burgher. On the whole the upper stratum of the young bourgeoisie blended in with the "aristocratic" tenor of "conventional" life.[96] When it separates off from the lower burgher groups, it partakes in its own fashion of the aesthetic life of conventions and etiquette. It shares the ideal of service.[97] Although its existence is preoccupied with *negotium*, its economic activities provide the surplus for the culturally necessary *otium*. The serious division between "cultured and uncultured" (*gebildet und ungebildet*), now beginning to cut across German society, finds at

---

[94] *D.G.*, IV, 116.

[95] *D.G.*, IV, 3–10, 32–48, 63–64, 114–21, 304–47. Lamprecht, in general, held to the opinion that the state is dependent upon the development of society; e.g., *D.G.*, IX, 3, 7, 300, 305. The nation-state was only possible in his opinion during the "subjectivistic" age.

[96] ". . . sie haben nach Ritters Art gelebt" (*D.G.*, III, 180); see also *D.G.*, III, 12–13.

[97] *D.G.*, IV, 247.

least a considerable sector of the bourgeois actively on the side of an educated and refined (*feinsinnig*) life.[98]

The guild, as a social form typical of the burgher class in general, entailed for Lamprecht the same binding quality of a collective existence which had been characteristic of the *Markgenossenschaft* and the tightly interdependent village community.[99] He was convinced that every new form of economic life needs a "collective" organization in order to maintain itself at first.[100] Thus capitalism begins as *Gemeinwirtschaft*, communal economy; the community regulates its economic life so that advantages of the new system accrue to all members.[101] Capital is primarily still viewed as a "work fund" (*Arbeitskapital*), and the more or less equal guarantee of access to this new productive agency is one of the guild's functions.[102] As the constitutive cell of the larger corporate guild, the burgher family mirrors these collective ties. In the sense that the family has "rescued" its members from the larger and more oppressive kinship group (*Geschlecht*), it represents economic emancipation.[103] But during the "conventional" age it holds the person tightly within the family collective. It forms a strictly unified social body, geared to common production and consumption.[104] Property is family property, and capital belongs to the generations. Embedded in such cells, where only he is lord who has a smoking chim-

---

[98] *D.G.*, III, 180; ". . . eine geistig belebte Gesellschaft, eine Aristokratie der aesthetischen Bildung . . ." (*D.G.*, III, 12).

[99] *D.G.*, III, 27.

[100] *D.G.*, III, 25, IV, 178, V, 116, 136, XI, 352; *Einf.*, p. 118.

[101] *D.G.*, III, 25, IV, 178, IV, 192–201.

[102] ". . . sozialistisch gefärbte Produktivgenossenschaft . . . genossenschaftlich im Sinne rationeller Ausgleichung der ungleichen individuellen Produktionsaussichten" (*D.G.*, III, 25–26). For Lamprecht's conviction that *genossenschaftliche Formen* of economic and social life are peculiarly German, see *D.G.*, IV, 247, Erg. Bd. II, Pt. 1, pp. 471, 474, 482, 519, Erg. Bd. II, Pt. 2, pp. 459, 611.

[103] *D.G.*, IV, 244.

[104] ". . . in sich geschlossene Produktions- und Konsumtionskörper" (*D.G.*, IV, 245–46), while the modern family is only a "Konsumtionskörper."

ney, and absorbed by the corporate town life, the burgher rarely thinks of himself as an interesting personal microcosm.[105] And yet, he finds within this "bound" existence the conditions for a further differentiation of his psyche which produces the individualistic man of the next cultural age of German development.

Historical change has, for Lamprecht, its true origin in a changing condition of man himself, in the structure and the desires of his soul. An inner necessity of growth and evolution drives a people out of one cultural phase into the next. Each cultural age is essentially the inescapable sequel to the age that went before it. The state of transition is characterized by two phenomena which are only two aspects of one process. A new dominant announces itself — sporadically and vaguely at the beginning — as soon as the ruling dominant has succeeded in harmonizing the total existence of the nation and giving to all the apposite forms of life the opportunity for full deployment. In other words, when one particular process of psychic differentiation has worked itself out in full, the next necessary step in the nation's development calls for a new dominant to give force and direction to further differentiation. On the other side, men simultaneously experience the existing dominant as a series of progressively disharmonious tones. Thus a process of dissociation set in, in which new forms of life, out of tune with the ruling harmony, force themselves into independent existence.[106] Institutions, manners, and mental attitudes, once appropriate expressions of a psychic condition, now are felt to hold back and stifle those emerging forces that are striving toward their realization. During this dissociative phase of a dominant, external factors may play a large role. It is as if the "ear of the soul" became receptive now to various suggestions. This formed for Lam-

---

[105] D.G., IV, 260.
[106] D.G., X, 15, XI, 311–18, Erg. Bd. II, Pt. 1, pp. 11–12.

precht the problem of the exogenous and the endogenous "renaissance."[107] The stimuli (*Reizungen*) may come either from a different culture or from within, that is, from a people's recollections of earlier stages in the pilgrimage of its own soul.[108] Lamprecht saw an exogenous renaissance in the influences which reached the Germans at various moments from Rome and Greece; but also relevant to him were the stimuli exerted by knowledge of other national cultures such as the more advanced cultural life of France and England during the seventeenth and eighteenth centuries, or even the *chinoiserie* of the Enlightenment.[109] He spoke of an endogenous renaissance in connection with the transition from the "individualistic" to the "subjectivistic" age when the German psyche revived outlooks, values, and attitudes from the "bound" stage which had been muted during the "individualistic" phase.[110] Neither in an endogenous nor in an exogenous renaissance can the pristine forms of the stimuli be absorbed without a strong measure of transmutation demanded by the psychic needs of the moment. A renaissance, therefore, always is only a means toward an end determined by the state of the national psyche. The immanent psychogenetic cause is, in every age of transition, the really vital one.[111]

There remains one additional complication of the dynamic process. Although a psychic dominant pervades the life of the entire social body, the transition from one age to the other is not necessarily worked out by the people as a whole, with equal participation of all its strata. As the Germans move from the "symbolic" to the "typic" age, for instance, the transi-

---

[107] *Einf.*, pp. 139–64; see also *A.N.*, p. 79.

[108] The general phases are indicated in "Geschichte der Formen des Nationalbewusstseins," *D.G.*, I, 8, 11, 15, 31, 38, 41, 43.

[109] *D.G.*, II, 30, 80–82, 230 (discussion of the Carolingian Renaissance, which was not "eigenmächtig"), III, 189, IV, 3, V, 174–75, 200–14, 317–21, VI, 348, VII, 140, 336–39, VIII, 488–94, IX, 46, X, 343–47, 445; *Einf.*, pp. 145, 160–63.

[110] *D.G.*, VI, 332–35, VII, 3–30, 226. The "Ottonian Renaissance" also was "eigenmächtig" (*D.G.*, II, 65, 83).

[111] *Einf.*, p. 46.

tion is uniformly experienced by all, since their homogeneity permits no separate differentiation. In reverse, the cultural age which Lamprecht foresees beyond the "subjectivist" one will be the result of a similar common change, since it occurs in a society entirely composed of "subjective units." So, in two very different situations, the process can take a phenomenologically identical form. A people as a whole undergoes a change which touches all its members and leads them toward the beginning of individuation; and a people fully individuated (where each member experiences life in a subjective manner) can move forward, simultaneously toward its integration into a higher, but all-comprehensive social configuration. But in some phases of the evolution, for instance in the transition toward the "conventional" age, the differentiation creates new social subdivisions within the society[112] and the speed of cultural change may differ widely in each of these social groups; a culture lag will be the consequence.[113] During the dissolution of the "conventional" age, for instance, the German peasantry loses contact with the most significant changes in the cultural life and is only fully reintegrated during the "subjectivist" period. Lamprecht does not imply with this example that a large sector of society can stay back completely at an earlier stage of cultural development (while others march into the next) and then, jumping over, so to speak, one entire epoch of cultural development, join the rest of the nation at a later level. The peasantry does partake of one fundamental psychic change characteristic of the "individualistic" age: its new religious orientation (*Frömmigkeitssinn*).[114] But whereas some groups achieve a new life-orientation almost completely harmonized through a new psychic dominant, other sectors of society lag behind, slowed down by persistent influences from the previous age which

---

[112] *D.G.*, III, 90.
[113] For discussion of lag, see *D.G.*, I, 174, III, 180, IV, 176, V, 90, 555, VI, 62, 319, 396, VII, 695–700, 795, VIII, 219, IX, 4, 221, 281, XI, 18, 112, 142, 369, 670.
[114] *D.G.*, V, 10.

prevent their total adaptation to the new life. In the total German development, this phenomenon of "lag" is but temporary, since it occurs on a large scale only during the "middle" period.

The cultural age succeeding the "conventional" had to untie the German personality from its social bindings. The previous ages had prepared the way for this "solvent process" by loosening the hold of the most binding and uniform social structures. The "conventional" period contributed a stratification into smaller groups and thereby considerably diminished the direct impact of the society as a whole on each of its members. The smaller "professional" groups permitted gradually a much freer development of each person's potential, and consequently the conventions which at first confined the members of these smaller social cells were disrupted by a trend toward individuation. Two layers of society, in particular, furthered this development: the burghers and the "princes." Both had interests which, after an initial collectivist stage, drove them toward an individualistic form of life. The daily economic activities of the maturing burgher class reinforced the tendencies of a new age toward the molding of an individualistic human type.[115] Of special importance, according to Lamprecht, were such matters as the rationalization inherent in capitalistic enterprise, the particularism of city life, the changing relation to nature through more extensive travel, and the greater contact with the sea. In the political realm the ancient states made up of different ethnic grouping (*Völkerschaftsstaat* and *Stämmestaat*) had been decomposed through the emergence of large landholdings. In the absence of a genuine central power these had been consolidated under princes, a process bound to culminate in a host of more or less absolutist principalities during the "individualistic" age. This territorial segmentation, eventually to be re-fused in a nineteenth-century Germany, constituted a

---

[115] *D.G.*, VI, 26, 63, 100–101, VII, 3.

morphological parallel to the social stratification of the "conventional" age.

The change in religious attitudes is for Lamprecht the most portentous indicator of the shift from the "conventional" to the "individualistic" period.[116] Here, for the first time in his collectively conceived history, more than a hundred pages are given to a biographical sketch. Luther represents the new German whose life is dominated by the dual realities of a new "awareness-of-God" and an equally new "awareness-of-self" (*Gottesbewusstsein und Selbstbewusstsein*).[117] With this new state of mind the German individuum is generated and the "collectively fettered" man is left behind. In what manner then did Lamprecht see this psychic shift preparing itself in his treatment of the "conventional" age?

The German soul evolves from a condition internally unfree and ruled over by external realities to a situation in which man is internally free and dominates external reality. In the religious realm this reversal is the Protestant revolt. Here the German soul truly meets Christianity, the freest and most fully developed form of individualism in the ancient world.[118] But this encounter was not a sudden unprepared event. The Germans had earlier come into contact with Christianity in its "Roman form," that is, in the form of a legally defined and ecclesiastically institutionalized religion. To Lamprecht, a Lutheran minister's son, the Latinized church was characterized by dogma, miracle cults, canon law, and hierarchical order. Her chief commandment was obedience.[119] In his "fettered" stage, the German assimilated from this institutionalized religion whatever accorded with his psychic condition and his Germanic mythology. Such pronouncedly "external" Christianity was gradually replaced by a more internalized Christian attitude as the slow process

---

[116] *D.G.*, V, 6, 162, 246.
[117] *D.G.*, VI, 4, 30, 192, 196, VII, 65, 87–88, 102–3, 173, 249, VIII, 6.
[118] *D.G.*, III, 189, V, 246.
[119] *D.G.*, V, 247, 647, 657, VI, 180, VII, 390, VIII, 227.

of individuation gathered momentum during the "conventional" age. As this internalization advanced and spread, especially in the burgher class with its greater sense of self-discipline,[120] a differentiation occurred between ecclesiastic (*kirchlich*) and religious concerns, parallel to the growing distinction between law and morality in other aspects of life.[121] Ever larger circles of the bourgeoisie, by their stress on a spiritualized piety (*vergeistigte Frömmigkeit*), become critical of the church which they suspect of hostility toward an internalized religion (*das religionsfeindliche Treiben der Kirche*).[122] This growing aloofness among the educated layers of society finds its parallel in the church's failure to develop forms and expressions of piety appealing to the lower classes.[123] The burghers especially turn toward mysticism and practical charitable work. The *imitatio Christi*, the *devotio moderna*, the Rhineland mystics, the popularity of the mendicants (*Bussprediger*), all these express this shift to an internalized religion. Lamprecht takes particular interest in the sermons of Berthold of Ratisbon as an expression of burgher morality.[124] Most indicative of his concept of religious development is his discussion of mysticism. While contemplation and speculation free the mystic from the remaining "conventional" ties, his surrender to the Godhead prevents true individualism.[125] Yet, these late medieval phenomena prepare the German for the major Protestant experience: the encounter of the independent person with his God.[126]

Meanwhile other developments of burgher life support the gradual advent of individualism. Under the impact of in-

---

[120] *D.G.*, VI, 355, VII, 282.

[121] *D.G.*, III, 175–81, V, 153.

[122] *D.G.*, IV, 395.

[123] *D.G.*, IV, 263, 392.

[124] *D.G.*, III, 176, 212, 217, 261, IV, 44, 120, 251, 261.

[125] *D.G.*, I, 25–28, IV, 265–76 (esp., p. 271), V, 17–18, 159–61, 643, VII, 167.

[126] For Lamprecht's opinion that all subjectivist religion is "unkirchlich," see *D.G.*, VIII, 50, 270–71, 275, 277, 371.

creased travel the "conventionalized" typology breaks up.[127] The growing recognition of differences among men leads to the reverse insight of one's own specificity.[128] A different relation to nature is expressed by the artists in greater naturalism, more exact rendering of human anatomy, an increasing ability to catch the peculiarity of human physiognomy in the portrait, and the integration of natural objects into the landscapes.[129] The progressive rationalization of the burgher's life strikes Lamprecht even in such details as the clocks of Nuremberg which now sound every quarter-hour.[130] The exchange of ideas was quickened by the new trade in books and pamphlets. Vastly multiplied perceptions required new formulas to re-establish the collapsing balance of life for bewildered souls losing their stability and their hold on the world in the swirl of rapidly multiplying differentiation.[131] In particular, the growing art of letter writing indicates the nascent self-awareness and self-reporting.[132] On literally hundreds of pages Lamprecht traces the loosening of the fetters of tradition in art and music and the economic, political, and family life of the German people. In a wealth of learned observations about hundreds of changes occurring in the fourteenth and fifteenth centuries, the inner structure of the age as a whole is hardly

---

[127] D.G., V, 141–42.
[128] D.G., V, 147, VI, 6.
[129] D.G., V, 147, VI, 262.
[130] D.G., V, 68, and see also VI, 64.
[131] D.G., V, 148–49, VI, 100, 262, 317. To quote one nice exercise of Lamprecht's oversubtle writing: ". . . in Verfall geraten die alten Konvente und freieren geistigen Genossenschaften des 14. Jahrhunderts, und die Sprache bezeugt auch für andere Lebenskreise den Niedergang des alten genossenschaftlichen Ferments, indem sie aus dem Begriff Bursa 'studentische Genossenschaft' den individualistischen Begriff Bursche, aus dem Begriff Camerata, 'Stubengenossenschaft' den Sinn Kamerad, und endlich, wenn auch erst seit Beginn des 17. Jahrhunderts, aus dem Mittelhochdeutschen Vrouwenzimmer im Verstand von Gynäceum unsern individualistischen Begriff Frauenzimmer entwickelt" (D.G., V, 135).
[132] D.G., IV, 270, V, 132, VI, 98–99. Among the books which Lamprecht respected greatly is Georg Steinhausen, Geschichte des deutschen Briefes: zur Kulturgeschichte des deutschen Volkes (2 vols.; Berlin: Gaertner, 1889–91).

visible; only transitional elements seem to exist; no picture of a full life lived by human beings emerges.

Luther completes the break with tradition; his work and his person herald the appearance of the individualistic man. Lamprecht saw in him the "spiritual hero" [133] whose immense impact on history is the result of his personality, his actions, and his language, and, above all, of his new and genuine spiritual experience rather more than of any new system of theological thought. With Luther's awareness of his overwhelming personal experience (*Erlebnis*) of sinful man facing his wrathful and loving creator, the individual in a completely new sense was born.[134] He dared to look at the inescapable realities with unflinching eyes and tasted a new and fuller life with all his own organs. For him, man's individual existence, as this peculiar human being, was given in this new and indivisible experience of the God of Scripture and the "I" (*Selbstbewusstsein*) — God's enemy and God's child. This individualism, Lamprecht tells us, bears the marks of adolescent individuality: in all its consciousness of the separate and inexchangeable self, it still is directed by the leading-strings of an authoritative force, the Word.[135] Lamprecht shows the advantage of, even the need for, such a link with a superhuman authority for man during the early phase of individualism by contrasting Lutheranism with the *Schwärmertum*, the visionary left wing of Protestantism. Freed from tradition, but as yet without a fully developed inner discipline, the young individualism capsizes and becomes wildly arbitrary.[136] In this treatment of the sixteenth-century *Schwärmer*, as well as that of the later pietist, Lamprecht illustrates his concern with "anachronistic" phenomena of a cultural age.[137] Sebastian Franck, Kaspar

[133] *D.G.*, V, 229.

[134] *D.G.*, V, 238–39.

[135] *D.G.*, V, 249, 370 ("noch autoritativ gegängelter Individualismus").

[136] *D.G.*, V, 211, 326, 331. See also *D.G.*, VI, 355, and VII, 282, for the role of the burgher as the most disciplined factor.

[137] *D.G.*, V, 331, 370, VI, 235, VII, 162 ff.

Schwenckfeld, Herrmann Francke, and Nikolaus Zinzendorf are more precursors of the "subjectivist" age than representatives of the age of individualism, just as Charles V and especially Ignatius Loyola were out of step with their time in the "mistaken" attempt to force or lure men back into the ties that had bound the forms of medieval life.[138]

Luther and Kant mark for Lamprecht the emergence and the completion of the "individualistic" age of Germany. Where at the beginning man "leans" on biblical authority, he stands at the end as a free individual "who in the compass of his being gives himself his laws."[139] Midpoint between this early individualism and the transition to subjectivism stands Leibniz, who embodies the full realization of individualism in its prime.[140] Leibniz's monad reflects the individualistic personality, alone in its *Selbstbewusstsein* and its *Gottesbewusstsein*.[141] Where initially the biblical God formed one pole of the awareness, the age has assigned this place now to reason, the *lumen naturale*.[142] Individualism, Lamprecht asserts, has come fully into its own when the soul is defined as *ratio* and the cosmos as the unifying *sensorium* of all reasonable existence. In this way the self-contained (*in sich abgeschlossen*) individuum becomes the microcosmic expression of the macrocosm.[143] Lamprecht undertook to describe the culture built around this dominant element in six big volumes. The central features of this age are the emergence of modern science out of the pandynamism of the sixteenth century; of the arts as rational, learnable techniques; and of those social theories through which a sovereign individual

---

[138] *D.G.*, V, 647, 657, VI, 403.

[139] *D.G.*, V, 13; most of the discussion of Kant is to be found in Vol. VIII.

[140] Leibniz is central for Lamprecht's discussion of the "individualistic" age and constitutes a recurring theme throughout Vol. VII. In Vol. VIII Leibniz appears again as *the* thinker who prepared the shift to the "subjectivist" age.

[141] *D.G.*, VII, 92.

[142] *D.G.*, VI, 26, 100–101, 148, VII, 3, VIII, 11.

[143] *D.G.*, VI, 131, 189, VII, 92.

relates himself to a sovereign state. With ingenuous detail, Lamprecht brings this age to life for his readers, and while doing so, he again prepares the ground for the necessary transition to a new, "subjectivistic" age that succeeds the age of individualism after 1750.[144]

With a few words I can only try to do justice to Lamprecht's contribution to the struggle to establish a "cultural history." The nineteen volumes of his *Deutsche Geschichte* present the reader with an amorphous aggregate of quite ordinary, often quite unoriginal history. But embedded in this are often fascinating passages in which he seeks to give substance to his grand vision.

Lamprecht once recounts Herder's comparison of German culture to that fabled bird of paradise, which, deprived of feet, can remain alive only by flying without rest through the ethereal regions.[145] His own cultural history often resembles this bird. With vision and daring he establishes subtle relationships and meaningful contrasts among historical phenomena which are shunned by more cautious, or perhaps less imaginative, interpreters. There are sections in the *Deutsche Geschichte* where he deals with the phenomenon of the "human will" and where he traces it as a cultural manifestation which is at times submerged and at other times emerges as a manifest expression of the collective psyche.[146] Again and again he uses the different handling of light by the painters as an indicator of man's changing relations to nature. The contrast between the "individualistic" Rembrandt who had his figures illuminated by an imaginary source of light outside the picture, and light sensed as a coloristic ether in which all objects of the "subjectivist" impressionists are bathed, brings out for

---

[144] *D.G.*, VII, 158–60, 166, 171–85, 283–90, 331, 335, 350, 383–84, 390, 800.

[145] *D.G.*, IX, 40–41.

[146] *D.G.*, VIII, 5, 25, 41, 65, 362, XI, 311–18, 354–56, Erg. Bd. I, 387, Erg. Bd. II, Pt. 1, pp. 258–59, Erg. Bd. II, Pt. 2, p. 607.

Lamprecht some of the most basic differences between these ages.[147] He investigates the feasibility and the character of drama in terms of the conception of fate (*Schicksalsvorstellung*) appropriate for each form of *Seelenleben*.[148] Similarly he uses music as a "psychic" barometer and, especially in the later volumes, he discusses Schütz, Bach, Gluck, Haydn, Beethoven, Weber, Wagner, and Brahms at length as fitting expressions of their respective cultures. He establishes fascinating relations among the "subjectivist" burghers and the cult of the piano; [149] and, at other times, between the life the burgher leads and the furniture with which he surrounds himself.[150] He sees, as others have, a dependence of the "individualistic" political state on the emergence of mechanics,[151] and the inner connection of democracy and imperialism.[152] He describes the ties between democracy and the "graphic revolution" of cheap printing and lithography, as well as the affinity between the social prominence of burghers and the spread of reproductive techniques such as woodcuts, etching, engraving, and the paper silhouette.[153] He analyzes the educational theories of the *Sturm und Drang* and Romanticism as a necessary prelude to the conception of the state the Germans developed in the early nineteenth century.[154] He sees the relations between spatial conceptions, the modern voyageur,[155] and the reorientation of Germany's traffic pattern toward the sea.[156] He compares the humor and the mood of the medieval colonizer to that of the western pioneer in the United States.[157] And

---

[147] *D.G.*, VI, 288–95, 315–17, VII, 226, VIII, 15, X, 149, 165, Erg. Bd. I, 388.
[148] *D.G.*, VI, 108, 231, VII, 267, VIII, 554, X, 63, XI, 280–82, Erg. Bd. I, 320, 364.
[149] *D.G.*, VIII, 681.
[150] *D.G.*, IV, 242, Erg. Bd. I, 199–203.
[151] *D.G.*, VI, 64, 176–79, 387, VIII, 5, 12.
[152] *D.G.*, XI, 460–61, Erg. Bd. II, Pt. 2, pp. 593–606.
[153] *D.G.*, V, 134–35, 185–90, VIII, 589, 601, XI, 193.
[154] *D.G.*, IX, 8–9, 30, 39, 78, 104, 109, 113, 305, X, 456–60.
[155] *D.G.*, Erg. Bd. II, Pt. 1, pp. 173, 326 ff.
[156] *D.G.*, Erg. Bd. II, Pt. 1, pp. 161, 461.
[157] *D.G.*, III, 53, 313, 371, IV, 259, VII, 602, X, 362.

he draws attention to the similarities and differences in the "conventions" of Hohenstaufen knighthood and of the eighteenth century *salon*.[158] So he uses his comprehensive notion of culture to probe into every manifestation of civilized existence.

Lamprecht labored under enormous pressures. He must always have feared that time would not permit him to put his visions on paper. He composed the last parts of the German history before he wrote the middle sections. His combativeness and the pleasure he took in apodictic statements provoked quarrels in which he was involved with monotonous repetition until both audience and participants were worn out. He was a very popular teacher — "Endlich ein Herr Professor der nicht rostet!"[159] — and was sought as a public speaker. He established his Institut at Leipzig and simultaneously served as editor for the revised Heeren-Uckert series on world history and as secretary to the Historical Commission of the Saxon Academy. His chief work suffered from the haste with which he tried to meet all his commitments. The ideas gushed forth in the text whenever they broke loose in his mind and so they do not always appear in the place where they seem to belong. Some he flattened by too much attention, and others, crying for elaboration, are barely sketched. His language is often as uncontrolled as his composition.

Lamprecht lacked the very qualities which made Burckhardt such a master of cultural history. Lamprecht enjoyed a thorough humanistic education; late in life he was still able to conduct conversations in Latin;[160] yet he never attained a humanistic sense for style, for form, and for moderation. Everything this man touched revealed his inner lack of restraint. He hardly cultivated that inner sense of measure and delicacy which told Burckhardt when to stop and where to tread lightly or to run for shelter. Where Burckhardt merely

[158] *D.G.*, VII, 22, 44.
[159] Schmoller, pp. 39, 52.
[160] *Kindheitserinnerungen*, pp. 93–94.

hinted, Lamprecht wrote volumes. He staked out his claim as the discoverer of "the" scientific historical method and as the author of "the" definitive German history. The modest Swiss, his sight always trained on the manifestations of man's greatness and suffering, presented his works as mere essays — as the elaboration of only one of the numerous vistas that history opens before the eyes of the acute observer.

The "yes, . . . but" attitude which Lamprecht's great critic Huizinga[161] thought should be each historian's inner guide, will in the end lead to an essentially positive verdict on the total work of this great German fighter for cultural history. If few read Lamprecht nowadays, few escape his direct and indirect influence. His reception in Germany was hostile, but even antagonists like Walter Goetz, and later Friedrich Meinecke, acknowledged his significance. In spite of his blatant Teutonisms[162] foreign historians recognized his value. Lamprecht's impact on American historians can be traced in the "New History" cultivated at Columbia University, where he lectured during his sojourn in this country.[163] He fitted perfectly into an age which saw the birth of such journals as the *Revue de synthèse historique* and which struggled for steadily widening conceptions of history. What textbook today does not pretend, at least, to encompass social, economic, and cultural phenomena in addition to the customary political history? We have only to compare the old Oncken series, *Allgemeine Geschichte in Einzeldarstellungen*, with the *Propylaen Weltgeschichte*, or the 1902 version of the Cambridge

---

[161] For Huizinga's *Auseinandersetzung* with Lamprecht, see Johan Huizinga, *Verzamelde Werken* (Haarlem: H.D. Tjeenk Willink, 1948–53), II, 404–11, III, 262, IV, 268, 429, 486, VII, 5, 8–10, 23, 34, 47, 69, 73, 94–95, 117–18, 188, 233–34.

[162] For example, see *D.G.*, I, 165–66, Erg. Bd. II, Pt. 2, p. 593.

[163] This question deserves to be investigated by an expert in American historiography; George G. Iggers, "The Image of Ranke in American and German Historical Thought," *History and Theory*, II (1962), 24, seems to imply that Lamprecht had little influence, but Iggers' discussion centers on Lamprecht's contribution to Ranke's image in this country.

Modern History with the current revised edition, to see that the modern editors seem to be executing a vital part of Lamprecht's program. The view of one comprehensive configuration of culture — the culture of one epoch, one nation, of mankind — forces itself upon our consciousness, even while we tremble before the *hybris* of those who dare to give substance to our dream. Burckhardt, with his almost feminine sensitivity and his delicate sense of balance, remains the unrivaled master of cultural history; but he gives fragments only. Lamprecht throws at us a system of the totality of cultural history, conceived with boundless daring, ingenuity, virtuosity, and haste. His vision was needed as a complement even if he fails in a thousand details, even if hardly anybody any longer accepts his system as an analysis of man's pilgrimage through time. The tension between Lamprecht and Burckhardt symbolizes the — perhaps permanently hopeless — task the historian of culture has to face in our century.

5 : Huizinga

1872 - 1945

Johan Huizinga belonged to a generation once removed from Lamprecht. At the time when the Dutch Sanskritist shifted his scholarly interests from linguistics and Indian civilization to the history of medieval Haarlem,[1] Lamprecht had finished half his monumental German history and was steeped in the controversies of the *Methodenstreit*. Without openly participating in this professional feud, Huizinga revealed his lively interest in the issues and did not hide his personal leanings.[2] He sided largely with Lamprecht's opponents, but he reserved admiration for Lamprecht's courage in undertaking such a

---

[1] Huizinga was born in 1872 in Groningen, where his father was professor of physiology; he was trained as a linguist and Sanskritist at Groningen and Leipzig; after obtaining his doctorate in 1897 he became a high school teacher at Haarlem and *privaat docent* for Indic studies at Amsterdam; in 1905 his history professor P. J. Blok obtained the history chair for him at the University of Groningen; in 1915 Huizinga moved to the University of Leiden, where he taught until the Germans closed the university late in 1940; subsequently Huizinga was imprisoned in a camp for prominent Dutch hostages from which he was released for reasons of ill health through Swedish intervention in October, 1942, and forced to spend his last years in a small village, banished from students and his books; he died in De Steeg in February, 1945. For the work on Haarlem see *De Rechtsbronnen der stad Haarlem*, ed. J. Huizinga, Vol. XIII of the second series of *Werken der Vereeniging tot uitgaaf der bronnen van het Oud-Vaderlandsche Recht*, and also *Verzamelde Werken*, I, 203–411 for smaller writings (hereafter cited *V.W.*).

[2] For Huizinga's major writings on theoretical historical problems, see the collection in *V.W.*, VII, 1–258; the principal ones are: "Het aesthetische bestanddeel van geschiedkundige voorstellingen" (1905); "De taak der cultuurgeschiedenis" (1929), which is included in *Men and Ideas*; "Over een definitie van het begrip geschiedenis" (1929); "De wetenschap der geschiedenis" (1934); and "Over vormverandering der geschiedenis" (1941). For Huizinga's reaction to Lamprecht see *V.W.*, II, 404–11, III, 262, IV, 268, 429, 486, VII, 5, 8, 9, 10, 17, 23, 34, 47, 69, 73, 94–95, 117–18, 188, and 233–34.

comprehensive task. Throughout his life, Huizinga expressed respect for the "wrestlers with the Angel," those historical adventurers who struggled to present integrated visions of large segments of the past.[3] And almost every time he rejected their product. His stands on other issues of this methodological quarrel over the nature and task of history were similarly ambivalent. Was history a science or an art? Huizinga acknowledged the importance of a critical method for the historian and frequently insisted that modern scholars were bound to respect the "scientific" standards of their inheritance. Yet his own methodological writings were concentrated on the aesthetic aspects of historical work. He dismissed the demands that history adopt the more exacting methods and aspirations of the natural sciences, insisting that history was always inexact and a mere extension of common sense. Yet, in discussions of subtler epistemological issues, Huizinga would proudly point to the achievements of Wilhelm Dilthey, Heinrich Rickert, or Wilhelm Windelband, who founded in Huizinga's opinion a reliable method for the cultural sciences or *Geisteswissenschaften*.[4] He readily acknowledged the progress made by such new disciplines as psychology and sociology but doubted that they had much to contribute to the historian's work. He valued the new understanding opened up by an economic interpretation of history; yet his own work must largely be seen as an attack on what he considered a deterministic approach to the past.[5]

This introductory paragraph is not meant to suggest that Huizinga was an especially inconsistent historian, or that he was not correct in maintaining such ambivalent positions re-

[3] "Twee worstelaars met den Engel," *V.W.*, IV, 441–96 (a review article on H. G. Wells and Oswald Spengler); see also *V.W.*, VII, 5, 94, 234.

[4] *V.W.*, VII, 5, 69, 118, 233. For other references to these and to Georg Simmel, Eduard Meyer, Eduard Spranger, *et al.*, see the excellent *Register van persoonsnamen*, Vol. IX of *V.W.*

[5] A typical instance of this is Huizinga's lecture "La valeur politique et militaire des idées de chevalerie à la fin du moyen âge" (1921), *V.W.*, III, 519–29. Other clear examples in *V.W.*, IV, 412, 446, 525, V, 223.

garding the theoretical aspects of historical scholarship. The wisdom of his "theoretical" writings rests precisely on this unwillingness to commit his chosen discipline too rigidly to any particular methodological demand. Huizinga was deeply convinced that human thinking vacillates between antinomies,[6] that is, that man is constantly forced to admit the validity of seemingly opposite points of view. History is the discipline closest to life; and life is rarely free of contradictions. The historian therefore fares best with the permanent reservation "yes, . . . but."[7] He must maintain the right balance between the subjective and objective attitude involved in all historical work; he, no less than many of us, is caught between nominalism and realism (used by Huizinga with the meaning given to the terms by medieval philosophy);[8] he is aware of the problematic quality of his causal explanations, and yet he cannot dispense with them; he gains knowledge through image-like visions, and yet needs abstract conceptions; he rigorously strives for certainty and precision, and knows that his discipline is the most inexact of all. With its "yes, . . . but" attitude the whole profession is engaged in a continuous corrective process, an everlasting task of interpreting and reinterpreting.

It is difficult to give a clear picture of the character of Huizinga's historical work because his thought was so deeply influenced by this awareness of inescapable antinomies. A precise summing-up should include all his subtle qualifications. A constant reminder would be desirable — "but Huizinga also said this." This basic conviction, reinforced by a remarkable sensitivity for the complexities of historical matter, occasionally results in the absence of a clear, straightforward argument. Most of his writings appear to be clearly focused and structured. Yet, a careful reading often reveals

[6] See especially *V.W.*, VII, 147 n. 2. Also see E. E. G. Vermeulen, *Huizinga over de wetenschap der geschiedenis*, pp. 36–54.

[7] See *V.W.*, III, 447, IV, 397, 479, V, 377–78, VII, 169, 385, 427.

[8] *V.W.*, IV, 278, 385, VII, 38, 134–35.

that the apparent simplicity entails a slight illusion. Sometimes Huizinga worked the contrasts of his conception directly into the theme: man and crowds in America, individualism and association, wild and tamed America, image of nature and image of history in the eighteenth century, patriotism and nationalism, the limits of play and earnest necessities, how did Alanus de Insulis fuse poetry and theology?[9] Once, attempting to clarify the meaning of romanticism, Huizinga resorted to dialogue as the most effective form for setting divergent opinions against one another.[10] In other writings the contrasting poles are worked in differently. Fully one-half of Huizinga's basic belief about a matter may be stated in one sentence, while the remaining hundreds of pages, which the reader chiefly remembers, contain the other half. A brief introduction to the *Homo Ludens*[11] makes clear that Huizinga thought of man as *homo sapiens* plus *homo faber* plus *homo ludens*; yet the book may leave the impression that man can be completely circumscribed as *homo ludens*. Economic realities were vital to his conception of culture; yet he rarely discusses them. Rationality is the bolt which locks out chaos;[12] yet the weight of his sentences plays down the importance of

---

[9] Major writings in which Huizinga elaborated this are *Mensch en menigte in Amerika: vier essays over moderne beschavingsgeschiedenis* (1918; originally lectures at Leiden, 1917–18), in *V.W.*, V, 249–417; "Natuurbeeld en historiebeeld in de achttiende eeuw" (1933), *V.W.*, IV, 341–59; "Über die Verknüpfung des Poetischen mit dem Theologischen bei Alanus de Insulis" (1932), *V.W.*, IV, 3–84; *Patriotisme en nationalisme in de Europeesche geschiedenis tot het einde der 19e eeuw* (1940), *V.W.*, IV, 497–554, also included in *Men and Ideas*; "Over de grenzen van spel en ernst in de cultuur" (1933), *V.W.*, V, 3–25, the lecture out of which grew the *Homo Ludens*.

[10] "Kleine samenspraak over de thema's der Romantiek" (1929), *V.W.*, IV, 381–91.

[11] *Homo Ludens: proeve eener bepaling van het spel-element der cultuur* (1938), *V.W.*, V, 26–246 (also available in a Beacon Press paperback volume published in 1950).

[12] "[Die Vernunft] ist uns gegeben als ein Massstab der Dinge und ein Riegel vor dem Wahnsinn und dem Chaos," in *Der Mensch und die Kultur* (a lecture Huizinga was meant to give in Vienna in 1938 but did not because of the *Anschluss*), *V.W.*, VII, 456.

rationality. The entire description of the French-Burgundian culture during the "waning of the Middle Ages" has to be read against the background of the one initial chapter.[13] Thus Huizinga achieved unity and structure of argument often by elaborating only one aspect of his complete opinion. Usually this meant that Huizinga concentrated upon those aspects which he thought insufficiently treated by the profession as a whole. Much of his work has the quality of a correction of prevailing historiographic trends. He reacted in particular to the demand that history meet the rigorous conceptual and logical standards of the natural sciences. He fought the deterministic schemes of the scientists, the biologists, the psychologists, and above all the economic materialists — at least as schemes of historical interpretation. And he turned against the idea that man is *primarily* a rational creature, moved by utilitarian persuasions. This "correcting" Huizinga, the historian who sought descriptive forms for the "supra-logical," the playing and dreaming man, is the subject of the following discussion. His greatest contributions to the development of cultural history lie in that realm. But it is necessary to remember that the same man had profound respect for the great accomplishments of human reason, enduring devotion to careful and critically sound scholarship, and even in his darkest hours a trust in man's ability to lead a sane life.

What did culture mean for this great historian of culture? The years after 1924, when Huizinga had already gained great renown for his work on the Burgundian "civilization" and had completed his biography of Erasmus, were marked by a

---

[13] *Herfsttij der Middeleeuwen: studie over levens- en gedachtenvormen der veertiende en vijftiende eeuw in Frankrijk en de Nederlanden* (1919), *V.W.*, III, 3–435 (available in English as *The Waning of the Middle Ages* [London: Arnolds, 1942] and in Anchor Books [New York, 1954]; the English version is not a precise translation of the original but "the result of a work of adaptation, reduction and consolidation under the author's directions"; see introduction to paperback edition, p. 6). The translation, in my opinion, is a very inferior, crippled version of the Dutch original.

growing concern with writings of a more pronounced "theoretical" character. Huizinga was at that time more than fifty years old and no noticeable shift seems to have occurred in the major concepts by which the "practicing" historian could be differentiated from the historian who reflected upon his craft and the world around him. The mature scholar now presented his thoughts in more systematic and more reflective form on matters which had preoccupied him for a long time.[14] And as the malaise of Europe quickened after 1933, revealing ever more clearly the barbarian underneath a thin and quickly corroding layer of culture, the historian turned away from his promising work on the culture of the twelfth century and became involved in the analysis of the pathology of modern life. In rapid succession he produced *In de schaduwen van morgen, Homo Ludens,* and *Geschonden wereld.*[15] Until his incarceration in 1943 by the German occupiers of his land, he accepted more and more invitations to speak and write on the subject of conditions for the recovery of civilization.

Huizinga's numerous reflections on culture never grew into a closed system. In the last analysis he felt unable to define the

---

[14] A clear example of this is the *Homo Ludens.* In the foreword (*V.W.,* V, 26) Huizinga clearly states that he had been concerned with the interrelation of play and culture since 1903. Similarly, he also explains in the later chapter "on culture and epochs *sub specie ludi*" that he had already dealt with this problem in the context of the *Waning of the Middle Ages* (*V.W.,* V, 211).

[15] The work on the twelfth century was foreshadowed in the series of lectures at the Sorbonne in 1930, "Trois esprits prégothiques"; these appeared later in various forms as lectures and articles on Alanus de Insulis, Abelard, and John of Salisbury (*V.W.,* IV, 3–84, 85–103, 104–22). The major writings on Europe's crisis are *In de schaduwen van morgen: een diagnose van het geestelijk lijden van onzen tijd* (1935), *V.W.,* VII, 313–428 (also available in English as *In the Shadows of Tomorrow: A Diagnosis of the Spiritual Distemper of Our Time* [London: Heineman, 1936]); *Geschonden wereld: een beschouwing over de kansen op herstel van onze beschaving* (posthumously published in 1945), *V.W.,* VII, 477–606; *Der Menschund die Kultur* (1938), *V.W.,* VII, 442–59; *Neutraliteit en vrijheid, waarheid en beschaving* (1939), *V.W.,* VII, 460–66; *Conditions for a Recovery of Civilization* (1940), *V.W.,* VII, 467–76 (also in *Fortnightly Review,* CXLVII [1940], 390–400); *Nederland's geestesmerk* (1935), V.W., VII, 279–312.

concept and acquiesced in confining himself to a mere circumscription of the problem.[16] Always mindful of his linguistic training, he sought help from a verbal approach to the subject. What terms were used for the idea of culture? What were the differences? Did all the terms even try to cover the same phenomenon? And which term was preferable?[17] Huizinga looked for a term which could denote the totality of "cultural" phenomena. For this reason he avoided overly narrow denotations. The Dutch term *beschaving* was too closely tied to the original meaning of "polishing," the *humaniora* and erudition; it presented, in many ways, the same difficulties as the use of the German *Bildung*. The French word *culture* and the English *culture* were similarly narrow. The German word *Kultur* came closer to Huizinga's intentions, but he was perturbed by some of the connotations it had acquired through Burckhardt's distinction of the term from *Staat* and *Religion*, Virchow's slogan, "*Kulturkampf*," and especially Spengler's separation of *Kultur* and *Zivilisation*, an older distinction which Spengler, in Huizinga's opinion, greatly exaggerated.[18] The derivations from the Latin base *colere* were thus either too close to the original agricultural notion, too much associated with the cultivation of the "finer things in life," or, on the other extreme, too reminiscent of Edward Tylor's *Primitive Culture*. The formation of the noun *civilisation* from the verb *civiliser* offended Huizinga's linguistic sensibilities. Like Dr. Johnson he preferred the word "civilty."[19] He especially lamented the fact that Europeans had failed to adopt the Tuscan form *civiltà*, which

---

[16] *V.W.*, VII, 45, 165, 328, 480, 489, 500, 511.

[17] *V.W.*, VII, 481–91. A similar example for Huizinga's predilection for tackling a problem first by analysis of language is the second chapter of the *Homo Ludens*, "The Play Concept as Expressed in Language."

[18] The main discussion of the problem in *V.W.*, VIII, 443–45, 485–87; but see also IV, 483–84, VIII, 454.

[19] *V.W.*, VII, 482; for Samuel Johnson's reaction see *Civilisation: le mot et l'idée* (Paris: Centre International de Synthèse, Première semaine internationale, fasc. 2, 1929), pp. 6–8.

Dante had filled with such powerful meaning.[20] This term characterized a vital part of any comprehensive notion of a non-barbarian existence. "The high value of the Latin *civilitas* did not fully speak to Spengler. Although the full meaning of this word as 'cultured existence' [*beschaving*] developed only in Italian, the highest quality of human communal life was aptly indicated in the Latin word which in that sense was the equivalent of the Greek *paideia*. Spengler quite unjustly 'heard' something lower in contrast to something higher when he placed *Zivilisation* against *Kultur*. *Civilisation* speaks of man as a citizen, as a companion in justice, it speaks of a man fully conscious of his true worth. It speaks of order, law, and justice, and excludes barbarity."[21] But the same word is unfortunately weak in connoting those aspects of life which culture overemphasizes. The difficulty of the terms had accompanied European consciousness since the eighteenth century when Voltaire and his fellow *philosophes* "discovered" a human treasure they could not name. Huizinga could not resolve the issue by coining yet another term or defining one of the existing ones more precisely. So he used the relatively "unshaped" Dutch form *cultuur* and the ugly, but least compromised, English and French *civilisation*. His discussion of the terms suggests that all his thinking on the subject revolved around the right blending of those two root terms, *colere* and *civiliser*.

Culture (in this comprehensive sense which includes derivations from both *colere* and *civiliser*), though indefinable and even unnamable, did yet sufficiently point in the direction of a phenomenon familiar to everyone through his life experience, a phenomenon whose dimensions and conditions could be investigated. It seemed primary to Huizinga that a culture should preserve its spiritual (*geestelijk*) as well as its material

---

[20] Huizinga spoke repeatedly about the richness of Dante's concept and deplored the fact that it had never gained sufficient currency (*V.W.*, IV, 144, VII, 452, 459, 483–84, 489, 517–18).

[21] *V.W.*, VII, 488.

values. The realities of economic life, of power, of technology, of everything conducive to man's material well-being, must be balanced by strongly developed spiritual, intellectual, moral, and aesthetic values.[22] "The balance exists above all in the fact that each of the various cultural activities enjoys as vital a function as is possible in the context of the whole. If such harmony of cultural functions is present, it will reveal itself as order, strong structure, style, and rhythmic life of the society in question."[23] Clearly, this is an instance in which Huizinga acknowledged the importance of those economic and technological factors which he often seemed to ignore in his treatment of cultural history. But after a few lines it appears that some of the values seem "more necessary" to Huizinga than others. "A culture can reach lofty heights though it produces neither a scientifically developed technology nor sculpture, but not if it misses charity."[24] Ethical and spiritual values are necessary in an absolute, an indispensable sense. But culture also flounders without political and social order, stability, and a minimal measure of freedom. Man must control nature: external nature by his abilities as *homo faber*, and human nature by his self-restraint as a moral and civil being.[25] This concern with cultural balance, and with man's ability to control himself as well as his surroundings, was one main cause for Huizinga's critique of modern life. In sections of his study on American civilization Huizinga had sketched a problem of all civilized life: *de verwerktuigelijking van het leven*, the process whereby life is increasingly molded by man's own tools.[26] Man's dependence on tools entails a double prob-

[22] *V.W.*, VII, 328–29.

[23] *V.W.*, VII, 329; see also VII, 163, 490, V, 4.

[24] *V.W.*, VII, 329; see also "Lettre à M. Julien Benda" (1934), *V.W.*, VII, 269–78, and II, 507, V, 408, VII, 561, 573–74, 606.

[25] *V.W.*, VII, 330–31, 521–23.

[26] One of the essays on America was similarly entitled (see *V.W.*, V, 292–335). For Huizinga the "process of ennobling or refining [*veredeling*] culture is inseparable from the process whereby tools encroach on life [i.e., *verwerktuigelijking*]; . . . Each tool and each organization is endowed with [*geladen*

lem: first, the attempt to control nature may destroy the harmony of a culture by occupying too large a sector of life; and,
second, *homo faber* is always in danger of losing control over
his tools, and life is therefore constantly threatened by mechanization. The sorcerer's apprentice is at the mercy of his
broom. But the modern disharmony is also caused by hyper-
trophy of power. The modern state is a wolf to the state (Huizinga's variation of Plautus' *homo homini lupus*).[27] The im-
moderate claims of overgrown nationalism, unbounded
demands for power and the discarding of moral limitations
make the modern state (strengthened by modern technology
and propaganda) a voracious beast.[28] Instead of functioning as
a part of culture, the state is captured by the ever lurking
barbarian. In his war book, *Geschonden wereld*, Huizinga
above all concerned himself with the chances of reducing the
state to its proper place within the whole of culture. Without
such a rebalancing of its major components, culture seemed
doomed. And while the modern world was threatened by an
unbalanced concern with its material factors (technology,
power, wealth), Huizinga hinted that other ages had suffered
from an inability to progress materially, technologically, and
politically (e.g., the late Roman empire), while others (e.g., the
late Middle Ages) had never succeeded in integrating the
necessary material concerns into their dream world of aesthetically pleasing play.[29] Yet, in his various considerations of the

---

met] its own activity, which forces man to make the tool work, to let the organization function. Without such mechanization, culture [*beschaving*] does not
exist. . . . No image comes to mind more frequently when reflecting on cultural
history than Goethe's *Zauberlehrling*. The much used phrase '*die ich rief,
die Geister, werd ich nun nicht los*' remains the pre-eminent text for all great
movements of culture. And the image of the dumb broom which staggers in
with more and more water is more relevant today than ever. Poor humanity
always seems to remain the magician's little apprentice, the Master returns
seldom in history" (*V.W.*, V, 335). For Huizinga's concerns with the detri-
mental aspects of "mechanization," see *V.W.*, IV, 376, V, 290–91, VII, 294–95,
411.
   [27] *V.W.*, VII, 379–85, 472.
   [28] *V.W.*, VII, 292–99, 457, 523–24.
   [29] *V.W.*, VII, 325, 515–18.

problem of a cultural balance, Huizinga placed the emphasis overwhelmingly upon the need for balancing material concerns with spiritual values; for only when matter is ennobled by the spirit is it a genuine element of culture.

An inherent characteristic of culture is its teleological quality: ". . . all culture contains a striving. Culture is directedness [gerichtheid]. . . ."[30] It inevitably points toward an ideal, a vision of life shared by a community. It must be acknowledged as a shared ideal, a common consensus on a *summum bonum* amid the inevitable and desirable diversity of individuals.[31] And in a nationalistic, race-conscious age, when voices began to speak of "national cultures,"[32] Huizinga demanded that culture transcend the limitations of any narrow human group. The ideals and values which give a culture its direction, its teleological character, must entail aspirations beyond the merely selfish objectives of a particular community. "Culture must be metaphysically directed, or it will not be."[33] The existence, and certainly the strength and wellbeing, of any culture becomes problematic whenever its transcendent striving is surrendered. Huizinga stated the same, less abstractly, when he insisted that culture must contain the idea of service (*dienst*), the acceptance of high obligations.[34] It need not be work *ad maiorem Dei gloriam* (though Huizinga seemed to have a predilection for this); it can be devotion to any ideal by which the individual can truly serve mankind. Let it be old fashioned "metaphysical" ideas such as justice, wisdom, virtue, as long as man, in serving such ideals, raises himself above the limitations of his selfish material interests. For power, wealth, and security must be "ennobled by the spirit."[35] In a sense Huizinga had said this when

---

[30] *V.W.*, VII, 329; see also V, 3.
[31] *V.W.*, VII, 457, 596.
[32] *V.W.*, VII, 447–51, 551–54, 583–91.
[33] *V.W.*, VII, 33, 475; see also II, 531, V, 104.
[34] *V.W.*, VII, 331; see also IV, 272, 421, V. 4, 476–78.
[35] *V.W.*, VII, 365–71, 445.

he insisted that man control nature in its double aspect. Thus moral values are indispensable to culture. Ideals of life, service to a *summum bonum*, though they alone do not shape a culture, are yet the core elements which "direct" it. Huizinga summed up his notion of culture: "A community is in the state of culture when the domination of nature in the material, moral, and spiritual [*geestelijk*] realms permits a state of existence which is *higher* and *better* than the given natural conditions; and when this state of existence is further-more characterized by a harmonious balance of material and spiritual values and is guided by an ideal (in principle homo-geneously derived) toward which the different activities of the community are directed." [36]

No wonder Huizinga's critique of modern life revolved around these issues: the predominance of that puerile men-tality which considers the world its oyster without accepting responsibilities; [37] the forsaking of standards of truth and soberness; [38] the misuse of science and knowledge for power and infantile joys; [39] the illusions about man's potentialities; inflated heroism [40] and intoxication with such myths as "inevi-table progress." [41] Nor is it surprising that Huizinga, when looking for a cure, placed his hopes on a moral attitude: *askesis*, self-restraint which eschews the temptations of super-abundance. [42] A culture which no longer can integrate the diverse pursuits of men into a whole, which cannot restrain

---

[36] *V.W.*, VII, 332 (the closest Huizinga came to "defining" his concept of culture; but see also VII, 163, 165).

[37] *V.W.*, VII, 393–99, 544.

[38] *V.W.*, VII, 343–54, 400–402.

[39] *V.W.*, VII, 292–99, 355–60.

[40] *V.W.*, VII, 386–92; against such inflated heroism Huizinga placed such good Dutch burgher qualities as soberness (see VII, 285, 287–88, 576–78).

[41] *V.W.*, VII, 403–12, 416, 469. Huizinga was much preoccupied with the rising and declining (*stijging en daling*) of cultures and with the notion of "cultural loss" (*cultuurverlies*) (see VII, 511–20, 521–47).

[42] *V.W.*, VII, 412, 414, 424–28, 456–57, 475–76, 578–80. The idea that the welfare of culture necessitated man's restriction to essentials was, of course, a major theme in the life of the older Jacob Burckhardt.

men through a guiding set of norms, has lost its center and has lost its style.[43] It is threatened by the exuberant overgrowth of its separate components. It then needs a pruning knife, a human decision to focus once again on the essentials of culture and cut back the luxuriant but dispensable. Late medieval men had succumbed under the suffocating wealth of cultural forms. Could modern culture restrengthen itself through *askesis*? Could the sorcerer's apprentice acquire control again over the forces he had released? Huizinga hesitated; but he was unwilling to subscribe to an all-pervasive theory of determinism which left men no choice. So he clung to the hope for a revived moral commitment which might give us some control over ourselves and our surroundings. With his own sober pessimism he fought Spengler's hopeless pessimism from the moment that the *Untergang des Abendlandes* appeared. "We do not *want* to go down. With all its misery, this world is too beautiful to let it sink into a night of human degeneration and blindness of the spirit."[44] And, as a historian, Huizinga hoped that a sober view of the past might contribute substantially to the cleaning of the Augean stable of our culture.[45]

The central idea of culture, expressed in the context of Huizinga's critique of modern life, assigned a necessary but subordinate position to man's "utilitarian interests." What he called material values (e.g., security, wealth, power), the necessities which support biological existence, are never sufficient for culture, however basic they may be for life. They are necessary, but they do not truly shape a culture.[46] In his greatest study of a culture, *The Waning of the Middle Ages*, Huizinga had already analyzed a society characterized more by its aesthetic aspirations than its utilitarian concerns. *Homo faber* might be an interesting creature, but Huizinga found

---

[43] See Huizinga's discussion of the "loss of style" in *V.W.*, VII, 410–12.
[44] *V.W.*, VII, 418.
[45] *V.W.*, VII, 464, 549, and also 322.
[46] *V.W.*, VII, 420.

it impossible to account for man's varied doings by any theory that focused on needs and utility. Similarly, he wished to counteract and correct the thesis that the past could best be understood as a gradual movement toward indefinite progress wrought by *homo sapiens*. Huizinga opposed to these schemes of interpretation his own fascination with the supra-logical and unnecessary world of play: *Homo Ludens*.

Not until the middle thirties did Huizinga work out in book form the question which had long interested him: To what extent can and must man's world be explained by play? [47] The fundamental question was not what elements of culture can be viewed as play (as the subtitle to the English translation implies), but, To what extent must human culture be understood to result from play and to what extent does culture express itself in the forms of play? [48] And behind this lies the

---

[47] In 1933 Huizinga gave as his rectorate lecture the speech "Over de grenzen van spel en ernst in de cultuur" (*V.W.*, V, 3–25) in which he stated that the topic had preoccupied him for thirty years; in the *Homo Ludens* (*V.W.*, V, 26) he pinpointed 1903 as the year in which he first became concerned with the question.

[48] The Dutch subtitle is *Proeve eener bepaling van het spel-element der cultuur* or "Test of Delimiting [or circumscribing] the Play Element of Culture." In the foreword Huizinga states: "For many years the conviction has grown upon me that culture arises and unfolds itself in and as play. Traces of such an opinion are to be found in my writings ever since 1903. I took it as the theme for my address as rector of Leiden University in 1933, entitled *Over de grenzen van spel en ernst in de cultuur*. When I subsequently reworked this lecture, first for an address at Zurich and then Vienna (1934) and afterwards in London (1937), I gave it the title *Das Spielelement der Kultur*, 'The play-element of culture. Both times my hosts corrected it to *in der Kultur*, 'in culture' and both times I crossed out the preposition and re-established the genitive. After all, it was not my question which place play occupies among the other cultural phenomena, but in how far culture itself has the character of play." To this the English translator adds the cryptic note (see foreword in the *Homo Ludens* edition put out by Beacon Press): "Logically, of course, Huizinga is correct; but as English prepositions are not governed by logic, I have retained the more euphonious ablative in this title." One wonders why "The Play Element *of* Culture" is unacceptable, since Huizinga explicitly preferred it. The confusion lies in Huizinga's choice of the word *element*, which is not to be considered an element (i.e., a part) of the more comprehensive term and entity "culture," but as a phenomenological factor, as char-

latent, less precise, but broader question, What in the human existence accounts for the diversity of structured life, for this richness of forms so insufficiently explained by responses to biological needs or by the demands of rationality? For Voltaire also culture had many of the marks of "play." But Voltaire had treasured the ideal of that one form of existence which most perfectly adhered to the dictates of reason and utility; perhaps he even tolerated the diversity which he could not deny, those "many rooms in my Father's mansion," only for the sake of his ideal of toleration. Huizinga, like Burckhardt before him, was fascinated exactly by the "not-needed" richness of forms and by their supra-logical and non-utilitarian aspects.[49] And what appears less necessary, less predictable, and more arbitrary than play?

Play is non-earnest.[50] Human life can subsist without it. It is unnecessary for survival. From the point of view of our material needs and the immediate utility of our actions, play is a useless squandering of vital energy.[51] Play lies outside our highest moral commands and is neither sin nor virtue.[52] It lies outside the distinction of true or false.[53] Its nature is neither biological nor logical nor ethical.[54] Yet it occupies a large part of man's life. It expresses the superabundance and adornment of life. It may be useless; yet play has its own meaning — *zwecklos aber doch sinnvoll*.[55] It fulfils a social function and possesses its own forms, rules, and demands. It

---

acteristic of animals as of human beings. He clearly uses it as a phenomenon, a form of behavior, a function of organisms, which antedates culture.

[49] See, for example, *V.W.*, II, 442, IV, 343, V, 31, 48, 118, 158, 165, 169, 223, 270.

[50] *V.W.*, V, 5, 10, 32–33, 72–73 (all references to V, 26–246, are from the *Homo Ludens*).

[51] *V.W.*, V, 31.

[52] *V.W.*, V, 24.

[53] *V.W.*, V, 33.

[54] *V.W.*, V, 31, 169.

[55] *V.W.*, V, 47; Huizinga took the quotation from Romano Guardini, "Die Liturgie als Spiel," in *Vom Geist der Liturgie* (Freiburg, 1922), pp. 56–70. For further substantiation of the point see also *V.W.*, V, 28, 31, 77, 189.

is a freely accepted activity which submits the player to its own rigid order.[56] Play has its own ethics and its own seriousness which may even entail the question of life or death. It is always contest and strife.[57] Play demands intense concentration of body and mind and has as its rewards only satisfaction, possibly a prize, or glory. It is negated by dishonesty and unfairness, by disregard for its order.[58] It is meaningful only when its outcome is uncertain, when chance has a chance.[59] It must take place among equals, and yet it is profoundly "aristocratic" in "discovering" the best.[60] It expresses itself in styled forms and is always linked with our aesthetic sentiments.[61] It is strictly outlined and has a firm structure. It is repetitive in form, yet infinitely variable and unpredictable within its own order. It has rhythm and clear harmony.[62]

After thus circumscribing the nature of play and tracing its reflection in the major languages, Huizinga set himself the task of viewing culture *sub specie ludi*. Part of his discussion delves into the issue of the original relation of play and culture and is heavily based on anthropological material and his knowledge of early Hindu, Greek, and Germanic life. He concluded that play antedates formal culture,[63] but culture is not a fruit of play which gradually separates from the mother plant. Instead, Huizinga preferred the formulation that culture begins *in* play and develops *as* play.[64] It remains embedded in play and unfolds in the forms of play. In a series of chapters Huizinga then traced the detailed relationships of play and cultural forms: play and law, play and war, play and wisdom, play and poetry (which was for him, as for Vol-

---

[56] *V.W.*, V, 8, 35, 37, 117.
[57] *V.W.*, V, 6, 41, 117.
[58] *V.W.*, V, 39.
[59] *V.W.*, V, 38, 108.
[60] *V.W.*, V, 78.
[61] *V.W.*, V, 4–5, 7, 34, 36, 38, 91.
[62] *V.W.*, V, 38, 189.
[63] *V.W.*, V, 4, 28.
[64] *V.W.*, V, 103, 205; see also V, 26, 47, 76.

taire, perhaps the central issue),[65] play forms and art, and the function of imagination as a play of the human mind.[66] He explained numerous types of social action and cultural activities as the products of such forms of play as the contests of skill, the *agon*, the competition within circumscribed rules.[67] In this analysis Huizinga carefully avoided the conclusion that all culture is play,[68] thereby adding greatly to the value of the *Homo Ludens*, but also to its complexity. But neither did he restrict himself to plays, games, and contests as leisure-time activity, the frills of civilization. His focus remained the *ludique* factor of cultural activity, the "sportive" aspect of social behavior.[69] Thus, he sought to discover the penetration of this *ludique* factor into the "earnest" concerns of man, in the life of the state, religion, war, and economic institutions.[70] And so, the initial dichotomy of earnest necessity and play is not reflected in a similar division of culture. Instead, cultural manifestations are seen as fusions, each with its distinctive proportions, of the earnest and the *ludique*. Not only do such proportions vary from phenomenon to phenomenon; they vary within each phenomenon with the course of time. War or poetry or legal procedure may from time to time be more play or less play.[71] And similarly the ages themselves, in their total structure, can be viewed *sub specie ludi*, as Huizinga briefly indicated in a fascinating chapter.[72]

Play, for Huizinga, could enrich the life of a human com-

---

[65] "It is therefore desirable at this point to enquire into the nature of poetic creation. In a sense, this question forms the central theme for a discussion of the relation between play and culture" (*V.W.*, V, 148).

[66] "The imagination always functions as play" (*V.W.*, V, 14). See also *V.W.*, V, 166–76, and for references outside *Homo Ludens* (or the lecture *Over de grensen* . . .), see I, 164, IV, 71, 391.

[67] *V.W.*, V, 74–104, 130.

[68] *V.W.*, V, 23, 245–46.

[69] *V.W.*, V, 11. Huizinga felt self-conscious about forming the adjective *ludique*, but he desperately needed it.

[70] See chaps. 4–6 and 11–12 of *Homo Ludens*; special instances on pp. 18, 21, 32, 207, 243, and also *V.W.*, V, 286, 367 (essays on America).

[71] *V.W.*, V, 14–15.

[72] See chaps. 11–12 of *Homo Ludens* and also *V.W.*, V, 32, 74, 103, 159, 205–6.

munity by developing forms in which men could express their creativity. Huizinga took the major illustrations of play, as such a forming agent of cultural life, from the early phases of Hindu civilization, early Greek civilization, and the early stages in the life of Germanic societies.[73] As indicated above, the *Homo Ludens* largely involved a topical discussion of such themes as play and war, play and ritual, play and law, rather than an analysis of whole cultures under the aspect of play. This made it possible for Huizinga to trace chiefly the enriching quality of play. But he was also conscious of the perils which an excess of play involved for men's creativity. In his great study of Burgundian society he described how play could be an escape, how "play forms" could proliferate to such an extent that they suffocated other creative ways of men.

"Play is not the 'ordinary' or 'real' [*eigenlijk*] life. It involves a 'stepping-out' from that life into a temporary sphere of activity which has its own ends [*strekking*]."[74] If man does not control his play, then play "takes over," so to say, and the play forms hold man captive, just as man's technological apparatus can escape his control. "Play is a category which can devour everything, much as *Stultitia* [Folly], once she had taken form in Erasmus' mind, had to become Queen of the whole world."[75] When the *ludique* factor of life becomes so dominant that it stifles or falsifies man's concerns with the earnest demands and the ethical demands (which always stood outside play for Huizinga), a culture is in peril.[76] When play no longer fulfils a cultural function within the organic context of a whole society, when it exists merely for play's sake, it is no longer a "culturally creative" (*cultuurscheppende*), an enriching force. Of course, even then play may still be highly important in the life of a society by providing an

---

[73] See esp. chap. 3 of *Homo Ludens*.
[74] *V.W.*, V, 35. See also V, 5, 8.
[75] *V.W.*, V, 23. See also, V, 15, 244.
[76] *V.W.*, V, 208; Huizinga even used the words *verval van een beschaving* ("decay of a civilization") in this context.

escape from ordinary life, the dream world which may have become more important to men than the difficult task of maintaining a balance between play and earnest needs.

For Huizinga then, culture must be a well-balanced product of the *ludique* and the earnest. Play was in no sense for him the most valuable component of a culture. "On the other side of everything that passes as play lies all that of deepest value for man; pity and justice, suffering and hope." [77] But, without play, life is not worth living and true culture not possible. Play is the other necessary component of the "good life" which must be thoroughly fused with the "earnest" aspect. Play is an intrinsic part of the style of life. Through play men present their ideals and their interpretations of life.[78] And ultimately a culture as a whole possesses the basic qualities of play, especially since style itself is a "play form." [79] In his biography of Erasmus, Huizinga undertook a loving analysis of the *Praise of Folly*, acclaiming the humanist's insight that "he who is but earnest and reasonable cannot live." [80] Many of the good things in life may stem from folly. And man as "man-at-play," *homo ludens*, fulfils a large and indispensable part of his human role. Twice the Dutch scholar referred to Plato's *Laws*: "What I mean to say is that man is as a toy in the hands of God, and this ability to be a toy is in truth the best in him. Therefore, everyone, man or woman, contrary to ruling opinion, should aspire to this end and spend his life in playing the most beautiful play." [81] Huizinga hesitated; for this conception of play already transcends play. But man's greatest accomplishment, his culture, yet remains within the scope of play: ". . . real culture cannot exist without a certain content

[77] *V.W.*, V, 24; but see also V, 244–46.
[78] *V.W.*, V, 74.
[79] *V.W.*, V, 130, 134, 210, 217, 243 (all *Homo Ludens*), and also II, 445, V, 333.
[80] *Erasmus* (1924), *V.W.*, VI, 68. See also VI, 66–67, 71, 229–31, IV, 492–93 (in connection with H. G. Wells's trust in rational perfectibility). The Erasmus biography has been published in various English editions.
[81] The quoted passage in *V.W.*, V, 244–45; earlier references, pp. 46–47. See also VII, 592. The passage in Plato, *Laws*, Bk. VII, 803, 804.

of play [*spelgehalte*], for culture presupposes a measure of self-limitation and self-discipline, an ability for not confusing its own tendencies with the highest and most ultimate goals, a need to understand that it is enclosed within certain bounds which were voluntarily accepted." [82]

This concept of culture determined Huizinga's concept of history (i.e., knowledge of the past). History itself is a cultural phenomenon and thus shares the universal characteristics of culture as well as the specific qualities of a particular culture. [83] Culture is essentially a form, a structure. History also is a "form." "History is the mental form [*de geestelijke vorm*] by which a culture accounts to itself for its past." [84] As such a mental form, history is more inclusive than the term "scholarship" implies, for it leaves the possibility that certain societies account for their past in non-scholarly forms. The modern form of history, however, is scholarship and not mythology, or that adulteration of history, the belletristic *vie romancée*, "perfumed history." [85] Like theology, literature, and the natural sciences, history was for Huizinga a legitimate knowledge of the world. [86] Like all modern knowledge it must be "critical," resting on an undeviating commitment to the most honest and sober cognizance of things. More Huizinga did not want to say; for history was, strictly speaking, not a science but the most inexact of all forms of scholarship. [87] Yet with all its inexactness, its inevitable subjective components, and its tenuous method, history is indispensable to culture. "History

---

[82] *V.W.*, V, 244.

[83] *V.W.*, VII, 40, 98, 100.

[84] *V.W.*, VII, 102 ("Over een definite van het begrip geschiedenis"), which has been translated by D. R. Cousin as "A Definition of the Concept of History" in *Philosophy and History: Essays Presented to Ernst Cassirer*, ed. R. Klibansky (Oxford: Clarendon, 1936), pp. 1–10. Cousin translated: " . . . the intellectual form in which a civilization accounts . . ."; unfortunately the Dutch words *geestelijk* and *cultuur* have connotations other than *intellectual* and *civilization*. See also *V.W.*, VII, 125–26, 137, 162, 183, 185.

[85] *V.W.*, VII, 25, 57, 68, 158.

[86] *V.W.*, VII, 10, 41, 99, 164, 167.

[87] *V.W.*, VII, 182–85.

may at times seem less than scholarship because such a narrow range is left for its strict intellectual purity. But it is more than scholarship because it satisfies needs which transcend the sphere of a specific intellectual interest."[88] Since culture is a striving, a teleological process, self-orientation is a constant function. The "accounting for the past," that is, historical knowledge, fulfils a vital role in this act of orientation. "The life of a nation is history, as the life of the single individual is history. At each moment of living it has forms and meanings, significance and direction taken from that which has gone before. Whoever imagines himself cut off from memory of origin, development, and destiny, stands baffled before life."[89] In its contribution to self-understanding, history partakes of the teleological quality of culture.[90] The ideals by which a culture moves into the future are in part the "conceptions of excellence which man projects into the past."[91] Thus history, as the conception of the past, influences history, as the course of events. Among the images guiding man, the image of the past (het historiebeeld) plays its vital role in molding a culture.[92] Thus history is a cultural form and fulfils a function in culture.

But not only is history (and we are still speaking exclusively of the product of knowledge called history) a form and function of culture, it also understands that past in terms of form and function.[93] Huizinga thought historical epistemology a complex process interlinking the historian's search for knowl-

---

[88] V.W., VII, 105.

[89] V.W., VII, 280.

[90] V.W., VII, 53, 101, 138, 329; history has a teleological direction (finaal gericht) but is not definitive.

[91] V.W., IV, 414, quoted from one of his most fascinating articles, "Over historische levensidealen," which Huizinga gave as his inaugural lecture at Leiden in 1915 (included in Men and Ideas). See also V.W., IV, 411, 431, V, 392, VII, 58, 72–73, 102–3, 189.

[92] See the article "Natuurbeeld en historiebeeld in de achttiende eeuw" (1933), V.W., IV, 341–59, in which he analyzed the relative and the changing importance of these two images in the life of a culture.

[93] V.W., VII, 75–78, 99, 131, 185; also IV, 105–6, 277, 394, V, 418, 481–82.

edge of past realities and his desire to interpret them. "History presents the meaning which the past possesses for us. Implicit in the act of interpreting is the function of giving form. To understand a part of the past in the mirror of his own civilization, the historian must always and everywhere try to perceive the past's form and function. History always speaks in terms of form and function." [94] Huizinga's intense desire for visually concrete and image-like knowledge of the past is reminiscent of Burckhardt. Like the great Swiss, this Dutchman wanted to "see" the past, even if it was only a vague seeing "by the moonlight of memory." [95] His epistemological master-word was *verbeelden*, to take account of a datum of the past by forming an image of it. Ideally, therefore, the historian views historical tableaux, "colored with graphic quality [*aanschouwlijkheid*] and irradiated with visionary suggestiveness," [96] by a gradual process made up of clear questioning, vague presentiments (*Ahnen*),[97] simultaneous analysis and synthesis, and the arranging and co-ordinating of accumulated data.[98] But this process is also the activity by which the historian interprets the significance of the particular segment of the past viewed. His mind holds "forms" of an earlier life (i.e., the forms in which a culture expressed itself) which are but the external signs of the "functions" which these "forms" fulfilled in their respective societies. Meaning comes to the historian as he perceives forms (which had a function) in relation to other

---

[94] *V.W.*, VII, 75.

[95] *V.W.*, VII, 599 (also VII, 25) for the quotation. See *V.W.*, VII, 11–27, and IV, 124–25, 472, for his thirst for *Anschauung*; interesting in addition is his remark that "thinking by visual images" (*denken in gezichtsvoorstellingen*) is one of the oldest and most persistent characteristics of the Dutch ("De betekenis van 1813 voor Nederland's geestelijke beschaving" [1913], *V.W.*, II, 532).

[96] *V.W.*, VII, 76, and also VII, 16.

[97] Huizinga greatly liked Wilhelm von Humboldt's notion of *ein Ahnen* (*V.W.*, VII, 13).

[98] *V.W.*, VII, 17–27, 30, 43, 70, 146, 182–85. I have tried to elaborate this complicated process of *verbeelden* in an unpublished dissertation, "The Thought of Johan Huizinga on the Nature of History" (University of Chicago, 1957).

forms (and thus in relation to other functions). "Each work of history constructs connections, designs forms, by which past realities can be understood. History creates the notion of understanding through the meaningful arrangement of data primarily, and only in a limited sense, through the discovery of strict causality."[99] Huizinga always clung to this "inexact method," a mixture of critical reflection and subjective (but disciplined) viewing and construction whereby the historian trained his visual ability to the point where with his mind's eye he could penetrate historical landscapes and see the sun shine on its details.[100] It did not distress him that history was not a science. At least it was the form of knowledge closest to life and to death. And it sufficed that the historian live, like his modest muse, "quietly and seriously gathering flowers from the asphodel meadows in the land of shadows."[101]

The ultimate object of the cultural historian is a culture as a whole, the broadest historical object. His knowledge consists in the perception of cultural forms and functions. Huizinga gave considerable thought to making this general proposition meaningful by elucidating its details. What did he mean by assigning the whole of culture as the historian's object? He did not hold that cultural historians, to earn their title, must describe entire epochs of cultural life. Even though he had great respect for a historian like Burckhardt who set himself such a task, Huizinga was dismayed by the always present danger of hypostatizing notions such as baroque or Renaissance which, by their very vagueness, might become mere myths.[102] But while it was not necessary for the cultural his-

---

[99] *V.W.*, VII, 73, and also VII, 137.

[100] *V.W.*, VII, 24.

[101] *V.W.*, VII, 157.

[102] *V.W.*, IV, 232, 269, 341, VII, 33, 81. He thought Burckhardt the wisest man of the nineteenth century and admired his sensitive probing of cultural complexities; each chapter of the Renaissance book was for Huizinga an ideal attempt at writing cultural history. But Huizinga fought long (and perhaps more with Burckhardt epigones than directly with the great historian) over the weakness of the Renaissance as a concept of a period (see esp. "Het probleem der Renaissance" [1920], *V.W.*, IV, 231–75, and "Renaissance en realisme"

torian to write the history of an entire culture, it was important that every worker in cultural history keep his eye trained on the fact that "culture exists only as a whole." [103] The specific subject of investigation must ever be seen in relation to the whole of a culture. The historian's basic question should always be concerned with the place and function of the separate subject in the broader cultural context. Otherwise cultural history deteriorates into the compilation of curiosa, or becomes indistinguishable from the subject matter of specialized disciplines like folklore, art history, or antiquities. The question itself may be small — when did men begin to eat with forks? how did dueling disappear from English life? — and yet be a legitimate question for the cultural historian who sees his subject matter as a part of the whole.[104] It may be the history of books, of inns, of roads, of hats, or dogs, but it is cultural history only when seen and treated as a cultural form and function.[105] Cultural history thus could be called the historical study of structures, or cultural morphology. And for as long as the historian was insufficiently prepared to determine the structures of the large entities, the whole cultures, Huizinga stressed the importance of "specialized morphology" (bijzondere vormenleer).[106]

The use of the concept "cultural morphology" raises a dif-

[1926], V.W., IV, 276–97 — both articles are included in Men and Ideas; and see also V.W., III, 389–402). This was not so much the "revolt of the medievalist" as a part of his general uneasiness about designating periods with descriptive terms; he later regretted the colorful and suggestive title Herfsttij de Middeleeuwen ("the autumnal season of the Middle Ages"). Since he recognized the need for period names, he preferred those like quattrocento, Elizabethan age. For him Spengler and Lamprecht provided examples of the danger of mythologizing history and culture, to which was added, in Lamprecht, the error of overextending vague psychological terms in the naming of cultural periods.

[103] V.W., VII, 45, 49, 58, 112.

[104] V.W., VII, 45.

[105] V.W., VII, 84; see also, IV, 419.

[106] V.W., VII, 80–84. I have always wondered that Huizinga did not recollect at this point his own criticism of any historical labor which sought to justify itself as mere preparatory work (voorarbeid) for the broader task.

ferent question. What distinguishes cultural history from such a science as sociology? Huizinga resorted to the distinction that "cultural history considers phenomena in their own striking significance [within a larger cultural context], while for sociology they are nothing but paradigms. The cultural historian has only in a remote sense the intention to deduce generally valid rules for society from the phenomena." [107] "For cultural history . . . the forms of the past are expressions of a spirit [*geest*], which it seeks to understand, but always by viewing them as a part of the stream of events. Cultural history turns to its objects, focuses its attention on them, but continually returns from these objects themselves to the world in which they had their place." [108] The cultural forms have interest for the historian only in so far as they "are viewed as scenes of the great world drama itself." [109] Historical work maintains its contact with its genetic, its developmental reality.

The forms seen by the cultural historian are to a greater degree dependent upon the individual historian than are the more readily "given" forms of the political or the economic historian.[110] Because its object is not so definite as a specific institution, a war, or a parliament, "cultural history is to such a high degree the product of the free spirit" [111] of its practi-

---

[107] *V.W.*, VII, 76; see also VII, 82.

[108] *V.W.*, VII, 83, and see also I, 240, II, 525, III, 485, IV, 298, VI, 398, 402, VII, 135, 158. Huizinga has "suffered" considerably at the hands of Carlo Antoni, whose book *Dalla storicismo alla sociologia* contains a chapter on the Dutch historian. I am quoting this work from Hayden V. White's translation, *From History to Sociology*, pp. 185–206. However valuable I find this book in many respects, I consider it full of subtle untruth in its chapters on Huizinga and Wölfflin particularly. Even the inclusion of Huizinga in a treatise of this nature bothers me. In view of Antoni's reputation and influence it would be desirable to write a careful commentary on his Huizinga chapter, but this is beyond the present scope. One should place the above references against Antoni's general thesis and such statements as: Huizinga "often spoke of his research as sociological investigation" (p. 187), an assertion for which I can find no evidence.

[109] *V.W.*, VII, 83; see also VII, 119, 144.

[110] *V.W.*, VII, 76.

[111] *V.W.*, VII, 46.

tioners. Its quality depends upon the quality of the historian's initial question and the sensitivity of his mind.[112] Huizinga himself had a predilection for the questions which lead to a clearer vision of past "forms of life, forms of creation, and forms of thought" (*levensvormen, scheppingsvormen, en denkvormen*).[113] Perhaps his most striking idea was to write the cultural history of the seven deadly sins. "If someone could write the history of vanity, he would command over half of cultural history. Who will give us the history of pride in the seventeenth century? The seven deadly sins are seven chapters of cultural history which await their treatment."[114] This fascinating subject demanded a more systematic treatment of a single theme than Huizinga thought characteristic of himself. He spoke of himself as "a spiritual vagabond."[115] His work, in his opinion, had "never been more than a slow drifting over the gardens of the spirit, touching on a blossom here and there, then moving on immediately."[116] He unsystematically found sources for his historical preoccupation in such cultural forms and functions as honor, service, loyalty, conceptions of death and love, the visual and the literary presentation of the world.[117] His object was to treat of "forms of thought," "forms

[112] *V.W.*, VII, 37–46.
[113] *V.W.*, VII, 46, 492; see also IV, 394.
[114] *V.W.*, VII, 83–84.
[115] *V.W.*, VII, 442.
[116] *V.W.*, I, 41; this is taken from Huizinga's charming autobiographical sketch, written late in life, "Mijn weg tot de historie." I do not think that Huizinga was merely modest when he made this remark, but rather that he touched upon a characteristic aspect of his work. Hoselitz (in his introduction to *Men and Ideas*, p. 14) correctly states: "Huizinga's reputation as an artist in the history of culture is based primarily on his larger works, most notably on the *Waning of the Middle Ages*. But his full skill and versatility become even more apparent in his shorter essays. . . . they provide, in their totality, the best insight into his genius." Huizinga, indeed, looks "naked" when seen only as the author of the famous books; he put much thought and ability into his vast array of essays.
[117] See the program he discusses in *V.W.*, VII, 83. A striking set of articles and lectures given by Huizinga in various forms are those in which he discussed Burgundy and later the Netherlands as the "middleman" among France, England, and Germany, a role which to him surely was a form of "national

of love," "forms of conduct," "forms of life" — and important forms are always expressions of play. And in one masterwork he viewed a society through its sentiments, its fears, its play, and its elaborate dreams of a better world.

The Waning of the Middle Ages resulted from Huizinga's preoccupation with the art of Van Eijck.[118] Was this the art of a culture which had run its course, or did it signify the beginning of a new age? Why are moderns still stirred by these paintings but not by the literature of the Burgundian world? And for the cultural historian who noted a growing inclination on the part of a modern public to build conceptions of past ages on impressions of the artistic remains,[119] there arose the interesting question whether the reconstruction of a culture from its pictorial remains might not distort former realities. It is clear from Huizinga's autobiographical remarks that he undertook the study of Burgundian culture as a correction to the opinions, voiced during the first decade of the twentieth century, that this period (especially when viewed through its art) was the beginning of a northern Renaissance.[120] The understanding of Van Eijck's art, and its usefulness as a cultural barometer, depended upon a cor-

---

service"; see, for example, "Die Mittlerstellung der Niederlande zwischen West- und Mitteleuropa" (1933), *V.W.*, II, 284–303; "How Holland Became a Nation . . . " (1924), *V.W.*, II, 266–83; "Der Einfluss Deutschland's in der Geschichte der niederländischen Kultur" (1926), *V.W.*, II, 304–31; "L'état bourguignon: ses rapports avec la France et les origines d'une nationalité néerlandaise" (1930) *V.W.*, II, 161–215; "Burgund, eine Krise des romanisch-germanischen Verhältnisses" (1933), *V.W.*, II, 238–65.

[118] *V.W.*, I, 38–39 (account in the autobiographical sketch), III, 4 (foreword to *Herfsttij*); the treatise which preceded the book was "De kunst der van Eijcks in het leven van hun tijd" (1916), *V.W.*, III, 436–82. For parallel concerns with the interrelation of art and the temper of a time see "Nederland's beschaving in de zeventiende eeuw" (final form, 1941), *V.W.*, II, 412–507 (see esp. pp. 489, 501); and IV, 22–25, 33, 39, 43, 398–403.

[119] *V.W.*, II, 436–37, IV, 195–96; this, of course, has nothing to do with his idea that the historian sees the past in visual impressions.

[120] *V.W.*, I, 39; see also III, 342, and the article on the Van Eijcks.

rect grasp of its place and function within the culture of which it was a part.

The book which Huizinga wove around these questions appears complex and has bewildered its admiring critics.[121] To some it is not even a work of cultural history but rather the observations of an ethnologist with sociological aspirations and misunderstandings.[122] In addition to being unnecessarily confused, it is allegedly unfocused, since it neglects the political and socioeconomic institutions of the period. And all too often, the book is seen primarily as a counterargument to Burckhardt's work on the Renaissance. But it is none of these things when seen in the context of Huizinga's conception of culture and cultural history.

Ideally, culture was a balance of man's material and spiritual concerns, a harmonious relation between the earnest preoccupations necessary for sustaining physical existence and the non-utilitarian occupations and creative functions.[123] When a historian has distinguished and analyzed a given material base of life for a certain society (i.e., its state, political institutions, economic forms, modes of warfare, and social structure), the question remains whether the ideas and conceptions held by the men of this society about life, their ideals, dreams, and sentiments, their varied forms of expression, reflect this material base. Is there a clear congruence between both realms of life, and, if not, what relation exists? In the essays on America (on which Huizinga worked at the same time), and in his later reflections upon the dilemma of modern culture, Huizinga discerned the imbalance of a predominantly "material" life. In such cases the pursuit of material interests clashed with the inherited spiritual conception of life and was likely to displace it. As a medievalist Huizinga

---

[121] See especially the essay by P. L. Ward, "Huizinga's Approach to the Middle Ages," in *Teachers of History*, ed. H. Stuart Hughes (Ithaca: Cornell University Press, 1954), pp. 168–95.

[122] See Antoni, *From History to Sociology, passim*, and esp. p. 193.

[123] *V.W.*, VII, 490.

was especially impressed by the discrepancy between medieval man's conception of his life as a high vision of beauty and excellence and his apparent lack of concern for integrating his material activities into this vision. Huizinga saw men preoccupied with a "dream of life" which bore little resemblance to the harsh realities.[124] The ideals of life, had, in many ways, lost contact with its realities, or they were deceptively used to hide reality. "The tension between the forms of life [levensvorm] and reality has become extraordinarily strong; the light is false and painful to the eye."[125] How could such a cultural phenomenon be explained?

Huizinga suggests in his second chapter that men have three basic reactions to a surrounding reality which they wish better and more beautiful.[126] They can, as most societies have done at some stage, reject (verzaken) the world and hope for a more beautiful life beyond this terrestrial one. Second, they can devote their existence to the constant improvement and beautification of this life; in other words, they can hope for progress, a solution impossible for medieval men who were convinced of the insurmountable obstacle of human sinfulness. "The third path to a more beautiful life is that of the dream. It is the easiest path, but also the one which leaves the goal as unattainable as before. If earthly reality is so hopelessly miserable, and the renunciation of the world so difficult, let us color life with a beautiful appearance, let us live away in the dreamland of bright fancy, let us temper reality with the ecstasies of the ideal."[127] Every age has to some extent incorporated in its fancy the ideal themes of the great heroes of yesteryear, the wise men with good counsel, the peace and comfort of a bucolic life. But in this Burgundian age the tension between reality and dream reached immense proportions and seemed to Huizinga the dominant aspect of a cultural period.

---

[124] V.W., III, 20–21, 112, 119, 123, 127, 144, 152, 161, 165, 167, 213, 266, 287, 295, 438.
[125] V.W., III, 43.
[126] V.W., III, 40–45, 134.
[127] V.W., III, 41.

For the elaboration of this theme, the bulk of the book traces the multifaceted expressions of men's dream. But it is erroneous to think that realities are not considered by Huizinga. The first chapter speaks of "life's harsh and violent tenor" and sets the background for the study. The middle chapter on Death's macabre intrusion into the world of the dream serves as another reminder of the inescapable realities. And even though these realities are rarely described thereafter, they make their "compresence" felt at every moment. The initial tension between reality and dream which had been Huizinga's point of departure, persists throughout the entire book.[128] The play forms of life are not seen in rarified isolation but always in the specific manner in which they transform, envelop, and even oppress the real world. Huizinga neither argued in his theoretical treatises that culture was altogether the creation of *homo ludens* nor did he seek to exemplify in this book a culture which was pure play. Cultural history *sub specie ludi* studies play in relation to other realities which, by the very nature of that relationship, are always present, even when they are not explicitly mentioned.

Huizinga gave structure to his total view of this particular culture of fifteenth-century Burgundy and northern France through several related subviews. In one of these, he analyzed and described the idealized style of knighthood, and especially its social function, its conception of love, and its relation to nature. This dream of a noble and idyllic life is counterbalanced by a powerful chapter on the macabre awareness that Death pitilessly interrupts the play. This segment is followed by the religious conceptions which emphasize the visual, the symbolic, and the allegorical nature of such "thought forms." To this Huizinga added the imagery of daily life and of an art which served a decorative function. The main part of the concluding section centers on the rela-

---

[128] Again it seems to me that Huizinga's basic point is not the separation of reality and dream (as Antoni seems to imply) but the tensions; see *V.W.*, III, 112, 119, 123, 127, 152, 161, 165, 266, 287–304, and also III, 438, 449, 529.

tion of image to word, and involves a comparison of plastic and verbal expression. At first these chapters seem to be a strange addendum to the book. Huizinga returned here to the starting point of his investigation: the relative value of art and literature as expressive forms through which men reveal their values, sentiments, and views of life. He concluded there the argument which had come to be central to the book: in what sense did the forms in which men expressed their conception of life reflect both the tension between reality and dream and the end phase of a culture, a dead end in which the old forms had become inadequate? This last argument contains the dynamic vector in a book which might otherwise appear to be a static picture of a static society.

Huizinga presented this view of culture through an analysis of the expressive forms employed by the late medieval men themselves.[129] This meant, on the one hand, that he did not describe events, institutions, and the like; and, on the other hand, he was restricted to the expressive layer of society which left a record of its thoughts, ideals, and sentiments. In vital respects Huizinga described a "courtly culture" the forms of which, however, pervade the hierarchically ordered society.[130] The basic conception of aristocratic life was expressed in the ideal of knighthood and its concomitant feature of courtly love. The realities of warfare and economic life, especially in the heavily urbanized Flanders and Brabant, should have made this medieval institution obsolete. Yet it flourished in this whole Burgundian realm, a state created by an act of knightly folly.[131] Huizinga saw the ultimate reason for the longevity of knighthood not in any accident or perversity but in its high ideals. "Chivalry would never have been the cen-

---

[129] *V.W.*, III, 4, 5, 93, 108, 111, 130, 134, 137, 146, 162, 219, 249, 307, 390, 401–2, and also III, 444, 524.

[130] *V.W.*, III, 66–67, 112, 327, IV, 422–23.

[131] In 1363 King John of France gave the Duchy of Burgundy to his son Philip in reward for his courageous loyalty during the battle of Poitiers, thereby creating a power which, in alliance with England, almost ruined France and her dynasty.

turies' ideal of life if it had not contained high values for the development of society, if it had not been necessary ethically, socially, and aesthetically. The strength of this ideal had rested in its beautiful excesses. It seems as if the passionate and ferocious spirit of the Middle Ages could only be guided by placing the ideal far too high; the church acted thus, thus also acted the chivalric idea." [132] This society saw in the knight its pillar and protector. His code of honor, personal loyalty, and devotion to service had met no rival formulation in any other social ideal. And, as a matter of fact, "all higher forms of the burgher life of modern times rest on an imitation of those aristocratic forms of life." [133] But Huizinga knew that a cultural ideal which demanded too many virtues was likely to result in a profound disharmony between reality and the adopted forms of life.[134] As a consequence, knighthood, in its last phase, became illusion and sheer play.[135] In the first half of the book Huizinga concentrated upon the description of this play, its rules, and its forms. From these pages emerges the great panorama of late chivalry: the tournament, the conduct on the battlefield where others no longer adhered to a knightly mode of warfare, the vows to go on crusades about which no one in Europe cared, the excessive stylization of love, the imitation of old heroes whose examples were no longer relevant, the search for a bucolic and pastoral adornment of life by people who were tired of the artifices of court life, the search for maidens to be rescued when even pilgrimages were standing invitations for amorous adventures, and the instituting of 'the Golden Fleece and the hundred-fold multiplication of chivalric orders to include solid burghers.

---

[132] V.W., III, 127.

[133] This was a matter of great importance to Huizinga, who in later years lamented the decline of such values as honor, loyalty, and service. He attributed much of the weakness of modern society to neglect of such values. It is good to remember, in this context, that his conception of culture included the ideal of service as a necessary condition.

[134] V.W., III, 127.

[135] V.W., III, 78, 91, 95–96, 98, 104, 123, 157, and also III, 524.

And occasionally there appear even brief quotations in which a writer betrays the ironic smile behind the mask — the sign that at least some of the players understood the unreality of the play. On the whole, Huizinga presented in the first major section of the book a carefully drawn tableau of the intensive activities of an entire class of men and women who sought in play a grandiose ornamentation and beautification of life.

In the second half of the book Huizinga studied above all the religious forms of life and through them focused even more clearly on the central theme. He portrayed a daily life deeply pervaded by religious modes of thought. While Huizinga again delved into the specific description of forms of thought and forms of action, he employed the analysis of religious life to elaborate the underlying theme of the whole work more clearly: the image-like quality of all late medieval thinking and dreaming. The chivalric life found expression in actions and descriptions of high symbolic content and eminently visual concreteness. Huizinga was struck even more by the intense effort of this society to sanctify every part of life (*das Heiligen aller Lebensbeziehungen* — the phrase is Burckhardt's) [136] and to do so by means of imagery (*ver-beelden*). "One feels an unrestrained need to form images of everything sacred, to endow each conception of a religious sort with a well-rounded form, so that it stands out in the mind as a sharply impressed etching." [137] Consequently the mental life and functions became congested with images which multiplied almost mechanically. And since the images were derived from the objects and actions of daily life, the concrete world pervaded religion as much as, if not more than, religion pervaded the world. [138] The concrete visualization of religious events, say, the Passion of the Holy Mother, coupled with the

---

[136] *V.W.*, III, 180; the passage is taken from Burckhardt, *Weltgeschichtliche Betrachtungen* (Bern: Hallwag, 1941), p. 167.

[137] *V.W.*, III, 180, and also 245–52.

[138] See for example *V.W.*, III, 186–98, 205, 210.

desire to make them personally real through an act of imitation, contributed enormously to the emotional quality of religion. In a fascinating chapter Huizinga analyzed the mystics' great struggle to climb out of this necropolis of forms and images to the image-less reality of the Godhead, only to become hopelessly entangled again in the imagery of their visions.[139] Men found no escape, at this time, from the symbolic tradition built over centuries.

In the course of development of the symbolic form of thought and expression lay Huizinga's deepest explanation of this culture. Symbolism had been the architect of the Middle Ages. "Medieval men never forgot that all things would be absurd if their meaning were exhausted in their immediate function and in their phenomenal forms, that all things reach into a world beyond this with a part of themselves."[140] And the more man related all of his experience to a divine reality, the more support the symbolic attitude gained. "When we see all things in God and refer all things to him, we read in common matters superior expressions of meaning."[141] "Roses, white and red, blossom among thorns. The medieval mind immediately sees symbolic meaning: maidens and martyrs shining in their glory among their persecutors."[142] Things, thoughts, and actions found their place in hierarchical relationships and were interlinked by multiple bonds of meaning. "Thus resulted that great and noble imagery of the world as one great symbolic unity, a cathedral of ideas, the richest rhythmic and polyphonic expression of the mind."[143]

But symbolism, especially if it is allegorical, has the imminent danger of dissolving thought into imagery. Thought cannot cut its bond to the image, and the image is limited by

---

[139] *V.W.*, III, 240–44, 261–78.
[140] *V.W.*, III, 246, and also III, 180.
[141] *V.W.*, III, 246 (Huizinga took this quotation from William James, *Varieties of Religious Experience* [London, 1903], p. 475).
[142] *V.W.*, III, 248.
[143] *V.W.*, III, 247.

its tie to the thought.[144] Once the image is accepted as the basic instrument for understanding the world, it "clings to thought like a rankling weed."[145] Symbolic and allegorical thinking so easily deteriorates into a mechanical process.[146] If the twelve months are the twelve apostles, and the four seasons the four evangelists, then the whole year must be Christ. The mystic Suso could not eat an apple without cutting it into four parts; one of which was eaten in memory of the fact that the mother Mary lovingly gave her son an apple; the other three are consumed in the name of the Trinity. He emptied his cup in five drafts in memory of the fact that our Lord had five wounds, "but since blood and water flowed from Christ's side, he drank the last draft twice."[147] Symbolism was fading through overuse in all realms of life; its vitality escaped, and its forms began to petrify:[148] ". . . it was a time of over-ripeness and withering. Thought had become too dependent on images; the visual ability, so germane to the late Middle Ages, had won the upper hand. All potentiality of thought had become plastic and pictorial. The conception of the world had attained the tranquility of a cathedral in the moonlight in which thought could go to sleep."[149] Perhaps it is strange to express it thus; but the element of movement in the tragic drama of this late medieval Burgundian world (and in consequence the "developmental" factor of this book) is to be found in Huizinga's vision of men caught in this labyrinth of images, forced to use a form of play which is daily losing its meaning, finding it less and less possible to cut their way through to living realities.

---

[144] *V.W.*, III, 385, and esp. 461, but also III, 247, 255, 293, 296, VII, 403–9 (the latter reference in relation to the modern situation).

[145] *V.W.*, III, 252, and also III, 385.

[146] *V.W.*, III, 183, 198, 205.

[147] *V.W.*, III, 181.

[148] *V.W.*, III, 245–60 (esp. 252), 312, 330–31, 343.

[149] *V.W.*, III, 260. See also the introduction to the *Herfsttij*: "The main content of these pages is the luxuriant growth of old and compelling forms of thought over the living kernel of thought, the desiccation and paralysis of a rich culture."

There remains Huizinga's initial question, Why do the paintings of the period speak to us while the words have lost their interest? The Burgundian culture had two basic ways for expressing and communicating its life: the word and the picture. Since so much of the content which these art forms were to express consisted of images, symbols, and visions, it was the artist's task to give the appropriate image-like form to such content. When a late medieval writer addressed himself to this task he became the victim of rankling symbolism; one image led him to the next, and then to an additional labor of adornment by another little image here and there, with nothing to stop him in his vagarious act of embroidery.[150] Only where the artist gave up the attempt to beautify life by incessant adornment, where he resorted to direct reporting of realities, where he even expressed his understanding of make-believe (i.e., in satire and the comical), there the literature of the age seemed readable to Huizinga.[151] The painter profited (though not in the eyes of his contemporaries who still saw meaning in the written word) from the spatial limitations of his canvas and the prescribed content of his subject matter. The frame became an insurmountable barrier for the painter, who, like the writer, saw his objective in the careful rendition of visual detail. Since most of the paintings which survived have a religious content, we know chiefly the art in which the artist's freely imaginative inclinations were restrained by the traditional mode of representing holy objects and events.[152] Bound to the frame and the moderately variable nature of his themes, the painter was protected from the writer's temptation to sacrifice the artistic unity to the interminable decorative "afterplay on hackneyed themes."[153] The

---

[150] *V.W.*, III, 343, 349, 366, and also III, 472 (Van Eijck).

[151] *V.W.*, III, 366–70, 371–83, and also III, 473–75 (Van Eijck).

[152] *V.W.*, III, 349, 353, 363, and also III, 451–55 (Van Eijck). Huizinga made a special point of noting that the artistic attempts which were not tied to a traditional conception of the subject resulted in ludicrous products (see *V.W.*, III, 385).

[153] *V.W.*, III, 344.

ever-so-refined decorative detail of Van Eijck is absorbed in the totality and retains its decorative character better than the descriptive detail of the poet, who, moreover, must arrange these sequentially while the painter can make them part of one view.[154]

And finally, the epoch was predominantly visual. "In periods where the creation of beauty limits itself to the mere description and expression of a body of thought already established and thought over, the fine arts have a deeper value than literature. . . . If the painter does nothing but render an external object simply in color and line, he yet places behind this purely formal reproduction an unexpressed and inexpressible remainder. But if the poet aims no higher than to express in words a visible or already familiar [*doordachte*] reality, then he exhausts in his words the whole treasure of the ineffable."[155] For men within this culture the poet's words invoked associations of great meaning because the thought expressed was still an integral part of the life shared by reader and writer. Once that thought no longer stirred men, the literature of the age had no future. "The painter of the same epoch and of the same mentality as the poet will have nothing to fear from time. For the inexpressible which he has put into his work will be as fresh as on the first day."[156] The painter could, in part at least, rise beyond the limitation of his culture. The writer was caught in the nets of his aging culture. Symbolism was played out; the habit of thinking in images forced thought to move within the old familiar grounds. Huizinga had to his own satisfaction explained his initial query. There was indeed great danger in interpreting an age by relying primarily on its pictorial remains. The deepest concerns and the truest attitudes of the Burgundian man could not be fathomed from a mere study of art. What looked to the historically untrained like a new departure in the realm of paint-

---

[154] *V.W.*, III, 476 (Van Eijck).
[155] *V.W.*, III, 343.
[156] *V.W.*, III, 344.

ing, the beginning of a northern Renaissance, was in reality still an integral part of a waning of the Middle Ages. The search in answer to his query had led Huizinga into a fascinating study of the characteristic "forms of life, forms of creation, and forms of thought" produced by a dying civilization.

Unlike his precursor Lamprecht, Johan Huizinga was the first to admit that he had not found the one and only approach to cultural history. He amply praised predecessors whom he admired: Viollet-le-Duc, Leslie Stephen, and, above all, Jacob Burckhardt.[157] Nor did he claim that his preferred mode of studying a culture by focusing on the function of play, of sentiments, of man's dreams, and supra-logical attitudes led to complete understanding. Henri Pirenne, whom Huizinga greatly admired, took another way of contributing to the historical understanding of culture and centered his questions on aspects which Huizinga usually neglected.[158] Huizinga thought it characteristic of his countrymen that they lacked the German inclination to build systems.[159] Surely he himself, with his irrepressible "yes, . . . but" attitude, laid no claims to systematic treatment of something as complex as culture.[160] But he was part of a revolt, which had started long before him, against the overrating of rationality, of man's utilitarian interests, and of material and technological progress. Like all great cultural historians, he wished to perceive past human life in all its richness and diversity and yet make it intellectually comprehensible. He found one way of reaching this aim by revealing man as a free creator and imaginative player with forms, a creature touched by magnificent folly. Culture itself, and the struggle for its creation and preservation, was an extraordinarily serious matter for Huizinga. But his earnestness was moderated by his insight that play, and therefore also

---

[157] For instance *V.W.*, VII, 77. There are many laudatory references, especially to Burckhardt (see *V.W.*, Vol. IX, *Register van persoonsnamen*).

[158] *V.W.*, VI, 501–7 ("Henri Pirenne, Verviers 1862–Ukkel 1935"), and VII, 71.

[159] *V.W.*, II, 325, VIII, 462.

[160] *V.W.*, I, 39–40, VII, 6, 15, 19, 113, 123, 169, 172.

culture, was serious without ceasing to be play. And as a historian he knew that the long view of man, which is history, serves best for seeing man in his true proportions. "For what is better for man than to see the confines of his narrow personality in the perspective of time and space, than to feel himself bound to all that preceded and shall come? What is more wholesome than to perceive his imperfection and his eternal aspirations, the limitations of all human endeavor . . .?"[161]

---

[161] *V.W.*, VII, 154; see also VII, 217.

6 : *Ortega y Gasset*
1883 - 1955

Our thinking about history and the development of culture has been enriched by suggestions more often from the non-historian than from the historians themselves. Augustine gave the basic framework of interpretation for the historians of the Christian centuries. And an encyclopedic mind like Voltaire's intervened with new conceptions of historical reality when those older foundations of providential history crumbled. Hegel's idealism fructified historical thought during the nineteenth century even through the opposition he evoked. Modern historiography has been profoundly modified by the interpretative schemes of Comte, Marx, and Dilthey, the critique of Nietzsche, and the evolutionary ideas of Darwin. And in the current century, historians must cope with the themes and theories suggested by a sociologist like Max Weber, a theologian like Troeltsch, philosophers like Bergson, Croce, or Whitehead, and psychologists like Freud and Jung. And often the modern historian looks to the social scientists for fresh knowledge which might deepen his own understanding of man.

The most problematic relation has been that of historian and philosopher. They oppose each other even in their basic questions: "What was this man and this society like?" "What, in general, is Man and Society?" Where the one strives for a complete view of man within the cosmos, the other pursues the ineffable specificity of the "unique." The urge of the one to transcend time and appearances by speculation runs counter to the other's desire to recapture, even if only by the moonlight of memory, the moment in its elusive quality. And yet, philosopher and historian need one another. Their thought is interlinked and complementary, though marked by high tension.

When a philosopher takes history as seriously as did Ortega y Gasset, his philosophy should be of special interest to the historian.[1] "I hope that in our age of curiosity about the eternal and invariable which is philosophy and the curiosity about the inconstant and changing which is history may come together and embrace."[2] Ortega was often harsh with historians. Although it would be feasible to construct Ortega's view of western history by compiling his numerous observations on our past, strewn through his numerous writings,[3] Ortega cannot be considered a historian. He never steeped himself in the detailed labors of historical research. He borrowed from the works of great historians and let them speak on historical matters. He wrote no cultural history and is an outsider among the cultural historians of this study. The presentation of his thought, therefore, differs from that pursued in the previous five chapters. While the others fused theory and practice of cultural history, Ortega presented chiefly a philosophical framework and the theoretical tools for historians of culture. He has no claim as a pioneer in this field, but he continued in his theoretical reflections a certain line of development central to this book. For, like the five previous

---

[1] In contrast to the preceding essays, this one was not worked from the original texts but merely from translations. It is therefore plagued by all the difficulties which beset work based on translation. The basic text employed in this study has been the German edition for which Ortega himself selected his writings: José Ortega y Gasset, *Gesammelte Werke* (hereafter cited as *G.W.*). It was based on the incomplete Spanish *Obras completas* published by the Revista de Occidente in Madrid off and on since 1946.

[2] *What Is Philosophy?* p. 27 (hereafter cited as *W.I.P.*).

[3] If the mere elaboration of Ortega's theories could be shortened more than I have been able to do, interesting historical analyses could be extrapolated from the following of his writings (all in *G.W.*): Notas del vago estio; Meditación del Escorial; Hegel y América; Intimidades; España invertebrada; El ocaso de las revoluciones; Las Atlántidas; Etica de los griegos; Mirabeau o el político; La rebelión de las masas; En cuanto al pacifismo; En torno a Galileo; Vives; Epílogo al libro "De Francesca a Beatrice"; Del Imperio romano; A "Aventuras del Capitán Alonso de Contreras."

representatives, Ortega's philosophy also suggests answers to these questions: What is the historian's object of study? What is the structure of culture? How can this complex entity be analyzed and described, especially if culture has a constantly changing structure?

Ortega y Gasset was born in 1883 in Madrid; he was educated by Jesuits but received his final training in philosophy at the Neo-Kantian school of Marburg University in Germany. Much of his life was concerned with reconciling his Spanish tradition and the German thought which had so deeply impressed him. From the chair of metaphysics, which he occupied at Madrid from the age of twenty-seven until the outbreak of the Spanish Civil War in 1936, Ortega propounded his own philosophy. Through his frequent contributions to journals, and through his many public lectures, he reached a larger public than just his students and fellow professionals. His influence in the Spanish-speaking world was enormous, though he steadily complained that no one would listen to him. After a period of self-imposed exile which took him to Paris, Holland, Portugal, Argentina, and back to Portugal, Ortega returned to Spain in 1945. Forbidden to assume his university chair, he occupied himself with lecturing at the Instituto de Humanidades, which he and his students founded in 1948, until he died in 1955. "My vocation was thought, the eagerness to make things clear."[4] He tried to awaken his country to its inescapable tasks; he sought to fulfil his role as a European intellectual by pinpointing that cultural crisis which had preoccupied him since his student days. It will presumably take years to assess his thought adequately; some crucial writings (such as his study on Leibniz) are only now being published, and much supporting evidence for his basic ideas is buried in notes, as yet inaccessible. On many recurring issues of modern thought Ortega's position

---

[4] Quoted in Christian Ceplecha, *The Historical Thought of José Ortega y Gasset*, pp. 30–31.

parallels that of such others as Bergson, Husserl, Dilthey, Nietzsche, Simmel, Heidegger, Whitehead, and Toynbee.[5] On other issues he went his own separate way. He always had a unique mode of expression and a characteristic formulation of problems. He addressed himself to the educated reader and not merely to the expert, and he surely is one of the most readable modern philosophers. His style has generally been admired but has also been harshly condemned; it was characterized by a penchant for paradox and heavy use of metaphor, especially during his earlier years. His formulation often tended to be aphoristic and the essay was his favorite form.[6] He hardly provided a system of solutions but concentrated rather on the initial phases of stating a problem. Usually he projected a problem and then attacked it by drawing ever narrowing circles of argument around it, much like the tactic of the Israelites in their siege of Jericho.[7] And often, before the problem is taken by conquest, Ortega abandons his reader, leaving merely a suggestion for a solution. Pointing a way to truth was always more important to him than providing easily repeatable formulations.[8] The act of philosophizing was always more important to Ortega than the obtained result.

---

[5] A very special problem is involved in Ortega's relation to Wilhelm Dilthey's work. To those who know and value Dilthey, Ortega's work may appear to be merely secondary labors which restate what Dilthey had already stated. Ortega encountered Dilthey's writings at a late date; he was at first so impressed that he thought all he wanted to say had been said; but gradually he became conscious of many differences between himself and the German thinker. See, for example, "A Chapter from the History of Ideas — Wilhelm Dilthey and the Idea of Life," in *Concord and Liberty*, pp. 131–82 (hereafter cited as *C.A.L.*); *G.W.*, III, 416, IV, 128, 400; Ceplecha, pp. 5, 103, 161–62; José Sánchez Villaseñor, *Ortega y Gasset, Existentialist*, pp. 62–63, 80, 99, 145–46, 151–56, 158–70. Ortega had a similar experience in relation to Heidegger (for which see note in *G.W.*, III, 277–79). Many of these problems involving his relations to the thought of contemporary thinkers need to be straightened out by someone who has access to notes and private papers.

[6] *Meditations on Quixote*, p. 40 (hereafter cited as *M.O.Q.*).

[7] *M.O.Q.*, p. 52; *W.I.P.*, pp. 17, 30.

[8] *M.O.Q.*, p. 67. E. R. Curtius, "Ortega," *Partisan Review*, XVII (1950), 260, goes very far in making a comparison of Ortega and Socrates in this respect.

"Cervantes knew that 'the road is always better than the inn." [9] Ortega will always be a more stimulating philosopher for those who like to fence with problems than for those who expect a system of answers. It is a struggle to extricate a coherent order of thought from his many suggestions.

Before it is possible to present Ortega's thinking on culture in relation to history, a rough sketch of his most basic ideas about man's position in the cosmos is called for. This outline does not presume to summarize his many, and often quite diverse, philosophical concerns. But it should provide a brief introduction to his (often idiosyncratic) terminology.

Philosophers, in Ortega's opinion, search for the *radical reality*, the "root reality," which presupposes no other. [10] Was this radical reality, as western man had proposed at several times, in the nature of things, or in the nature of thought, or in man's consciousness? Was thought the result of the true being of things, and knowledge therefore discovery, the unveiling of the radical reality behind the appearances? [11] Or was the primary reality for man his own consciousness and was the reality of things problematic for him, if not chaotic? [12] Ortega sought to resolve the contradiction between realism (as he understood it) and idealism (as he understood it) not by rejecting either position but by assimilating the truth from each and superseding both. "In the life of the spirit only that is superseded which is conserved — as the third step rises above the first two merely because it has them beneath it. If they should disappear, the third step would fall back to being only the first." [13] Ortega thought it his task — "the modern

---

[9] *G.W.*, III, 24, and also I, 382.

[10] *W.I.P.*, pp. 54, 101.

[11] *W.I.P.*, pp. 111, 154, 166–68, 206, 235–36; *Man and People*, p. 100 (hereafter cited as *M.A.P.*); *G.W.*, I, 262, II, 419, IV, 23.

[12] *W.I.P.*, pp. 149, 151–53, 179; *G.W.*, II, 431, 448–51, IV, 237.

[13] *W.I.P.*, p. 150. The aim of transcending previous positions by subsuming them in a new conception was one of Ortega's vital concerns; see *W.I.P.*, p. 201 ("all surpassing is conserving"), and *G.W.*, I, 54, 292, II, 415, 430, III, 82 ("we

theme" — to find a root reality which includes what is tenable about both the reality of things and the reality of thought, but in such a manner that the primary reality is neither solely thought nor solely the nature of things. This radical datum was for him "my life,"[14] a more fundamental and more inclusive reality than either thought or natural being. "The basic datum of the universe is not simply that either thought exists or I, the thinker, exist. . . . I am not a substantial being, nor is the world, but we both are in active correlation. I am that which sees the world and the world is that which is seen by me. I exist for the world, and the world exists for me."[15] "Therefore, the basic and undeniable fact is not my existence, but my co-existence with the world."[16] In his first major book, Ortega had already formulated his position through a favorite expression of the radical reality: "I am myself and my circumstances."[17]

In this proposition, "I myself" is probably the vaguest component, yet most "vital," that is, the one most involved in the process of living. In general terms it signifies an inner center of experience. It is distinguished from that which is on the outside, or "ex-ists," that which "stands around," that is, *circumstantia*. It is the center to which is related all that happens in the process of "my life."[18] But it is not identical

---

are entirely free to abandon our true task, but only at the risk of becoming prisoners of the lower floors of our destiny"), 375, 382, and IV, 402–3.

[14] "Calling it 'radical reality' does not mean that it is the only reality, nor even the highest, worthiest or most sublime, nor yet the supreme reality, but simply that it is the root of all other realities, in the sense that they — any of them — in order to be reality to us must in some way make themselves present, or at least announce themselves, within the shaken confines of our life" (*M.A.P.*, p. 40).

[15] *W.I.P.*, p. 199. See also *M.O.Q.*, p. 41, and *M.A.P.*, p. 87.

[16] *W.I.P.*, pp. 199–200. See also *W.I.P.*, pp. 208–9, and *G.W.*, II, 452–54, and III, 274.

[17] *M.O.Q.*, p. 45; and also p. 13, quoted in the introduction by Julian Marías: "This expression which appears in my first book and which sums up my philosophical thought."

[18] *W.I.P.*, p. 216; *M.O.Q.*, p. 41; *G.W.*, I, 329, 334, III, 428 ("the main thing to note in considering man is that his 'Life' is the substantive noun and all the rest are mere adjectives"), and IV, 366, 389.

with "my thought," "my body," "my feelings," "my psycho-somatic makeup," or "my soul."[19] It is not that which lives in the *biological* sense, but the center of life in the *biographical* sense.[20] In other words: the center of my life, the true "I" for Ortega, is that which is *least* transferable, that which can be said to be the *most* its very own, that which is essentially radical solitude.[21]

Yet this center is related to all that is part of my life. It is surrounded by circumstances and therefore part of a configuration — "I myself and my circumstances" — with a center, a "vital horizon," and beyond that a region of "cosmic" reality known only by its "compresence."[22] It is the focal point of a coexistence and is understood by means of a relation. Conceptually it is intelligible as an "occasional concept,"[23] one

---

[19] *M.A.P.*, p. 124, and *G.W.*, III, 272–73, 281. The most concerted effort Ortega made to clarify the problem of the various layers of "zones" of a personality is to be found in an essay written in 1927, "Vitalidad, alma, espíritu," included in *G.W.*, I, 317–50, as "Vitalität, Seele, Geist."

[20] *M.A.P.*, p. 44; *W.I.P.*, p. 165; and *G.W.*, I, 198, II, 150, III, 263. Note also the statement in *M.A.P.*, p. 166: ". . . the concrete and unique I that each one of us feels himself to be is not something that we possess and know from the outset but something that gradually appears to us . . . step by step, by virtue of a series of experiences that have their fixed order."

[21] *W.I.P.*, pp. 174, 202–3; *M.A.P.*, pp. 46, 48, 58. See also the remark: "We are more than anything else a natural system of preferring and rejecting" (*G.W.*, II, 336), and other statements substantiating the same in *G.W.*, I, 32, 104, 187, 218, 322–40, 411, II, 116–17, 175, 431, III, 329, and *W.I.P.*, p. 245.

[22] *M.A.P.*, pp. 66, 77 (". . . how much it is of man's essence to feel that he is in a regionalized world in which he encounters each thing as belonging to a region . . ."), 80, 112; and *G.W.*, I, 364 ("the human mind has only a limited capacity; only a limited number of things have room in it . . ."), and II, 183, 370. The concept of "compresence" Ortega took from Husserl and used it extensively to indicate a presence which is not immediately to be experienced and is yet present in a specific sense; for instance, the other side of the apple before me which is strictly speaking not present to my experience until I turn it around; see *M.A.P.*, pp. 63–66, and *G.W.*, I, 365 (where Ortega characterizes the agnostic as a person unwilling to cope with the problem of "compresence").

[23] ". . . there are concepts which some call 'occasional concepts,' thus, for instance, the concept 'here,' the concept 'I,' the concept 'this one.' Such concepts or designations have a formal identity which enables them to assert the constitutive non-identity of the matter designated or thought by them. All concepts through which the genuine reality which is life can be thought must

tied to a specific here and now. The living "I" "always finds itself amid certain circumstances, in a surrounding arrangement filled with things and people. . . . constitutionally the vital world is circumstance, . . . this world here and now."[24]

The living "I" is thrown amid specific circumstances. It is thus forced from the beginning to "take account of the world," to find itself, and to justify itself.[25] Coexistence with the circumstances is, therefore, not a state but a process. It necessitates constant interaction with "things" which, therefore, are mere *pragmata* for the individual.[26] The characteristic state of being is "being shipwrecked" amid circumstances, and life for the self consists in "saving itself and its circumstances."[27] Life thus is a constant process of deciding and implementing the future.[28] "Life is not a static persistent thing, it is an activity which consumes itself."[29] Life in this sense is a "project," a scheme, a purposeful action projected from the now upon the future.[30] It is not ready made, but must

in this sense be 'occasional concepts' [*Gelegenheitsbegriffe*]," *G.W.*, IV, 393, and see also IV, 394, III, 587 (where Ortega again uses the idea of Nicolas of Cusa that man is a *deus occasionatus*); and *W.I.P.*, pp. 236, 247.

[24] *W.I.P.*, p. 241. See also *G.W.*, III, 31, 48, IV, 84. Much of Ortega's critique of modern man addresses itself to man's unwillingness to accept limitation as a precondition for life.

[25] *G.W.*, I, 428, III, 518, IV, 140; *M.A.P.*, p. 41.

[26] *M.A.P.*, pp. 79–80; *W.I.P.*, 218–19 ("the important thing is not whether things are or are not bodies, but that they affect us, interest us, caress us, threaten us, and torment us . . ."); *G.W.*, III, 106, 231.

[27] *M.O.Q.*, pp. 31, 45 ("I am myself and my circumstance, and if I do not save it, I cannot save myself"); *W.I.P.*, p. 211 ("let us save ourselves in the world, save ourselves in things"), 220, 226; *G.W.*, I, 38, III, 127, 270, 445, 570, IV, 140, 582; Ortega almost identifies this act of saving with the justification of one's existence.

[28] *W.I.P.*, pp. 224–25 (". . . our life is a constant series of collisions with the future. . . . Life is an activity executed in relation to the future"), 243 (". . . the living being begins by being the creature over there, the one that comes afterwards"), 249; and *G.W.*, III, 473.

[29] Quoted by Julian Marías, in *Dublin Review*, CCXXII, 69, Ortega apparently took the phrase from Simmel (see *G.W.*, II, 102). See also *G.W.*, I, 490 ("to live is a transitive verb"), II, 224, 421 ("One lives as much as one wishes to live more").

[30] *G.W.*, I, 473 ("fundamentally life is project"), III, 110 ("for life means

be made from moment to moment; thus man is necessarily free, he has no choice but to make choices.[31] Life is therefore a coexistence with a purpose (project) *and* a reason (a causal relation). Or, as Ortega preferred to phrase it: life is drama, with a plot and characteristics made by the interactions of self and circumstances.[32] The most remarkable aspect of man then is not that he is a biological datum but a biographical one. And the decisive issue in understanding human life is that man has no nature but has a history.[33]

Ortega y Gasset was too committed to the western philosophical tradition to opt for life at the cost of reason.[34] He did not follow Bergson, Unamuno, or Spengler, who leaned toward irrationalism in their defense of life. Instead he labored to reconcile life and reason through a tool he called "vital reason" or "historical reason."

Every theory of thought involves, for Ortega, a simultaneous assumption about the nature of things and of thought. Every epistemology is at once ontology.[35] Central to the issue of knowledge is the old problem of the relation between

---

fulfilling of a task"), 276 ("for life is not a thing, but is through and through problematic and a task"), IV, 54 ("man as such is a program"), 55 ("I am no thing but a drama, a struggle for the realization of that which I must become"), 366, 390–91 ("But man must not only create himself, his hardest task is to determine what he desires to be. . . . this plan of life is the true I of a human being").

[31] *G.W.*, IV, 392. See also *W.I.P.*, pp. 221–22; *M.A.P.*, pp. 43, 45, 58; and *G.W.*, III, 36, 61, 400–401.

[32] *M.A.P.*, p. 25; *G.W.*, III, 62, 273, 408, 444, 518, IV, 55, 106, 389.

[33] See esp. *G.W.*, IV, 401; but also III, 62, 231, and IV, 197, 380 ("it is false to speak of man's nature, for man has no nature").

[34] See esp. *M.O.Q.*, pp. 87–93 ("This very opposition between reason and life, so much used to-day by those who do not want to work, is in itself open to suspicion. As if reason were not a vital and spontaneous function! . . . Not everything is thought, but without thought we do not possess anything fully," pp. 91–93), 98 ("Man has a mission of clarity upon earth"); also *W.I.P.*, pp. 110 ("my objection to mysticism is that out of the mystic vision no intellectual benefit redounds to mankind"), 147. See also Marías, p. 73.

[35] *G.W.*, II, 422 (in his article "Kant, Betrachtung zur Jahrhundertfeier" written in 1924); Ortega repeatedly struggled with Kant's "ontophobia" (see the article "Reine Philosophie," *G.W.*, II, 440–54; also relevant, IV, 386).

intellect and things, the *adaequatio rei et intellectus*.[36] Ortega rejected the simple relativist position that truth does not exist in an absolute sense but only as a truth relative to the subject. At first glance such relativism might seem to serve the historians who learned that men have changed their positions throughout history; but Ortega disagreed. "History's profound assumption, . . . is the complete opposite of a basic relativism."[37] The historian must at least assume that former men "thought with meaning" (which was Ortega's redefinition of man as a rational animal). On the other hand, Ortega was not prepared to accept the rationalistic *adaequatio*: being is of the same nature and function as thinking. The real coincides with the rational. Truth is one, it is absolute, unchangeable, and through reason (Descartes's *ratio* and Kant's *intelligiblen Charakter*) we partake of an unchanging reality.[38] By that view, history is essentially accumulated error.

Ortega sought to save both the notion of truth (or reason) and the uniqueness of all life by a third position, namely, that which assumes that thinking and being coincide only in part and which therefore attempts to trace the line of coincidence and discrepancy between thought and the universe.[39] The eternal and unchanging things — thought, values, transcend-

[36] *W.I.P.*, p. 85; see also *G.W.*, II, 101.

[37] *W.I.P.*, p. 27.

[38] *G.W.*, II, 93, and IV, 387–89. See also *W.I.P.*, p. 87, and *G.W.*, II, 105, III, 356; *M.A.P.*, pp. 30, 129 (where Ortega suddenly inveighs against rationalism: ". . . rationalism is a form of intellectual bigotry which, in thinking about reality, tries to take it into account as little as possible").

[39] *W.I.P.*, p. 88. See also *W.I.P.*, pp. 64 ("philosophy . . . admits from the start that the world may be a problem which in itself is insoluble"), 69–70, 78 (". . . nor do we know . . . whether or not it [the universe] will be basically knowable"), 97, 143 ("what philosophy says is only this: neither the existence nor the non-existence of the world about us is certain . . ."); *G.W.*, II, 97 (". . . neither rationalistic absolutism which saves reason and destroys life, nor relativistic absolutism which saves life while reason breaks into pieces"), III, 351–59 (a short, but interesting essay, "Reform der Intelligenz"), 382; and Ceplecha, p. 40 (quoting Ortega: "Reason is a brief zone of analytical clarity which opens between two unfathomable strata of irrationality" from an article written in 1924, "Ni vitalismo ni racionalismo").

ent realities — must be seen in terms of the radical reality of our life. Thrown amid circumstances which do not simply explain themselves (either in the form of the one great metaphor which thinks of the mind as a wax tablet in which things impress their seal or the other metaphor of the container which holds reality as idea),[40] man must pose himself the problem of his situation. Our reason then becomes "in the true and rigorous sense, every intellectual action which puts us in contact with reality, by means of which we come upon the transcendent."[41] It therefore does not prejudge whether reality is rational or irrational. It is not reason *sub specie aeternitatis*, a standpoint which does not exist according to Ortega,[42] but it is "vital reason," reason as a function of "my life."[43] Vital reason is the tool of the shipwrecked: "to live is to have no help for it but to reason in the face of inexorable circumstance."[44] But that conception of reason, which fulfils such

[40] See the essay "Die beiden grossen Metaphern" (1925) ("Las dos grandes metáforas"), *G.W.*, I, 249–65.

[41] *G.W.*, IV, 408. See also *W.I.P.*, pp. 21–25; *G.W.*, II, 135, 251, IV, 237–41 (in one of Ortega's most interesting essays, written in 1940: "Über das Denken, seine Thëurgie und seine Demiurgie"). Ortega was much concerned with the notion that "we think with the things" and with Hegel's position that "Die Vernunft in ihrer Bestimmung gefasst, das ist erst die Sache" (see *G.W.*, III, 380–83, from the essay "Hegel's Philosophie der Geschichte und die Historiologie").

[42] *G.W.*, II, 137, and also III, 293, IV, 417.

[43] *M.A.P.*, pp. 20, 23 ("we think in order that we may succeed in surviving"), 99; *G.W.*, II, 99 ("thinking . . . is an instrument, an organ of my life, and is regulated and directed by it"), 114–15, IV, 224, 250 ("Cognition is no 'natural' and inevitable process of man, but a purely historical form of life [*Lebensform*] at which he arrived through specific experiences and which he may surrender in view of other experiences"), 259 ("Cognition is nothing substantial in itself, but a function of life, which in turn is a task"), and 259–63.

[44] Quoted by Marías, p. 76; see also *M.O.Q.*, p. 73 ("to think is to ask for trouble"); *M.A.P.*, p. 28; *W.I.P.*, pp. 65–66 ("To live is certainly to deal with the world, to turn toward it, to act within it, to be occupied with it. Hence it is literally impossible for man . . . to renounce the attempt to possess a complete idea of the world, an integral idea of the universe. Be it crude or refined, with our consent or without it, that trans-scientific picture of the world is embodied in every spirit; it comes to govern our existence much more effectively than does scientific truth"), 74; and *G.W.*, III, 398–99.

a broad scope of living, must be understood broadly. Thus, vital reason, for Ortega, is not a specific mode of reason, but reason as such without qualification; while "pure reason," or logical reason, physico-mathematical reason, and the like are most specific varieties. Whereas vital reason is the immediate contact established between most concrete situations, namely, between "I myself and my circumstances," the specific reasons are more abstract forms which posit theories or symbolic equations between intellectual modes and possible realities.

Since "vital reason" is, for Ortega, the most concrete manner of taking account of the most immediate realities, each life takes cognizance of that part of truth and cosmic reality which constitutes its circumstances. It is therefore a function of each subject ("my life") to be a receptive organ, a net, for those parts of cosmic reality which are its circumstances and can be caught in its nets.[45] Any knowledge and understanding is tied to a "here" and a "now." All truth is seen in perspective. "Cosmic reality is such that it is given only from a specific perspective. The perspective is thus a component of reality. It is not the distortion of reality; it is the ordering scheme of reality. A reality which is the same from all standpoints is a non-sense."[46] Thus divergence between two separate subjective worlds does not imply the falsity of one or both. Rather, each life is one perspective of the universe. "Each individuum, be it a person, a people, or an epoch, is an irreplaceable organ for the conquest of truth. . . . Without the unfolding, the constant change and the inexhaustible adventure known as life, the universe, the ever valid truth, would remain unknown."[47] Only that perspective which claims to be the only one is false, for it is utopian to claim to stand nowhere or everywhere.

---

[45] G.W., I, 17, 202, II, 136.

[46] G.W., II, 137; see also I, 15–16, 240, II, 129, III, 276. Ortega admitted he took the notion of perspectivism from German thinkers (see W.I.P., p. 28).

[47] G.W., II, 138; see also II, 183, 208 ("cultures are the organs which succeed in grasping a small piece of the absolute yonder"), 370; see also II, 73 ("historical changes are chiefly changes in perspective").

Thus human life is understood only by accounting for the particular manner of coexistence between a subject and its circumstances. We have no recourse but to tell a story: the story of this subject and the situation in which it found itself, its long struggle to master a problematic coexistence with its own realities, the projection of a life by which it sought to prevail over its circumstances. We have only the act of re-experiencing as a road to understanding, and it is an imperfect, foreshortened acquaintance with the reality of another.[48] That is to say, we can understand human life only historically. Vital reason is historical reason.[49] Man is not an eternal first man, an Adam in Paradise, but a member of a society with a past. He exists at the "historical level" of his generation. His circumstances include the ingredients of what has happened to man before, "a reality transcending the theories of man, and which is he beneath his theories."[50]

Much in Ortega's thought about culture and history revolved about his conviction that life is a dialogue between "I myself" and my circumstances.[51] As such a dialogue, life can have two aspects. Man can live an "authentic life" (i.e., that which one does by oneself) when he turns within (*ensimismamiento*) and from there turns to the task of personalizing, or humanizing (strictly speaking, 'I-zing' — however horrible a word) his circumstances.[52] As a second aspect, life is "possession

---

[48] *G.W.*, II, 201–6, III, 408, 439. See also *M.A.P.*, p. 158 ("Beyond the men within the horizon that is our environment, there are many, many more; they are latent lives — they are Antiquity. History is the effort that we make to recognize Antiquity — because it is a technique of intercourse with the dead, a curious modification of the present, genuine social relation").

[49] This is the main point of Ortega's centrally important essay, "Die Aufgabe unserer Zeit" ("El tema de nuestro tiempo") written in 1923 (*G.W.*, II, 79–141); see also *G.W.*, IV, 251–54.

[50] *G.W.*, IV, 412; see also III, 394–95, and IV, 403.

[51] *G.W.*, I, 98, II, 182.

[52] *M.A.P.*, pp. 20, 59; *M.O.Q.*, pp. 41, 45; *G.W.*, I, 87, II, 108, III, 149, 215, 291, 294 ("One discovers how raw and inhospitable, even hostile, the circumstances of this world are. This encounter either suppresses forever the heroic intent to be what we secretly are, and then the philistine is born in us; or our self reaches clarity about itself through this collision with the 'against-us' which

of all that is other" (*alteración* or "otheration," an equally impossible word).[53] Man lives on a plateau, on something not made by himself, on an inheritance, at the level of his generation.[54] The authentic life is limited by the power of custom (i.e., a binding observance or *vigencia*) which socializes, automatizes, mechanizes, and dehumanizes life in some sense.[55] But at the same time, this world of binding observances, which is such a large part of our social circumstance, is a great liberating force; for it settles parts of life which otherwise would be problematic. Thereby it frees man to "project" his authentic life on other (unsettled) zones of his existence.[56]

In one line of his argument, Ortega suggested that the world around us is basically problematic; that is to say, we do not know what things are; they present a puzzle and a task to us.[57] We are compelled to act within these problem-offering circumstances. We have to create our world as a projection which we seek to realize in interrelation with our circumstances. While Ortega inquired if such a task could be fulfilled, he became more and more interested in a part

is the universe, and decides to be itself, to effectuate itself, and to imprint its image on destiny"), 409, 535, 572, IV, 58.

[53] The two terms *ensimismamiento* and *alteración* were among Ortega's most basic concepts for describing the human reality; see especially the essay "Insichselbstversenkung und Selbstentfremdung" ("Ensimismamiento y alteración") written in 1939 (*G.W.*, IV, 7–31), which subsequently became the first chapter of *Man and People*. The terms are his modifications of the older ideas of *vita contemplativa* (or *theoretikos bios*) and *vita activa* (see *W.I.P.*, pp. 45, 178, 238; *M.A.P.*, p. 23). See also *M.A.P.*, p. 104, and *G.W.*, III, 414, 461–64.

[54] *M.A.P.*, pp. 144–45 ("even in the case of maximum genuineness, the human individual lives the greater part of his life in the pseudo-living of the surrounding or social, conventionality"), 147; *G.W.*, III, 21–28, 76–77, 329, 414–15, 461, 535, and the essay "Phrase und Aufrichtigkeit" ("Fraseología y sinceridad") written in 1927 (*G.W.*, I, 351–62).

[55] *M.A.P.*, pp. 17, 174–75, 212, 259; *G.W.*, I, 533–37, II, 475, 599.

[56] *G.W.*, I, 69, 360, III, 56–57 ("norms are the foundation of culture. . . . there is no culture when there are no norms for which we and our enemies can reach. . . . Barbarism is the absence of norms and authorities of appeal"), 60, 102–3, 178, 414, 419, 519, 579.

[57] *M.O.Q.*, p. 19 ("circumstance: the mute things which are all around us"); and *W.I.P.*, p. 64.

of man's vital reality which he called *creencias*. Man cannot live in radical uncertainty about himself and every one of his circumstances.[58] Although the philosopher can postulate such a complete shipwreck *in abstracto*, a look at concrete human existence reveals that life is always a tentative solution to the shipwreck. That is to say, every life has some certainty. Every perspective of vital reality rests on a part of reality which, in relation to iself, is a firm *locus* or *topos*. This zone of stability which each radical reality "has" in relation to itself is a "certainty of faith," a *Glaubensgewissheit*, a *creencia*.[59]

Creencias are firm beliefs about a part of reality. They are such fundamental conceptions about our realities that we identify them with reality. In contrast to "ideas" (which are only tentative theories about reality), *creencias* are "fundamental ideas" (*Grundideen*) which have become absolute certainties. Or, as Ortega put it: "they are not ideas which we *have*, but ideas which we *are*."[60] We formulate ideas through a mental activity by which we respond to the problems posed by circumstance; but we *find* ourselves in *creencias*. We think ideas; we reckon with and count upon *creencias*.

We can say about those thoughts upon which we come and which we make our own — and I repeat that I count among these the most rigorous scientific insights — that we produce them, support them, argue them, spread them, that we fight for them, yes even that we are willing to die for them. But

---

[58] See esp. *G.W.*, III, 104, 402–3, 458–61, IV, 97, 126, 366.

[59] *G.W.*, IV, 97. The most important writings in which Ortega elaborated his notion of *creencias* are "Ideen und Glaubensgewissheiten" ("Ideas y creencias"), written in 1934 (*G.W.*, IV, 96–129), "Vives," written in 1940 (*G.W.*, IV, 195–212), "Geschichte als System" ("Historia como sistema"), written in 1941 (*G.W.*, IV, 366–412), "Über das römische Imperium" ("Del Imperio romano"), written in 1940 (*G.W.*, IV, 414–60), "Zum Thema Pazifismus" ("En cuanto al pacifismo"), 1937 (*G.W.*, III, 163–95), "Im Geiste Galileis" ("En torno a Galileo"), written in 1933 (*G.W.*, III, 386–567).

[60] *G.W.*, IV, 97, and see also III, 231, IV, 101, 104, 110, 117, 120, 124, 372, 425.

what we cannot do, is to live "from" or "out of" them. They are our work and therefore already presuppose our life, which in turn founds itself on those *creencias* we do not produce,[61] for which we cannot even account normally, and which we neither argue, nor spread, nor support. Ultimately we do nothing at all to these certainties of faith, we simply live "in" them . . . ; with a sure sense, popular language found the expression "to live in the faith." Indeed, one *is* in faith and one *has* and maintains a thought; but faith is that which "has" us and maintains us. There are therefore ideas *with* which we encounter ourselves . . . and there are *creencias in* which we encounter ourselves, which seem to be present before we begin to think.[62]

Creencias originate as ideas which some man formed about human reality. They started their career as suggestions, as tentative solutions to the problems of reality. But it is exactly characteristic of them that they, at some point, lost this tentative quality and that they exchanged their problematic nature for an unquestioned identification with reality.[63] Ortega was especially interested in the *creencias* which have become the assumed realities by which whole groups of human beings live. The truly noteworthy quality of *creencias* appears in such instances as when a whole society lives in the conviction that the biblical God is an unquestioned reality, or that the physical world is an ordered, intelligible cosmos, or that the physical world is a hostile force in human life, or that there is a naturally ordained hierarchy in human relations, or that the universe is open rather than closed, and so on, and so on. In principle, there may be as many *creencias* as there are firm points of view.[64] In actuality, their number is limited. *Creencias* are social realities, common features of society,

---

[61] See also *G.W.*, IV, 107, 372–73, and *M.A.P.*, pp. 97–98, 262–63.

[62] *G.W.*, IV, 97–98; see also III, 551–52, IV, 127, 428, and *W.I.P.*, p. 49.

[63] *G.W.*, I, 125, 450, II, 91, III, 478, IV, 102, 119, 120, 124, 213, and *M.A.P.*, pp. 197–98.

[64] *G.W.*, IV, 126, 208–9.

which are not "made" in each life separately but rather communicated to each life as a part of its circumstances. Thus, *creencias* share some of the characteristics of usage and custom, since the latter are the actual forms in which societies express their basic convictions.[65] This collective faith, which does not depend on your or my acceptance, imposes itself on us because it has become a part of reality with which we must reckon. Usually we take it for granted, we do not account for it, we do not reduce it to a problematic aspect of existence; we live in it without making thoughts about it.

Our life consists then in part of those places or positions in which we already are, of realities which are given to us as realities. We have been placed within the repertory of convictions, the faiths of our fathers, which remain convictions for us to the degree to which they do not become problematic. We are heirs who live with a capital of unquestioned reality, that is, an inherited experience of life.[66] That which we already are, the settled part of our existence, the only possession which we have, the one thing which has been determined for us and not by us, is our past.[67] We have history. And it is *our*

---

[65] *G.W.*, IV, 109, 117, 170, and esp. *M.A.P.*, pp. 192–221, 222–57, which contain Ortega's most systematic attempt to explain what he meant by *usage*. He was much concerned with language as a form of usage: ". . . language is the fact in which the characters of social reality are given most clearly and purely, and hence the being of a society is manifested in it with incalculable precision" (*M.A.P.*, p. 228). "Words do not have etymologies because they are words, but because they are usages. . . . man is constitutively . . .. the 'etymological animal.' Accordingly history would be only a vast etymology, the grandiose system of etymologies. That is why history exists and why man needs it; it is the only discipline that can discover the meaning of what man does and hence of what he is" (*M.A.P.*, p. 203).

[66] *G.W.*, II, 83 ("The work of others, which is done and completed, comes to us with a strange halo; it seems to be sanctified, and since we did not do it ourselves, we are inclined to consider it no one's work, which means we accept it as reality itself"), IV, 114, 117 ("above all else man is heir . . . and to know that one is heir, means to have historical consciousness"); see also *W.I.P.*, p. 128, on "experience."

[67] *G.W.*, III, 585; see also III, 268–69, 283, 592–93, IV, 117, 401; *W.I.P.*, p. 244 ("My future then makes me discover my past in order to realize that future.

past because we carry it with us. "Man is that which has happened to him, what he has made. Other things could have happened to him, he might have made other things, but that which actually happened to him and that which he actually made, presents an unchangeable line of experience which he carries on his back as the vagabond carries his possessions. Man is the pilgrim of his being, he is substantially a wanderer. . . . there is only one fixed line which is determined and given beforehand, which can orient or direct us: the past. The experiences which man made limit his future." [68] Man is *res gestae*, things done, just as God, in Augustine's word, is that which He has made (*deus cui hoc est natura quod fecerit*).[69]

Our *creencias* are the parts of the past which do not appear as error, those which have remained viable, those which still support us. But, our lives are not what we are, and what we have, but that which we do and will be. With that which we are and have, we work at our authentic life, at our task. That is, we live *in* our *creencias* but *with* the project, ideas, activities which preoccupy us. Because one zone of our circumstances is settled for us, we work on that zone of our circumstance which is problematic. We live as problem solvers, as decipherers of enigmas, as "the divine beast weighted with problems," but can do so only because we do not doubt every

---

The past is now real because I am re-living it, and it is when I find in the past the means of realizing my future that I discover my present"); *M.A.P.*, p. 133 ("the antique formula could not be improved: *fata ducunt non trahunt* — destiny directs it does not drag. For great as is the radius of our freedom, there is a limit to it — we cannot escape the need of maintaining continuity with the past").

[68] *G.W.*, IV, 401. See also III, 484–85, 562, 585, IV, 395 ("Before us open up the various possibilities of being, but behind us lies what we have been. And that which we were acts negatively on that which we can be"), 398 ("The past is the moment of identity in man, that which is thing-like in him, the inexorable and fateful"); and *M.O.Q.*, p. 103 ("The individual cannot get his bearings in the universe except through his race [i.e., a *historical* manner of interpreting reality], because he is immersed in it like the drop of water in the passing cloud").

[69] *G.W.*, IV, 401.

part of our coexistence with circumstance.[70] We can progress (which simply means to take a step into the future and does not imply that this step will be superior in value to those which went before) because we egress from an already fixed point. Our life can be a project because we can use something given to mold something to come.

Life at any given time, therefore, possessed a definite structure for Ortega y Gasset.[71] It has *certain* zones. There always is a firm area, the realm occupied by *creencias*. Beyond this lies the segment of reality upon which man works, on which he spends his energies in the attempt to control it by his projected plan of life. Here is the realm of ideas, of experiment, of uncertainty which man attempts to make certainty. From within a core of realities, man lives toward the problematic peripheries of his circumstances. And beyond this horizon toward which he moves lies a transcendent world known only by its "compresence." It is the world which, at some later time and some other place, may become man's circumstance. And these zones are supplemented by a structure of activities and relationships. Man can turn within, or he can turn without. He turns within as he searches for the certainties of life with which to tackle the problems. He turns to the active life, and toward the horizon, from his certainties. In any large social group, there are some, moreover, who actively engage in solving problems and upholding norms; and there are others who merely live within the zone of certainties, neither venturing forth on the ocean of problems nor turning actively within themselves.[72] In other words, there are elites who live

___

[70] *M.A.P.*, pp. 143, 212; *W.I.P.*, pp. 83, 135; *G.W.*, III, 474–75, IV, 59, 110, 231, 542. The "divine beast weighted with problems" is, of course, Plato's statement on man.

[71] *G.W.*, III, 179 ("the historical reality is the only thing in this world which inherently [*schon von sich aus*] possesses structure and organization"), IV, 368.

[72] *G.W.*, I, 121, II, 42, 44, III, 9, 14–15, 210, 346–48, IV, 217–21, 451. This is, of course, the theme of Ortega's most widely known work, *The Revolt of the Masses*.

life to the fullest and strenuously, who make projects and affirm norms, men who accept life as a task, as a responsible process of continuous decision-making. Such elites are determined exclusively by an attitude toward life, the essence of which is expressed in the idea of *noblesse oblige*.[73] And there are the others — the mass, not because they are many (which tends to be the case), but because they are inert. They use the given without feeling obliged to maintain it, or to go beyond it. They live irresponsibly with the inherited capital. They live at a minimal rate; they move into the problematic zone at a minimal pace; and they live among the certainties without turning within, without ever realizing that they live off the labors of others.[74]

Culture, for Ortega y Gasset, was such an ordered group life. *Cultura* is the totality of ideas and *creencias*, the system of convictions and thoughts which men have about the reality which surrounds them.[75] Culture, in this sense, is the repertory of solutions which men advance in response to the problems of their lives. "It is the conception of the world or the universe which serves as the plan, riskily elaborated by man, for orienting himself among things, for coping with his life, and for finding a direction amid the chaos of his situation." [76]

---

[73] *G.W.*, I, 286, 474, II, 46, 53–58, 81, III, 11, 49, 51, 70, 117, 459. It should be kept in mind that Ortega considered the presence of a mass as vital as the presence of an elite (see *W.I.P.*, p. 117, and Ceplecha, p. 78). Ortega suggested through the example of ancient Greece that a society is unstable if it does not possess a sufficient mass; see *G.W.*, II, 58, which is taken from an essay "España invertebrada," written in 1921, nine years before *The Revolt of the Masses*. "There are peoples where an almost frightening surplus of eminent personalities stands on the base of a very thin, inadequate, and unadaptable mass. This was the case of Greece and this is the reason for its historical instability. . . . a genius as a culture, Greece was unstable as a social structure and state."

[74] *G.W.*, I, 66, III, 38, 51, 54, 201, IV, 115; *W.I.P.*, p. 232; *M.O.Q.*, pp. 44 ("Acquired culture has value only as the instrument and weapon for new conquests"), 154.

[75] Esp. *G.W.*, III, 207; see also II, 90, 108, III, 230, 233–34, 251, 293, and *M.O.Q.*, pp. 141–42, 145.

[76] *G.W.*, III, 403–4; and also II, 207, III, 411.

"Culture is only the interpretation which man gives to his life, the series of more or less satisfying solutions he finds in order to meet the problems and necessities of life, as well those which belong to the material order as the so-called spiritual ones."[77] It is always the total world view and the accompanying usages and techniques of the society.[78] But it has structure: it has a zone of *creencias* and another realm of ideas, tentative solutions. It has a horizon beyond which lies the possibility of another reality which is excluded for the present.[79] It is a system with clear relations between the various zones: an ordered relation in which the core of *creencias* determines the character of the tentative ideas, and all compressed within a given set of circumstances (i.e., it has a vital horizon). And, in addition, every culture has its dominant minority and its mass.

The structure of a culture is fundamentally determined by the repertory of convictions men have about themselves and their circumstances. Every cultural institution, every project of life, every activity, thought, and sentiment is dependent on this core zone of *creencias* from which each culture lives.[80] Political life, economic activity, the sciences and religious beliefs, the arts, the love life of a society, are expressions of this deepest stratum of trusted reality. It would be erroneous, however, to assume that these core *creencias* are a

---

[77] *G.W.*, II, 464; see also III, 490, 504, 585, IV, 399, and *M.O.Q.*, p. 98.

[78] Ortega used the notion of technique in a very broad sense; see especially the essay "Betrachtungen über die Technik" ("Meditación de la técnica"), written in 1933 (*G.W.*, IV, 32–95). See also *G.W.*, I, 308 ("technique is what provides solutions"), III, 65 (where Ortega, in an aside against Spengler's distinction between *Kultur* and *Zivilisation*, pleads for a broader cultural conception of techniques), III, 95, 132–33 (where he speaks of the state as technique), 165 (on war as technique). Thinking, similarly, is a technique for Ortega; and life is made possible by a whole repertory of techniques for coping with circumstances.

[79] *G.W.*, II, 185–86, taken from a very interesting essay "Atlantiden" ("Las Atlántidas") from the year 1924 (*G.W.*, II, 173–209) in which the whole concept of the "vital horizon" is a major topic.

[80] *G.W.*, II, 80, 88, 90, 422, III, 195, IV, 372.

logically coherent system and that, consequently, all expressions of these convictions form a logically consistent pattern. Ortega y Gasset spoke of a *repertory* to indicate that the series of *creencias* possessed by a man, a people, an epoch, never has a completely logical structure; this is to say, it never forms a system of ideas like that to which philosophy aspires. The *creencias* which coexist in a human life, which inspire and guide it, occasionally do not fit one another; they contradict one another or, at least, are logically unrelated.[81] For instance, the ideas which a culture forms about the behavior of physical things, based on its convictions about the relation of cognizance and knowable object, may be only loosely related to its ideas of inter-individual behavior, based on convictions of "the other's" nature. On the other hand, it may also be that physics and interpersonal relations depend on *creencias* which are closely affiliated. Ortega did not imply that every aspect of a culture can be explained by reference to one all-pervading conviction. He argued, moreover, that *creencias* may be of different ages and strengths. Thus a culture may live from very strong convictions about the nature of political and social life but very undeveloped and weak ones about physical realities.[82] Because the prevailing *creencias* form no more than a repertory, cultures are self-consistent, to some degree, and, to some degree, filled with tensions. The repertory of faiths is not a mere conglomerate, however; it has structure in so far as it is composed of weaker and stronger *creencias*. Its architectonic form stems from the fact that some convictions are of greater weight and value for a culture than others. Some *creencias* are, in that sense, more "vital" than others. Some are in the ascendance, and thus of greater significance for the future, while others are losing their vitality, their hold upon men; ". . . the decisive changes in human life are the changes in

---

[81] *G.W.*, IV, 367; see also IV, 396.
[82] Ortega's conception of Rome might fit this example; see "Über das römische Imperium" (*G.W.*, IV, 413–60).

creencias, their strengthening and their weakening." [83] In other words, men have living faiths and dead, inert faiths (which nonetheless exercise strong effects on a culture), growing faiths and dying faiths. Consequently, men experience certain aspects of their culture, certain institutions, modes of behavior, and ideas, as dead weight. To the extent that culture becomes the expression of dying faiths, it becomes a burden men seek to escape. [84] Then preachers of the simple life appear and turn man against culture, unmindful that man cannot live without a configuration of beliefs. At other times, the classical ages, men live essentially out of a living faith and thus experience their culture as a harmonious reality, something that fits like a skin. These golden ages have their own peril: men may become worshippers of culture, unmindful that they create cultures to live in, instead of living for their culture. [85] Culture without life is Byzantinism, but life without culture is barbarism. [86]

---

[83] *G.W.*, IV, 367. See also I, 450, III, 424, 441, 454–57, 588, IV, 206 ("If one has once understood the meaning of a firm and at the same time rich faith for human existence, there is nothing which equals as drama the dissipation of the same"); and Ceplecha, p. 112 ("Decisive historical changes do not come from great wars, terrible cataclysms, or ingenious inventions; 'it is enough that the heart of man incline its sensitive crown to one side or the other of the horizon, toward optimism or toward pessimism, toward heroism or toward utility, toward combat or toward peace' ").

[84] *G.W.*, I, 69–70, 292, III, 62–63, 464–68, 563, 586, 588, IV, 370–71; and *M.O.Q.*, p. 43. Culture always provides some restraint for all who actively pursue the "authentic" life.

[85] *G.W.*, II, 170 ("the traditionalistic soul is a mechanism of faith [*Vertrauensmechanismus*]"), 416 ("Life meant for those men: leaning on a fixed order and letting the collective ideal of style prevail in their innermost"), III, 288 ("The consciousness of being secure kills life; this accounts for the repeated decline of aristocracies"), 293, 464–65 ("But simple acceptance, unrelated to the exertion involved in creation, has the disadvantage of leading to an inactive, a vegetative life"), 468, IV, 460. Ortega often warned against the seductive dangers of "classics" in an age of crisis.

[86] *G.W.*, II, 104–5; see also I, 362 (man's struggle is always a two-front war against "phrase" and barbarism), II, 108–9, III, 477 (the double danger is always idolization of culture [*Kulturvergötzung*] and despising culture [*Kulturverachtung*]), IV, 116; and *M.A.P.*, p. 32 (". . . thus the essence of man is

Ortega's lesson for the historian lay in his insistence that past life is unintelligible without knowledge of the *creencias* on which that life was built. The diagnosis of any culture rests on the historian's ability to reconstruct the repertory of *creencias*, the core reality of any culture.[87] The understanding of varied forms of life depends upon insight into the structure of their zone of *creencias*, the relative strength of each conviction, the power it exerts upon the project men seek to realize.[88] There, for Ortega, lies the fundamental historical reality. This clearly meant that the historian could not explain his subject merely through an investigation of the zone lying outside the *creencias*. With few exceptions, Ortega thought, the historians had committed exactly this error. They wrote the histories of states, of artistic production, of customs, of techniques, of ideas, of institutions, and so on. But what did this mean in Ortega's scheme? States, works of art, ideas, customs, are secondary realities below which lie more fundamental realities.[89] An idea, for instance, is a theorem applied by man to a part of his circumstance. It possesses a "vital" reality only because it is being thought by something with a more

always purely and simply 'danger.' Man always travels along precipices and, whether he will or not, his truest obligation is to keep his balance").

[87] *G.W.*, III, 101, 104, IV, 126, 202–3 ("History thus becomes history of preconditions. . . . And the first thing a historian must establish about a man or period is this system of *creencias*. Thus history becomes inquiry in depth"), 368.

[88] The historian, according to Ortega, must always be conscious of the fact that *creencias* are the things least immediately expressed by a people, and that he therefore must go behind the immediate expressions; see "Glanz und Elend der Übersetzung" ("Miseria y esplendor de la traducción") written in 1937 (*G.W.*, IV, 152–77), esp. pp. 166–67 ("Each people keeps silent on some matters, so that it can express others") 246 ("Each thought-out philosophy, when put into words, moves in the haze of an ante-philosophy or conviction which remains silent, because in its full value it is reality itself for the individual"). Jacob Burckhardt may have expressed much the same in his *Griechische Kulturgeschichte*, I, 400: "Everywhere in the past we encounter things which remain unexplained only because they were completely self-understood in their time and, like all daily matters, were not thought necessary to write down."

[89] *G.W.*, II, 181, IV, 99, 134, 367–68, 458.

radical reality, that is, a man living in a specific faith. An idea is not self-explanatory; at best it rests on another idea. A history of ideas, of what has been thought, is a history in a vacuum, a history of an abstraction. As a reality, an "idea is an action taken by a man in view of a definite situation and for a definite purpose."[90] It is deprived of its vital reality when separated from the man and those basic convictions which led him to this specific thought. One and the same idea may fulfil quite different functions in two radically different lives; it possesses its significance only in relation to a concrete situation.[91] The true account of the idea can only be given by "discovery" (Ortega liked the Platonic term *aletheia*) of its living context. The history of ideas is meaningful, and truly intelligible, when it is an integral part of history of culture. Similarly, the history of any separate part of the total human world (i.e., a culture) requires the study of "history as a system"[92] whereby the major segments of life are seen as an interrelated whole.

The error of the traditional historians was their satisfaction with facts. Ranke's famous dictum, that history merely states "how it actually was" (*wie es eigentlich gewesen*), was justifiable, for Ortega, only in so far as it countered the excessive claims of Hegel's philosophy of history.[93] But when historians thought they possessed a science by virtue of having critically

---

[90] "Prologue to a History of Philosophy" in *Concord and Liberty*, p. 99; the whole essay is an argument against a history of ideas which is not adequately based on a study of *creencias*.

[91] Esp. *G.W.*, III, 394. See also I, 357–58, II, 442–43, III, 386–87, 600–601, IV, 101, 106; and *W.I.P.*, p. 25 ("And yet the fundamental task of history, if it wishes in all seriousness to be a science, must be to show how this philosophy, or that political system, could only have been discovered, developed, and in short, lived by a particular type of man who lived at a particular date").

[92] See *G.W.*, II, 198–99, III, 77, 486, 579.

[93] *G.W.*, III, 364–65. A centrally important paper for Ortega's idea of historical method is the essay "Hegel's Philosophie der Geschichte und die Historiologie" ("La 'Filosofía de la historia' de Hegel y la historiología"), written in 1928, originally as an introduction to the translation of Hegel commissioned by Ortega (*G.W.*, III, 360–85).

verified facts, they sorely misunderstood what a science is and what history ought to be. True science begins beyond the facts, beyond its method for ascertaining facts. It is construction *a priori*, verified by knowledge *a posteriori*.[94] History thus must be more than the aggregate of data; more than "document and critique." The ultimate realities the historian must understand are not the *facta* but the processes of life. "Life is a gerund and not a participle, a *faciendum* not a *factum*."[95] History therefore must be re-creation of the dramatic events which constituted man's coexistence with his circumstances. It explains, in so far as it accounts for, a *status nascendi* in terms of what preceded. "We have understood a situation historically when we have seen it emerging by necessity out of another, an earlier one."[96] "In short, the explanatory consideration, the *reason* consists then in a story. Over against mathematical-physical reason there stands a 'telling reason.' In order to understand something human, personal or collective, one must tell a story."[97] Yet it is never sufficient for history to recount that a man thought this or acted thus. For a story of a human deed must be more than a meaningless event. "A human datum is thus never a mere happening, a purely accidental process. It is a function of an entire human life, an individual or a collective one. It belongs to an organism of facts which all, without exception, play an active and effective part therein. Strictly speaking, only one thing happens to man: his biological existence; everything else is inner process, which releases counteractions in the inner life and finds a value and meaning in it. The importance of the fact thus does not lie in itself, but in the indivisible unity of each life."[98]

---

[94] See, for example, *G.W.*, IV, 393, 397, and III, 367, 375.

[95] *G.W.*, IV, 390.

[96] *G.W.*, II, 88; and III, 144, 165, 439, IV, 72, 198. See also I, 128, and Ceplecha, pp. 49–50.

[97] *G.W.*, IV, 399, and see also IV, 459 (there are facts "which we cannot reason out like a concept, but which someone must tell us").

[98] *G.W.*, III, 394–95; see also II, 192, III, 438–39.

History then cannot fulfil its function through a mere concern for the realm of the problematic, that zone of life into which man moves from his *creencias*. It must see that whole human reality, the whole culture, which man constructs as his "world." [99] The historian must go beyond the thoughts men describe, the acts which they leave as evidence. He must rather relate these to that reality of which men never speak because it is self-evident to themselves. He must account for ideas, institutions, and the like by *creencias*. But since these are what is "given" to men, their inheritance, the historian simply accounts for men's actions in terms of the past.

Thus then the reader should look at his life and should try to look through it as one looks through a glass container to see its infusoria. When he asks himself why his life is thus and not otherwise, he perceives that not a few singularities may be ascribed to an unintelligible accident. But the great lines of his reality will appear fully understandable when he sees that he is "such" because the society, the collective man of which he is a part, is "such." The mode of being of his society, in turn, explains itself when one uncovers in society what it was before , what was believed, felt, loved, and so on. This means that man sees the foreshortened form of the entire human past in his momentary now as something acting and continuing. For yesterday cannot be explained without the day before yesterday, and so on. History is a system, the system of human experiences which form an inexorable chain. Thus nothing in history is really clear so long as all is not clear. It is impossible to understand well what the rationalistic European man is when one does not really know what it was to be a Christian, and this, in turn, one does not really understand if one does not know what it meant to be a Stoic, and so on.[100]

---

[99] *G.W.*, II, 190, 193, 195, 230, 443, III, 375, 538, IV, 253; Ceplecha, p. 57 ("In reality the only history is universal history, all the rest is broken pieces and severed members"). For the following sentence in the text see n. 88 above.

[100] *G.W.*, IV, 403–4; see also the quotation from a review of Spengler in Ceplecha, p. 73.

So far, Ortega suggested a scheme for analyzing and understanding the horizontal structure of culture, a cross-cut through a static entity. In his choice of an ordering principle for such a structure he went further in the direction of an unconscious force inside man than did the authors discussed in the preceding chapters. The men of the past had to be understood in terms of *creencias* of which they themselves were least conscious. In addition, Ortega advocated one main tool for the understanding of man, historical reason, since man in his opinion had only history and no nature. Yet by the whole tenor and weight of his arguments he insisted that human reality is an everlasting process. What tool did he furnish then for understanding culture as perpetual change? Ortega attempted a solution through his notion of "the generation" — in his opinion, the most important tool for the historian. Even his early writings hint at the importance he attributed to this idea. It gained increasing importance for him as he became more involved in the discussion of historical change. In his *En torno a Galileo*, one of his most fascinating but also perplexing books, published in 1933, he elaborated the idea in most detail. Although he personally valued his conception of the generation, he treated it publicly as a suggestion. In all fairness to him, it will be best if the following is taken in the spirit of a suggestion.[101]

Man is characteristically a fabricator of "worlds."[102] In response to the problems posed by his circumstances, he shapes an interpretation of his reality and develops instruments and techniques for acting within this reality. The interpretations

---

[101] For a discussion of the background of the idea of the generation see Ceplecha, pp. 103–8, which also deals with Ortega's claims to originality and the subsequent elaboration of the idea of the generation by Ortega's pupil Marías. The treatise, of greatest importance for an understanding of Ortega's use of the notion of the generation, "Im Geiste Galileis," was started as a series of lectures in 1933 but was never completed because of the events in Spain (see *G.W.*, III, 387). For the "suggestive" character of the treatise, see *G.W.*, III, 420, 433, 538 (which I may have misread, however).

[102] *G.W.*, III, 411, and also III, 232, and *W.I.P.*, pp. 222–23.

of his reality, and his actions in and upon it, *are* his world. The human drama as a whole consists then of the following sequence: man finds himself amid circumstances — he builds his world out of these and out of his own activity — he thereby creates new circumstances — these again demand a response, a new creation, and so forth. "Each transformation of the world and its horizon brings a change in the structure of life's drama."[103]

A man is born into a world made by others. In the first phase of his life he absorbs this particular reality and orients himself within it. He discovers the world left to him by those ahead, by those who have lived in another stage of life.[104] Through their own response to the world they once inherited, these others have left him a world, a profile of reality, which differs from the circumstances which they once inherited from those ahead of themselves. Thus, a man's task involves building a world from realities which differ somewhat from the world which the others had to interpret.[105] But this means that three different profiles of reality coexist at one and the same time, carried, so to say, by men in different stages of life. There is the world of the young, the world of the mature, and the world of the old.[106] Within any existing society, every moment, every historical today, exhibits three different time stages of world-construction (i.e., life). Every man, therefore, has not simply a personal age but, more significantly, coexists with a world of a specific age. Each mode of life is placed between a preceding and a following one; it comes from one life and moves toward another.[107] Or, worlds (constructions of

---

[103] *G.W.*, III, 412, and also III, 20, 449.

[104] Not only the men ahead of him are in a stage of development but also their works; see *M.A.P.*, p. 216: "I am convinced that everything human — not only the person but his actions, what he constructs, what he fabricates — always has an age. That is, every human reality that presents itself to us is either in its infancy, or its youth, or its maturity, or its decline and decadence."

[105] *G.W.*, II, 85, 305, and esp. III, 414–23.

[106] *G.W.*, I, 436–39, III, 417; *W.I.P.*, p. 33.

[107] Life always stands at a specific level of time; *G.W.*, II, 83, III, 585, IV, 198, 589–90.

reality) succeed each other, not by existing in isolation for a while and then making place for the next, but by coexisting at one and the same time with the preceding and the following.[108]

Ortega sought to clarify this problem of the simultaneous existence of three world profiles by distinguishing between contemporaries and coevals.[109] All members of my society who live in this specific historical today are contemporaries. But the same today finds men at twenty in the process of forming their world, men of forty maintaining their world, and men of sixty seeing their world disappear in transformations. All who belong to one world profile, who share one task, Ortega called coevals. All contemporaries are thus grouped in three classes of coevals, which, like three different caravans, move through this today. Ortega called each coeval group a generation. Each generation therefore has its own profile, its own style, its own function, and its own time.[110]

> I once spoke of a generation as a caravan in which man moves along, but not without his secretly given consent, and not to his dissatisfaction. Once properly placed within this caravan, he holds loyally to the poets of his age, the political ideas of his time span, the female type who triumphed in the days of his youth, yes even to the specific manner of movement to which he became accustomed when twenty-five. Sometimes the strange silhouette of another caravan appears; it is the other generation. And at the occasional orgy of a feast day, it may occur that the two caravans are mixed up; but in the hours of our normal life the chaotic nod separates into organic parts. The individual recognizes in a mysterious manner who else belongs to his world, his community, analogous to the members of an ant heap recognizing their own. The discovery that we are bound by fate to a specific style of life and a specific

---

[108] *G.W.*, III, 425–29. Ortega did not state the obvious here about the quick change noticeable in periods of crisis; he believed in this coexistence of three slightly different world profiles in the most stable periods also.

[109] *G.W.*, II, 417–18, and *W.I.P.*, pp. 34–35.

[110] And it has its own elite and mass; see *G.W.*, II, 82.

age group is one of the melancholy experiences which every sensitive human being makes sooner or later. The belonging to a generation is an existential mode which affects all fields and imprints its ineradicable stamp on each individual. In wild tribes one can recognize the members of the different age groups by their tattoo. The ornaments which became fashionable when they grew up, have irrevocably grown into their nature.[111]

A generation is therefore a group with specific common characteristics, boxed in by two similar groups, one ahead and one behind itself. It was of utmost importance to Ortega that three such groups lived at one time and in specific interdependence, rather than as a mere succession in a genealogical sense. Historical change, that is, the modification of man's world, results from the encounter (or *Auseinandersetzung*) of the generations. "If all contemporaries were coevals, history would stand still and would stiffen in a petrified expression without any possibility of incisive renewal."[112] Each generation represents a level in the forward motion of time. Its world lies on a level beyond the preceding one, and yet each generation stands in the past and is to some extent its prisoner.[113] Each generation must contend with the world left by the preceding one, and it, in turn, will have to maintain its own conquest of a world in the contest with the following one. And it has a genuine contest on its hands because the contending generations are a living reality. Moreover, it must fight its fight from the level of its own time.[114] It has its own

---

[111] *G.W.*, III, 419; similarly II, 304, 459. See also II, 82.

[112] *G.W.*, III, 417. See also I, 364 (each generation shifts its attentions slightly, and such shifts in human attention are historical change), III, 431–32, 449, 531; *W.I.P.*, pp. 32–33.

[113] *G.W.*, III, 426 (". . . somewhat like the acrobats in the circus who form a pyramid. One on the shoulders of the other; he who stands on top thinks he surpasses the others, but should at the same time be conscious of being their captive").

[114] For a discussion of Ortega's conception of the "level of the time" see esp. *G.W.*, III, 21–28, and also III, 208, 384, 425.

situation and task in the total movement of man; it cannot exchange its place with any other and is itself irreplaceable.[115] Being present, between past and future, meant to Ortega to be at the level of one's time, which, in turn, meant to him to be the carrier of a certain world, to present a specific solution to the problem of life, to be one specific tone in a melody.

Ortega suggested some refinements to make such general ideas more immediately useful to the historian. Upon consideration of a number of schemes which subdivided human life into a sequence of stages, Ortega advocated the simple view of Aristotle, who discerned three basic ages: Youth, Fullness (or *acmé*), and Old Age. Three "vital" functions correspond to each of these ages: (1) to grow into a world, (2) to make and maintain a world, and (3) to have been responsible for a world. The generation representing the age of fullness is the dominant one among all contemporaries. Its world profile gives to the moment its dominant character. It has won its struggle against the old men and maintains itself as yet against the young. The two important ages for a historian to watch, therefore, are youth and fullness. What span of times does each such generation fill? Ortega suggested that the cryptic remark of Tacitus be taken seriously: life changes in terms of fifteen-year spans (*per quindecim annos grande mortalis aevi spatium*).[116] An average life of seventy-five years subdivides thus into fifteen years each of childhood, youth, introduction, fullness, and old age. Of these, childhood and youth form one generation, introduction and fullness another, and old age a third. The two important generations thus last thirty years each, but each generation passes through two phases.[117] To Ortega this two-phase structure of each generation was mainly important in the "dominant" generation.[118] The period of maturity, from thirty to sixty years, contains

---

[115] *G.W.*, III, 426, and W.I.P., p. 184.
[116] *G.W.*, II, 9, and III, 437. See also III, 431.
[117] *G.W.*, III, 74.
[118] *G.W.*, III, 429–32, and also I, 55.

two phases: one in which men seek to establish and to introduce their view of the world, in which they make propaganda
for their solutions, their ideas, their sentiments and inclinations. This is the period of introduction. It is followed by
another, from age 45 to 60, in which they maintain their
world. They change the world up to the age of forty-five and
then seek to preserve it against the new changers.[119]

This scheme in no way predetermines where a specific
individual may fit in. Some are young, that is, they still orient
themselves in relation to a world, while others, born in the
same year, may be already engaged in the work of introduction. Ortega was inclined to consider a man's "age" in terms
of his "vital" task rather than his exact chronological age.[120]
A generation lasted for Ortega through a "date zone" (*zona
de fechas*), a span of time characterized by a "vital" function.
One begins to be young and ceases to be young not at a fixed
year but during such a date zone. "Age is thus not a datum
but a 'date zone'; in the 'vital' and historical sense of age not
merely those belong to the same age who were born in the
same year but rather those who were born in a particular 'date
zone.'"[121] The man who reaches his thirtieth year in 1966
does not automatically know whether he belongs to the fifteen-
year zone which is just coming to an end, which has just begun,
or has run half its course; ". . . from the vantage point of
the individual, a man never knows exactly whether his chronological date of age forms the beginning of a generation, the
end, or the middle."[122]

By the notion of the generation Ortega had worked out a
scheme for the understanding of historical movement in general. He still faced the problem of co-ordinating this genera-

[119] *G.W.*, III, 74.
[120] *G.W.*, III, 416–17, 420–21, 427, 581; *W.I.P.*, p. 184 (". . . in the strictest
sense of the phrase, every period has its task, its mission, its demands for innovation. More than that . . . time is not, in the final analysis, what the clocks
measure, but time is quite literally a task, a mission, an innovation").
[121] *G.W.*, III, 421.
[122] *G.W.*, III, 433.

tion chronology with the actual course of development of a specific society. Ortega needed to demonstrate that actual changes in the structure of history concurred with the periodicity of the generations. But to understand Ortega's suggestion for resolving this problem, it is best to elaborate briefly on the different aspects of historical change.

The change produced by the interaction of generations results in differing versions of the reality which men experience as their world. But each such world has, according to Ortega, its own characteristic structure of zones. The all-important question is, therefore, Which of these zones are affected by change and to what extent? In relatively stable periods of a culture, generations possess a more or less common set of *creencias*.[123] After all, *creencias* are those *certain* aspects of an interpretation of reality unquestioned by men. They constitute the traditional answer to a set of problems which therefore have ceased to be problems. Men, not being forced to preoccupy themselves with these certainties, therefore concern themselves with the remaining problems — that area of their tasks and labors which is the zone of ideas and not the zone of *creencias*. The changed world profile which emerges, generation by generation, differs in terms of solutions to those problems which are problems only in relation to the fixed verities of *creencias*.[124] Thus men elaborate and specify their particular culture but do not change its *essential* character. Yet, with every new answer to previously unresolved problems, men add to their culture and thereby increase the cultural burden they must carry.[125] The more men push toward the horizon of a culture, the more they approach cosmic (transmundane) parts of reality which now become new circum-

---

[123] See *W.I.P.*, p. 37 ("Ordinarily the difference between sons and fathers is small, so that what predominates is the common nucleus in which they coincide, and the sons can see themselves as continuing and perfecting the type of life which their fathers led").

[124] *G.W.*, III, 455.

[125] *G.W.*, II, 256–57.

stances for men who cannot adequately resolve these new riddles in terms of the initial set of *creencias*.[126] The more actively men lead an "authentic" life of problem solving, the more they move away from their *creencias*. So it is the fate of active cultures to weaken their zone of absolute verities.[127] At a certain point, men lose the support of their faith and no longer experience certainties but doubts. These dramatic moments when *creencias* give way to doubts, the most dramatic occurrence in human life, Ortega called historical crises.[128] Now the world changes in a fundamental sense: men must struggle through to a new faith because the old one no longer supports them. Man's trust in the faith of the fathers crumbles and he is gradually overcome by despair. He again understands what it means to be shipwrecked. "A historical crisis exists when the modification of the world is such that the world, or the system of convictions of the preceding generation, is followed by a situation in which man is without the convictions, therefore without a 'world.' . . . It is a modification which, at first, is negative, critical." In a crisis, man, uncertain of his direction, moves hither and yon, tries this and that, without real conviction. "In ages of crisis one finds frequently false and hypocritical opinions. Whole generations falsify themselves, that is, they escape into artificial styles, into doctrines, into insincere political movements, merely to fill the emptiness left behind by the genuine convictions."[129] Very gradually, and chiefly through the work of those who

---

[126] *G.W.*, II, 181 ("No change in a culture is of more far-reaching importance than a shift in its horizon"). Indications of shifts announce themselves earliest in the realm of art and science; see *G.W.*, II, 255.

[127] *G.W.*, III, 71–72; it is the fate of western man, in Ortega's opinion.

[128] *G.W.*, II, 80, III, 454–57, 539–40, IV, 107, 367; *W.I.P.*, p. 38.

[129] All quotations from *G.W.*, III, 455. See also III, 441, 586–88, IV, 112–13 (where Ortega maintains that a new faith is usually on the way when an old one dies: "It is not possible that a *creencia* dies; it is then that a new one is born; for the same reasons that it is impossible to see an error without finding oneself, *ipso facto*, on the grounds of a new truth"). But the fact that a new faith has been forming itself among some, does not yet make it a social reality in the full sense.

withdraw within themselves (*ensimismamiento*) new certainties gain ground — until another set of basic verities is clearly formulated which can serve as the comfortable house of a new culture.

Ortega y Gasset suggested using such crisis generations to align his framework of generations with a historical chronology. The problem consisted in matching two co-ordinate systems of periodization until the one fit the other. For this, one needs an anchor point. Ortega proposed to find this by fixing on the life of one man who clearly represented the new set of convictions which would characterize the culture emerging from the crisis. In his example, the candidate for "eponym [name-giver] of the decisive generation,"[130] which represented the first truly "modern" generation, was Descartes. He was the representative of a "generation which for the first time thought the modern thoughts in full clarity and with full consciousness of their significance, a generation therefore which is no longer a pathfinder and is not yet a mere conservator . . . a decisive generation."[131] Descartes gave a clearly formulated expression to the new realities which members of the preceding generations had gradually developed. Having fixed a reference point with this eponym, Ortega proceeded schematically to superimpose his framework of generations upon the age. Descartes became thirty in 1626. This Ortega took as the midpoint of the decisive generation, which therefore stretches forward and backward by fifteen-year spans. Going backward, 1611 becomes the date for the preceding generation of Hobbes (born in 1588) and Grotius (1583); 1596 the date for the generation of Galileo (1564), Kepler (1571), and Bacon (1561); 1581 is the date of the generation of Giordano Bruno (1550), Tycho Brahe (1546), Cervantes (1547), Suárez (1548), and Sánchez (1550); 1566 becomes the date for the generation of Montaigne (1533) and

---

[130] *G.W.*, III, 435.
[131] *G.W.*, III, 434, and see also, III, 443, 541.

Bodin (1530). Each of these representatives of their generation attained his thirtieth birthday seven or eight years before or after the mid-date for each generation. More important for Ortega's scheme, however, was the question whether the actual thought of these men of different generations was related in the manner in which he believed it had to be. He therefore suggested, as a test, comparing the thought of Hobbes and Descartes. For, if the thought of both appeared to be on the same level of time, if it were to sound as the "speaking tube of one and the same structure of life," then the matrix of generations would have been improperly placed upon the historical reality. It seemed to Ortega that Hobbes's system of thought bordered exactly in the same manner upon that of Descartes as his generation touched on that of Descartes. The study of his works and the analysis of his total attitude toward problems of reality revealed to the Spanish philosopher a basic similarity, but not a congruence of both systems.

> Hobbes sees things almost as Descartes, but this "almost" is symptomatic. His distance from Descartes is almost insignificant, and is so in almost all questions. It is not that Hobbes coincides with Descartes in one point and differs in another; no, in order to circumscribe the very remarkable relation between both sharply, we would have to say that they coincide a bit in everything and that they differ a bit in everything. It is as if two men were looking at the same landscape from two levels separated by only a short distance. This is then a matter of difference in the relative height of one's position. But it is that difference in the "vital level" which I associate with the idea of the generation.[132]

Proceeding from the opposite direction, that is, coming from the past, Ortega ran a similar test with one single idea and its acceptance from generation to generation. Since he thought it characteristic of the modern approach to physical reality that modern man conceived of it in mathematical relations,

---

[132] G.W., III, 436.

he singled out the Copernican theorem and traced its gradual acceptance through the "generation dates" he had established.[133] Again, he felt assured that his scheme provided a useful tool for historical construction.

Ortega y Gasset considered himself a philosopher, not a cultural historian. He merely wished to suggest a method which seemed to him more promising than the standard approaches of the historian, but he himself wrote no cultural history. Yet in many writings he indicated the areas of concern which historians might select for making history more of a system, a structured whole. In accord with his entire manner of viewing human existence, he thought it especially fruitful to concentrate upon the great historical crises. For in the transition from one way of life, one culture, to another, the coherence of the entire western tradition emerges. Ortega especially selected the great crises in which western men profoundly altered their faith: the fourth century B.C., the age of Cicero and Saint Paul, the thirteenth to fifteenth centuries, and his own times. And since Ortega attributed particular prominence to the manner in which men conceive reality, he hinted at figures who illustrate different positions in the approach to reality *within* each culture; such men as Paul, Augustine, Anselm, Thomas Aquinas, Duns Scotus, Ockham, Nicolas of Cusa, or Descartes, Leibniz, Kant, Fichte, Husserl, and Einstein. Although he gave such prominence to representative thinkers, he never thought of history as the history of ideas or of philosophy.[134] For, genuine history must relate man's ideas to something more fundamental, namely, his core convictions, the mood in which he undertakes his task, the vitality with which he leads his problematic life. "History is inquiry in depth."[135]

Ortega y Gasset only hinted at the structure of historical

---

[133] *G.W.*, III, 449–54.
[134] See, for instance, *G.W.*, II, 442–43.
[135] *G.W.*, IV, 203–4.

reality, and merely urged the historians to take his suggestions as a starting point for their inquiries. He taught and wrote as a philosopher. The professionals will have to judge Ortega's philosophy. Did he work as fundamental a change in philosophy as he himself was inclined to think at times? To one superficially acquainted with the currents of modern philosophical thought, one who cannot account for the origins of certain intellectual trends, Ortega is reminiscent of positions encountered somewhere in one's education. For Ortega's own system this presents no serious issue; for an "authentic" thinker thinks at the "level of his times." Whether original or restating thoughts at second hand, this Spanish philosopher presented the historians a modern scheme of thought which can stimulate their own task.

Through his philosophical search for the ultimate human realities, Ortega arrived before the world of history. When he turned to the historians for further illumination, he despaired of the poverty of their work. He was above all overcome by the discrepancy between extensive historical research and the paucity of meaningful knowledge derived therefrom. "I firmly believe that God will not forgive the historians. Even the geologists have succeeded in awakening our interest in dead stones; but all that the historians, who have the most fascinating subject in their hands, have achieved is that less history is being read in Europe than before." [136] Thus he sought, in the spirit of Galileo, who had revolutionized one science, to direct the historian's concern to a promising method, another way. [137] He insisted that history must be the basic study of man. History is the science of the radical human reality, and historical reason the most concrete and fullest mode of understanding. To permit this, the historians must resolve the problem of the structure of historical reality and should seriously consider the task of making history an interdependent system.

---

[136] *G.W.*, III, 364. See also, I, 358, 476, III, 361.
[137] *G.W.*, III, 393.

Ortega elaborated certain suggestions to facilitate these many labors. He provided a manner for looking at the radical reality, our human life, as a historical reality. He suggested a way to understand the structure of society and its importance for the transmission of values and customs. He worked out a scheme for explaining the relations between a guiding minority and an indispensable mass. He analyzed the methodological difficulties of the historian and indicated a road toward a clearer conception of historical science. He proposed an idea for reducing the complexities of a culture to an intelligible entity. He made concrete suggestions for coping with the intricate problem of cultural development. Perhaps none of these will be considered helpful by the working majority of historians. Possibly more satisfactory schemes can be built on Ortega's foundations. "We see [our own philosophy] immersed in the stream of history like any other perishable product of the ages. . . . [It] shares in the fundamental feature of all human occupation: to be a promise that is never fulfilled. Man's doing is found to be wanting and it would be vain to expect of him full realization. . . . In the caravans that cross the parched deserts of Lybia we have heard an old adage: 'Drink from the well and make room for the next.' " [138]

Ortega y Gasset was a crisis philosopher [139] seeking to dispel illusions while retaining a living contact with the western achievement. His peculiar manner of philosophizing was shaped by his sense of urgency in the face of problems besetting modern man. He tried to direct men to their deepest problems *now* and wanted to cure them of a trust in sciences which postpone answers *ad calendas Graecas*. For life demands solutions to its problems now, and "the faith in progress which

---

[138] *C.A.L.*, pp. 127–28; see also *W.I.P.*, p. 37.

[139] Typical are remarks like these: "The sense of being shipwrecked, since it is the truth about life, already means a measure of rescue. I therefore believe only in the thoughts of the shipwrecked. One should place the classics before a tribunal of the shipwrecked and ask them certain fundamental questions about life" (*G.W.*, III, 270, taken from an essay, "Um einen Goethe von innen bittend" ["Pidiendo un Goethe desde dentro"], 1932).

postponed truth until a vague tomorrow has been the opiate which stupidified mankind."[140] None of the great model sciences has until today taken the study of man as the most serious issue. In that situation Ortega thought it better to dare solutions than to postpone them for fear of error. And he looked for help especially from that form of knowledge which makes the concrete life of man its proper subject. "Man asks himself: what is this one thing that remains to me, my life, my life without illusion? How did it happen that it alone has remained? And the answer is to discover the history of human development, that dialectic series of his experiences, which, I repeat, might have been otherwise but has been that which it was, and which we must know because it is *the* transcendent reality. Man, alienated from himself, finds himself again as reality, as history. And for the first time he sees himself forced to preoccupy himself with the past, not for curiosity's sake, or in order to find normative examples, but because he *has nothing else.*"[141]

---

[140] *G.W.*, IV, 377. See also, I, 429, II, 11, III, 233, IV, 389; and *M.A.P.*, p. 21.
[141] *G.W.*, IV, 411.

Conclusion

Six men from different societies, six different temperaments, different outlooks upon life, and differing views of history — each had his own way of treating civilization. But they all shared the problems of that distinguished band of historians who aim at nothing less than understanding human life in its full complexity. Despite all differences, their solutions are variations upon common themes.

They all come to their historical task with a genuine fascination for man's manifold cultural labors. But while some see humanity constantly struggling to attain the true model of civilized existence, others place the stress on the long, continuous process whereby men gradually elaborate the emerging pattern of the good life, and still others trace the formulation and then the dissolution of styles of life in which man, the Protean creature, expresses his manifold potential in ever changing combinations and emphases. The monist and the pluralist have different conceptions of culture and face different problems. Other variations in treatment stem from the extent to which a historian subscribes to deterministic genetic patterns. The less deterministic approach seems to have been more closely associated with works that restrict themselves to descriptions of separate cultural periods. This approach usually has the advantage of offering a richer picture of the many interrelations within one cultural complex and often, though not necessarily, de-emphasizes grand genetic schemes. The more deterministic outlook leads to a more coherent presentation of the linear succession of cultural phases, and those who take this approach, with some exceptions, show a tendency to curtail the full treatment of each separate period within this total progression of time. These are real differences; but since each historian faces the demands of the synchronic and the diachronic aspects of his subject matter, the differences, from a higher perspective, become matters of degree and emphasis.

While none of the historians treated here would deny that human affairs are in part conditioned by geography, climate, and external factors beyond human control, their main concern is man as the shaper of his civilization. Even when they lean more toward deterministic schemes of interpretation, the interaction of human creation and the realm of necessity emerges as an important issue. Certainly the historians of this study were deeply concerned with the relation between man and his culture. But it has been of particular interest to me that each focused upon different aspects of man as the decisive ones for understanding and presenting his total way of life. As one goes from historian to historian, a different facet of man himself, and of his self-made world, moves into the foreground, receiving the prime attention, and is clearly employed either as the central referral point for the organization of the whole picture or as a dominant explanatory device or as both. And the more modern these historians, the more they seem to prefer the less conscious regions of man's personality.

Voltaire, measuring the degree to which mankind approached the norm of truly civilized existence, had his eye on five cultural components: the state, material well-being, urbane sociability, sane philosophy, and good taste. As a *philosophe* he cared that all expressions of culture should follow the dictates of reason, and as a sensitive man he preferred that they adhere to the standards of good taste. Reasonable men with *esprit* and good taste were for him the mainstay of civilization. In a sense, Guizot retained this commitment to rationality. But he also placed great stress upon the idea that men follow the "higher reason" of history, or Providence. Such a mode of reason commands men to reconcile such antithetical principles as liberty and order, rationality and faith. Burckhardt, in the tradition of Herder and Goethe, looked at culture more as the expression of a *Geist* than of universal *ratio*. It is difficult to say whether this entailed a shift away from the stress on rationality; it is probably more important that it is a shift toward a more complex concept and thus fits in with Burckhardt's reliance upon a notion such as style for mastering this complexity. At any rate, he was always looking for the different styles, or types of men, and the spirit in which they gave a unique form to their total existence. He therefore focused upon the whole man, the harmony resulting from tensions, and did not single out one special aspect of "man-in-general" as the dominant factor. A particular human type, such as "Renaissance Man," might indeed possess individualism, for instance, as an outstanding trait. But the very same trait might appear, in a subordinate position, in another human type of another cultural age.

Lamprecht maintained a somewhat analogous position with his notion that the Germans of specific cultural phases gave coherence to their civilization by means of their particular "psychic dominant." But unlike Burckhardt, he insisted that these psychic dominants represent universally valid psychogenetic stages in the development of every *Volk*. Lamprecht did not focus so much upon the complete human being as upon certain psychological conditions, following fixed laws of development. And he employed these to explain the prevailing forms of rationality, the taste, the moods, the institutions, in short, all cultural phenomena. Huizinga shied away from all such scientific pretensions. But he had a penchant for such elusive matters as the moods of whole societies, their pursuit of beautiful dreams, the temper of aesthetic preferences, and the temperament of men. In so far as he looked for one key in the explanation of culture, he found this in man's play instinct, an unaccountable, unneeded, and suprarational element. And Ortega y Gasset selected *creencias* as the core reality giving structure to a cultural configuration. He thereby located the organizing principle, and the explanatory device, in such a "hidden layer" of man that the reconstructing historian must penetrate recesses of which the men who lived in that culture were not even fully conscious.

When one reaches the theory that culture must be understood as the product of the deepest sources of man's view of the self and the world, the question poses itself: what has the cultural historian gained by looking ever deeper into the human being while searching for a primary explanatory principle? Has this advance beyond Burckhardt's use of "personality types" enriched cultural history? I am almost certain that the cultural historian of the future will be wise to avoid any further splitting-up of man's motivations in ever more specialized causes and "causes of causes"; restricting himself to the explanatory principle of human types, he can then address himself to the more modest task of drawing an ever richer and more fully co-ordinated picture of cultural history as the explication, so to speak, of historically varying types in life and world. Cultural history could again become the history of styles of man and styles of life.

But where cultural history will go from here will depend in large part upon the motivation for writing it at all. The professional rewards for the historian do not lie in such monumental projects which bring him into constant danger of flying in the face of all the professional canons he was taught. To begin such a hazardous task, the historian needs a motivation akin to a sense of calling. Voltaire had such a motive in his desire to make life a bit more civilized. Guizot tied his whole political career to his interpretation of the past. Burckhardt and Huizinga struggled to preserve the cultural values of a world threatened with rebarbarization. And all of Ortega's thought turned on his idea that shipwrecked men could only cope with their crisis by understanding their culture and building upon it. Whatever the self-chosen task — be it to awaken man's cultural awareness and conscience, be it to furnish a justification and program for future action, be it merely the contemplative viewing of a cultural continuum and a sense of obligation toward its preservation, or be it to criticize current tendencies of civilization and to urge a re-balancing of its components — the historian who tackles a whole civilization must be a courageous man. Above all he needs the courage to undertake the task despite his ignorance and without hope of ever finding a perfect solution. As Huizinga saw it, "It is, after all, the lot of him who treats of cultural problems that he has to venture forth on many terrains which he insufficiently masters."[1] It is perhaps no para-dox that the great works of cultural history were written by men who had a genuine sense of the inadequacy of any human enterprise. That there were wrestlers with the angel, that men had the courage to face this seemingly hopeless task of writing the history of civilization, proves one fact: striving to understand the course of culture is not so much a matter of scholarly curiosity as a need growing out of living life itself.

---

[1] Johan Huizinga, *Homo Ludens: proeve eener bepaling van het spelele-ment der cultuur*, in *Verzamelde Werken* (Haarlem: Tjeenk Willink & Zoon, 1948–53), V, 27.

Bibliographical Notes

These lists are meant to be merely a guide to the texts and the editions cited in this study. They are neither exhaustive bibliographies of the works of the various authors nor a complete listing of all the works read for this study nor necessarily an enumeration of the best editions available. This working bibliography follows a simple subdivision of (1) works by the author, (2) biographical accounts, and (3) special studies cited in each chapter. Within the subdivision the arrangement is alphabetical and not according to importance of the texts.

CHAPTER 1: VOLTAIRE

Works by Voltaire
Candide and Other Writings. Edited by Haskell M. Block. New York: Random House, 1956.
Lettres choisies. Edited by Louis Moland. 2 vols. Paris: Garnier, 1883.
Mélanges. Edited by Jacques van den Heuvel. Bibliothèque de la Pléiade. Paris: Librairie Gallimard, 1961.
Oeuvres complètes. Edited by Louis Moland. 53 vols. Paris: Garnier, 1877–83.
  Vol. IX: *La Pucelle — Petits poëmes.*
  Vols. XI–XIII: *Essai sur les moeurs.*
  Vols. XVII–XX: *Dictionnaire philosophique.*
  Vols. XXII–XXIX: *Mélanges.*
Oeuvres historiques. Edited by René Pomeau. Bibliothèque de la Pléiade. Paris: Librairie Gallimard, 1957.
Romans et Contes. Edited by René Groos. Bibliothèque de la Pléiade. Paris: Librairie Gallimard, 1954.

Biographical Accounts
Brailsford, Henry N. *Voltaire.* New York: Holt, 1935 (also available as Oxford paperback, 1963).

Condorcet, Marquis de. *Vie de Voltaire*, in *Oeuvres de Condorcet*, IV, 1–186. Edited by A. Condorcet O'Connor and François Arago. 12 vols. Paris: Firmin-Didot, 1847–49.

Desnoiresterres, Gustave. *Voltaire et la société du XVIIIe siècle*. 8 vols. Paris: Didier, 1871–79.

Lanson, Gustave. *Voltaire*. Paris: Hachette, 1906.

Mahrenholtz, Richard. *Voltaire's Leben und Werke*. Oppeln: Franck, 1885.

Vries, Philip de. *Voltaire, burger en edelman*. Bussum: Kroonder, 1951.

Special Studies

Becker, Carl L. *The Heavenly City of the Eighteenth Century Philosophers*. New Haven: Yale University Press, 1932 (also available in Yale University Press paperback, 1959).

Black, John B. *The Art of History*. London: Methuen, 1926.

Brumfitt, John H. *Voltaire, Historian*. Oxford: Oxford University Press, 1958.

Cassirer, Ernst. *Die Philosophie der Aufklärung*. Tübingen, 1932 (also available in English: *The Philosophy of the Enlightenment*. Boston: Beacon Press, 1949).

Dilthey, Wilhelm. "Das 18. Jahrhundert und die geschichtliche Welt," *Deutsche Rundschau*, CVIII (1901), 241–61 and 350–80.

Gay, Peter. *Voltaire's Politics*. Princeton: Princeton University Press, 1959.

Kaegi, Werner. "Voltaire und der Zerfall des christlichen Geschichtbildes" in *Historische Meditationen*, I, 223–48. 2 vols. Zurich: Fretz & Wasmuth, 1942.

Loewith, Karl. *Meaning in History*. Chicago: University of Chicago Press, 1949 (also available in a Phoenix paperback).

Martin, Alfred von. "Motive und Tendenzen in Voltaire's Geschichtsschreibung," *Historische Zeitschrift*, CXVIII (1917), 1–45.

Meinecke, Friedrich. *Die Entstehung des Historismus*. Vol. III of *Werke*. Edited by Hans Herzfeld *et al.* Munich: Oldenbourg, 1959.

Naves, Raymond. *Le goût de Voltaire*. Paris: Garnier, 1938.

Romein, Jan. "Uit de voorhof der cultuurhistorie," in *Carillon der tijden*, pp. 88–130. Amsterdam: Querido, 1953.

Sakmann, Paul. "Die Probleme der historischen Methodik und Geschichtsphilosophie bei Voltaire," *Historische Zeitschrift*, XCVII (1906), 327–79.

———. "Universalgeschichte in Voltaire's Beleuchtung," *Zeitschrift für französische Sprache und Litteratur*, XXX (1906), 1–86.

———. *Voltaire's Geistesart und Gedankenwelt*. Stuttgart: Frommann, 1910.

Wade, Ira Owen. *Voltaire and Candide*. Princeton: Princeton University Press, 1959.

Chapter 2: Guizot

Works by Guizot

Essais sur l'histoire de France. 14th ed. Paris: Didier, 1878.

Gibbon. See Notes to Edward Gibbon.

Histoire de la civilisation en France depuis la chûte de l'empire romain. 2d ed. 4 vols. Paris: Didier, 1840.

Histoire des origines du gouvernement représentatif. 2 vols. Paris: Didier, 1856–57.

Histoire générale de la civilisation en Europe depuis la chûte de l'empire romain jusqu'à la Révolution française. 3d ed. Paris: Didier, 1840.

Histoire parlementaire; recueil complet des discours prononcés dans les Chambres de 1819 à 1848 par M. Guizot. 5 vols. Paris: n.p., 1863–64.

Letters. See *Monsieur Guizot in Private Life*.

Méditations sur l'essence de la religion chrétienne. 2d ed. 3 vols. Paris: Levy, 1866–68.

Mélanges politiques et historiques. Paris: Levy, 1869.

Mémoires pour servir à l'histoire de mon temps. 8 vols. Paris: Levy, 1858–67.

Monsieur Guizot in Private Life, 1787–1874. Edited by Henriette E. de Witt (née Guizot) and translated by M. Simpson. Boston: Estes & Lauriat, 1882. This is a collection of Guizot's letters.

Notes to Edward Gibbon, *The History of the Decline and Fall of the Roman Empire*. 6 vols. Philadelphia: Claxton, 1883. Contains also an introduction by Guizot.

Biographical Sketches
Bardoux, Benjamin J. *Guizot.* Paris: Hachette, 1894.
Pouthas, Charles H. *Guizot pendant la Restauration, préparation de l'homme d'état (1814–1830).* Paris: Plon, 1923.
————. *La jeunesse de Guizot (1787–1814).* Paris: Alcan, 1936.

Special Studies
Barzun, Jacques. *The French Race: Theories of Its Origins and Their Social and Political Implications prior to the Revolution.* New York: Columbia University Press, 1932.
————. "Romantic Historiography as a Political Force in France," *Journal of the History of Ideas,* II (1941), 318–29.
Keiser, Rut. *Guizot als Historiker.* Basel: n.p., 1925. Dissertation.
Mill, John Stuart. "Guizot's Essays and Lectures on History," in *Dissertations and Discussions: Political, Philosophical, and Historical,* II, 218–82. 3d ed. 4 vols. London: Longmans, Green, 1875.
O'Connor, Sister Mary Consolata. *The Historical Thought of François Guizot.* Washington, D.C.: Catholic University of America, 1955. A dissertation covering Guizot's career to 1830 only.
Pouthas, Charles H. *Essai critique sur les sources et la bibliographie de Guizot pendant la Restauration.* Paris: Plon, 1923.
Woodward, Ernest. *Three Studies in European Conservatism: Metternich, Guizot, the Catholic Church in the 19th Century.* London: Constable, 1929.

CHAPTER 3: BURCKHARDT

Works by Burckhardt
"Andeutungen zur Geschichte der christlichen Skulptur," *Italien: Monatsschrift fur Kultur, Kunst, und Literature,* October and December, 1929. This article appeared first in 1848 in Cotta's *Kunstblatt.*
Briefe. Edited by Fritz Kaphahn. Leipzig: Dieterichsche Verlagsbuchhandlung, n.d.
Der Cicerone: eine Anleitung zum Genuss der Kunstwerke Italiens. 2 vols. Leipzig: Seemann, 1893.

Erinnerungen aus Rubens. Vienna: Phaidon, 1938.
Frühe Schriften. Edited by Hans Trog *et al.* Basel: Schwabe, 1930.
Vol. I of the *Gesamtausgabe.* 14 vols.
Die Geschichte der Renaissance in Italien. Stuttgart: Neff, 1904.
This is also known as Vol. I of *Geschichte der neueren Bau-
kunst.* Edited by Jacob Burckhardt and Wilhelm Luebke. It was
first published in 1867.
Griechische Kulturgeschichte. Edited by Rudolf Marx. 3 vols.
Leipzig: Kroener, n.d.
*Historische Fragmente: aus dem Nachlass gesammelt von Emil
Duerr.* Stuttgart: Koehler, 1957.
Die Kultur der Renaissance in Italien. Vienna: Phaidon, n.d.
Vorträge. Basel: Schwabe, 1933. Vol. XIV of the *Gesamtausgabe.*
Weltgeschichtliche Betrachtungen. Edited by Werner Kaegi.
Bern: Hallwag, 1941.
Die Zeit Konstantins des Grossen. Vienna: Phaidon, n.d.

Biography
Kaegi, Werner. *Burckhardt, eine Biographie.* 3 vols. Basel:
Schwabe, 1947–57. This is, in all likelihood, the longest biography ever devoted to any single historian. It is of great value
for any study of Burckhardt, since it includes many quotations
from the unpublished writings in the *Nachlass.* It is incomplete
as of this date (1966), covering the years from 1818 to 1860; at
least one more volume is expected.

Special Studies
Ferguson, Wallace K. *The Renaissance in Historical Thought:
Five Centuries of Interpretation.* Boston: Houghton Mifflin,
1948.
Gilbert, Felix. "Cultural History and Its Problems," in *Rapports
of the International Congress of Historical Sciences, Stockholm,
1960,* I, 40–58.
Grisebach, Eberhard. *Jacob Burckhardt als Denker.* Bern: Haupt,
1943.
Kaegi, Werner. *Europäische Horizonte im Denken Jacob Burckhardts: drei Studien.* Basel: Schwabe, 1962.
Knittermeyer, Hinrich. *Jacob Burckhardt: Deutung und Beru-
fung des abendländischen Menschen.* Stuttgart: Hirzel, 1949.

Loewith, Karl. *Jacob Burckhardt: der Mensch inmitten der Geschichte*. Lucerne: Vita Nova, 1936.
Srbik, Heinrich Ritter von. *Geist und Geschichte vom deutschen Humanismus bis zur Gegenwart*. 2 vols. Salzburg: Mueller, 1951.

CHAPTER 4: LAMPRECHT

Works by Lamprecht
Alte und neue Richtungen in der Geschichtswissenschaft. Berlin: Gaertner, 1906.
Beiträge zur Geschichte des französischen Wirtschaftsleben im 11. Jahrhundert. Leipzig: Duncker & Humblot, 1878. This was Lamprecht's dissertation; it was also translated into French.
Deutsche Geschichte. 12 vols. and 2 Ergänzungsbände. The history of publication of this work is confused, since Lamprecht revised the volumes while still writing others. The edition available to me is a composite one of different imprints: Vol. I (Freiburg: Heyfelder, 1906); Vols. II–III (same publisher, 1904–6); Vols. IV (Berlin: Weidmann, 1911); Vols. V–VIII (Freiburg: Heyfelder, 1904–6); Vols. IX–XII (Berlin: Weidmann, 1907–9); Ergänzungsbände I and II (Freiburg: Heyfelder, 1905–6). Volumes V, VII, VIII, XI, and Ergänzungsband II, each appeared in two separate volumes, so that there is a total of nineteen volumes.
Deutsches Wirtschaftsleben im Mittelalter. 3 vols. Leipzig: Dürr, 1885–86.
Einführung in das historische Denken. Leipzig: Voigtländer, 1913.
Die Initialornamentik des 8.–13. Jahrhunderts. Leipzig: Dürr, 1882.
Kindheitserinnerungen. Gotha: Perthes, 1918.
Die Kulturhistorische Methode. Berlin: Gaertner, 1900.
Moderne Geschichtswissenschaft. Freiburg: n.p., 1905. This appeared as *What Is History?* New York: Macmillan, 1905.

Biographical Sketches
Bücher, Karl. "Worte zum Gedächtnis an Karl Lamprecht," *Berichte über die Verhandlungen der Königlich Sächsischen*

Gesellschaft der Wissenschaften zu Leipzig, Philologisch-Historische Klasse, LVII (1915), 93–104.

Popper, Annie M. "Karl Gotthard Lamprecht (1856–1915)," in *Some Historians of Modern Europe,* pp. 217–39. Edited by Bernadotte Schmitt. Chicago: University of Chicago Press, 1942.

Schmoller, Gustav. "Zur Würdigung von Karl Lamprecht," *Schmoller's Jahrbuch für Gesetzgebung, Verwaltung, und Volkswirtschaft im Deutschen Reiche,* XL (1916), Part 3, pp. 27–54.

Schoenebaum, Herbert. "Karl Lamprecht," *Archiv für Kulturgeschichte,* XXXVII (1955), 269–305.

Special Studies

Barth, Paul. *Die Philosophie der Geschichte.* Leipzig: Reisland, 1915.

Below, Georg von. "Die neue historische Methode," *Historische Zeitschrift,* LXXXI (1898), 193–273. This was one of the articles most hostile to Lamprecht.

Bernheim, Ernst. *Lehrbuch der historischen Methode und der Geschichtsphilosophie.* Leipzig: Duncker & Humblot, 1908.

Eulenburg, Franz. "Neuere Geschichtsphilosophie: kritische Analysen," *Archiv für Sozialwissenschaft und Sozialpolitik,* N.F., XXV (1907), 283–337.

Goetz, Walter. "Lamprecht's *Deutsche Geschichte*" and "Karl Lamprecht's Stellung in der Geschichtswissenschaft," in *Historiker in meiner Zeit; Gesammelte Aufsätze,* pp. 296–309, 309–13. Cologne: Boehlau, 1957.

Hintze, Otto. "Über individualistische und kollektivistische Geschichtsauffassung," *Historische Zeitschrift,* LXXVII (1897), 60–67.

Koetzschke, Rudolf. "Verzeichnis der Schriften Karl Lamprecht's," *Berichte über die Verhandlungen der Königlich Sächsischen Gesellschaft der Wissenschaften zu Leipzig, Philologisch-Historische Klasse,* LVII (1915), 105–19.

Kuhnert, Adolf. *Der Streit um die geschichtswissenschaftlichen Theorien Karl Lamprechts.* Gütersloh: Floettmann, 1906.

Spiess, Emil J. *Die Geschichtsphilosophie von Karl Lamprecht.* Erlangen: n.p., 1921.

Srbik, Heinrich Ritter von. *Geist und Geschichte vom deutschen Humanismus bis zur Gegenwart.* 2 vols. Salzburg: Mueller, 1951.

CHAPTER 5: HUIZINGA

Works by Huizinga
De Rechtsbronnen der stad Haarlem. Edited by Johan Huizinga. Ser. 2, Vol. XIII of *Werken der Vereeniging tot uitgaaf der bronnen van het Oud-Vaderlandsche Recht.* The Hague: Nijhoff, 1911.
Men and Ideas: Essays by Johan Huizinga. New York: Meridian Books, 1959.
Verzamelde Werken. Edited by L. Brummel, W. R. Juynboll, Th. J. G. Locher. 9 vols. Haarlem: Tjeenk Willink, 1948–53. Vol. IX of this edition has an excellent bibliography of Huizinga's writings, listing also translations of his works.

Biographical Sketches
Andreas, Willy. "Johan Huizinga, 7. Dezember 1872–1. Februar 1945," *Historische Zeitschrift,* CLXIX (1949), 88–104.
Gelder, H. A. Enno van. *Professor Dr. Johan Huizinga: Gedachten en beelden uit zijn werk.* Utrecht: Oosthoek, 1947.
Hoselitz, Bert. Introduction to *Men and Ideas: Essays by Johan Huizinga.* New York: Meridian Books, 1959.
Kaegi, Werner. "Johan Huizinga zum Gedächtnis," in *Historische Meditationen,* II, 9–42. 2 vols. Zurich: Fretz & Wasmuth, 1946.
Koester, Kurt. *Johan Huizinga, 1872–1945.* Oberursel: Europa Archiv, 1947.
Locher, Theodoor J. G. "Johan Huizinga," *Jaarboek van de Maatschappij der Nederlandsche Letterkunde 1947,* pp. 88–109. Leiden, 1948.
Valkenburg, C. T. van. *J. Huizinga: zijn leven en zijn persoonlijkheid.* Amsterdam: L. J. Veen, 1946.

Special Studies
Antoni, Carlo. *From History to Sociology: The Transition in German Historical Thinking.* Translated by Hayden V. White. Detroit: Wayne State University Press, 1959.

Kaegi, Werner. "Das historische Werk Johan Huizingas," *Schweizer Beiträge zur allgemeinen Geschichte*, IV (1946) 5–37.

Romein, Jan. "Huizinga als historicus," in *Tussen vrees en vrijheid; vijftien historische verhandelingen*, pp. 212–41. Amsterdam: Querido, 1950.

Vermeulen, Egidius E. G. *Huizinga over de wetenschap der geschiedenis*. Arnhem: Wiel, 1956.

CHAPTER 6: ORTEGA Y GASSET

"Concerning a Bicentennial Goethe," in *Goethe and the Modern Age: The International Convocation at Aspen, Colorado, 1949.* Edited by Arnold Bergsträsser. Chicago: Regnery, 1950.

Concord and Liberty. Translated by Helene Weyl. New York: Norton, 1946.

Gesammelte Werke. 4 vols. Stuttgart: Deutsche Verlagsanstalt, 1954–56. This is an excellent edition for readers without a knowledge of Spanish; it contains many essays not available in any other translation. The selection of works to be included was made by Ortega y Gasset himself.

Man and People. Translated by Willard R. Trask. New York: Norton, 1957.

Meditations on Quixote. Translated by Evelyn Rugg and Diego Marín. New York: Norton, 1961.

What Is Philosophy? Translated by Mildred Adams. New York: Norton, 1960.

Biographical Sketches

There are brief sketches in Ceplecha and also Borel (see below). For many works in Spanish see the bibliography in Borel.

Special Studies

Alluntis, J. "The Vital and Historical Reason of Ortega y Gasset," *Franciscan Studies*, XV (1955), 60–78.

Borel, Jean-Paul. *Raison et vie chez Ortega y Gasset.* Neuchâtel: Baconnière, 1959.

Cascalès, Charles. *L'Humanisme d'Ortega y Gasset*. Paris: Presses Universitaires de France, 1957.

Ceplecha, Christian, O.S.B. *The Historical Thought of José Ortega y Gasset*. Washington, D.C.: Catholic University of America, 1958.

Curtius, Ernst Robert. "Ortega," *Partisan Review*, XVII (1950), 259–71.

Ferrater Mora, José. *Ortega y Gasset: An Outline of His Philosophy*. New Haven: Yale University Press, 1963.

Loeser, Norbert. *Ortega y Gasset en de philosophie van het leven*. The Hague: Leopold, 1941.

Marías, Julian. "Ortega and the Idea of Vital Reason," *Dublin Review*, CCXXII (Spring, 1949), 56–79, and CCXXIII (Winter, 1949), 36–45. I regret, in particular, not having been able to read more of Marías' Spanish treatises; he was one of Ortega's main pupils and one of his chief interpreters.

Sánchez Villaseñor, José, S.J. *Ortega y Gasset, Existentialist: A Critical Study of His Thought and Its Sources*. Translated by J. Small, S.J. Chicago: Regnery, 1949.

Index

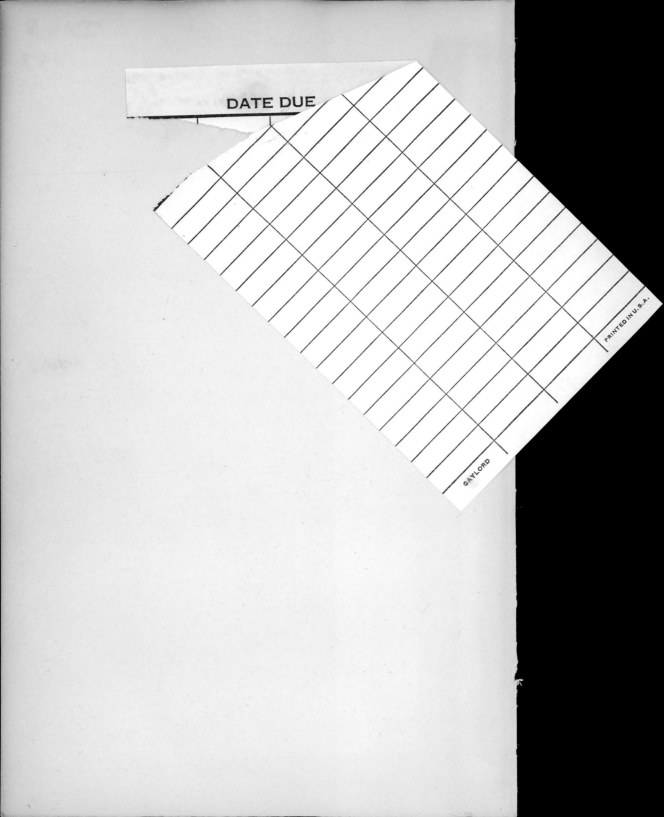

DATE DUE

GAYLORD

PRINTED IN U.S.A.